BENJAMIN S. JEFFRIES

VILE

Peeking Under the Skin of Murderers

Schiffer Publishing Ltd

4880 Lower Valley Road • Atglen, PA 19310

Other Schiffer Books by the Author:

Grim Shadows Falling:
Haunting Tales from Terrifying Places
ISBN: 978-0-7643-4708-5

Lost in the Darkness:
Life Inside the World's Most Haunted Prisons, Hospitals, and Asylums
ISBN: 978-0-7643-4319-3

Other Schiffer Books on Related Subjects:

Murder and Mayhem:
52 Crimes That Shocked Early California 1849-1949
Michael Thomas Barry.
ISBN: 978-0-7643-3968-4

Chesapeake Crimes II
Donna Andrews and Maria Y. Lim, Editors.
ISBN: 978-0-87033-582-2

Chicago Crime Stories: Rich Gone Wrong.

Bryan W. Alaspa.
ISBN: 978-0-7643-3114-5

Library of Congress Control Number: 2016936131

Published by Schiffer Publishing, Ltd.
4880 Lower Valley Road
Atglen, PA 19310
Phone: (610) 593-1777; Fax: (610) 593-2002
E-mail: Info@schifferbooks.com

Cover & Interior designed by Matthew Goodman
Type set in Incubus, Minion & Lucida Sans Typewriter

Cover background image:
grunge background © caesart. Courtesy www.bigstockphoto.com.

ISBN: 978-0-7643-5090-0
Printed in China

Dedicated To . . .

Michael Ralph Scaccia
(July 14, 1965–December 23, 2012)

Clive Ronald Burr
(March 8, 1957–March 12, 2013)

Jeffrey John Hanneman
(January 31, 1964–May 2, 2013)

David Murray Brockie
(August 30, 1963–March 23, 2014)

"But not all men seek rest and peace;
some are born with the spirit of the storm
in their blood."
–Robert E. Howard

Goodbye, my gods and monsters . . .

EPIGRAPH

"There is no real me, only an entity, something illusory,
and though I can hide my cold gaze and you can shake
my hand and feel flesh gripping yours and maybe you
can even sense our lifestyles are probably comparable:
I simply am not there."
–**Bret Easton Ellis**, *American Psycho*

"I've got to start eating at home more."
–**Jeffrey Dahmer**

CONTENTS

CHAPTER 1

ALBERT FISH

"THE GRAY MAN"

Brooklyn, New York

"On Sunday June the 3rd 1928 I called on you at 406 W 15 St.
Brought you pot cheese-strawberries. We had lunch.
Grace sat in my lap and kissed me. I made up my mind to eat her."
–**Albert Fish,** *In a letter to his victim's family*

The world in 1928 was naive, almost inculpable. The poor out-numbered the wealthy and it was not unusual for children to essentially raise themselves as their parents put in long hours of work for what could be considered menial pay. In the boroughs of New York, like Hell's Kitchen, Queens, and parts of Brooklyn, a lot of kids simply ran wild, hooking up with gangs, messing about with friends, or simply going to and from school. Reading how Albert Fish stole away with ten-year-old Grace Budd would infuriate most readers today; they would find fault in Grace's parents, mostly for allowing her to leave with someone who was basically a complete stranger. But that is what happened, and it's important to remember that, in those days, there were no terms such as "serial killer," and cannibals were often found on South Pacific islands, not on the Coney Island boardwalk. The "sick people" were all locked up and never discussed, and there were no monsters lurking in the dark. The true monsters were Poverty, Starvation, and Illiteracy—not a grandfather in a gray tweed suit. But after Albert Fish was executed, people would remember that monsters *do* exist and danger can be as close as your front door.

Albert Hamilton Fish first came to know the Budd Family after answering a classified advertisement placed in the Sunday edition of the *New York World* newspaper by the oldest son, Edward. He'd been looking for work, preferably in the countryside as a laborer, and Fish, who was fifty-eight at the time, came to call upon Edward and offer him a job in Farmingdale. Introducing himself as a farmer named Frank Howard, Fish was welcomed into the Budd household with open arms. He hardly seemed deadly in his gray suit, neatly coiffed hair and mustache, and slight, almost frail, frame. Even his light, watery eyes seemed to soften in their presence.

In truth, he had come to the Budd house to hire Edward and take him back to his place, where the young boy would be raped, tortured, maimed, and ultimately killed. But all of this changed when Fish saw Grace Budd, Edward's ten-year-old sister. He became smitten with her immediately, and she warmed up to him, as he treated her like a granddaughter, sitting on his lap and kissing his cheek. Later, Fish would say that, as she sat on his lap, he "made up his mind to eat her."

Fish would return to call on Edward one last time, agreeing to hire the boy. The family was overjoyed that Edward would be bringing money into what was primarily a low-income home. Fish used their happiness at Edward's good fortune to easily pry their daughter away. He'd been invited to a birthday party at his sister's house and he asked to take young Grace with him. It was a brilliant lie, one baited with good fortune for a downtrodden family. But while Grace's father, Albert Budd, quietly objected, her mother, Delia, relented and convinced her husband to let her go.

"She never gets to do anything special," Delia Budd reportedly told her husband.

Grace Budd was last seen walking down the sidewalk, hand in hand with The Gray Man, before turning a corner and disappearing forever. Not a single clue could be found for almost two years; the police turned up nothing in Grace's disappearance. But on September 5, 1930, police arrested Charles Edward Pope for the kidnapping of Grace Budd, an accusation lodged at him by his ex-wife. Between the accusation and Delia Budd positively identifying Pope as the man who took her daughter, Pope was charged and tried for the kidnapping. But during the trial, Delia Budd admitted she made a mistake in pointing the finger at Pope. That admission, and the fact that he was accused by a fairly vindictive ex-wife, got Charles Edward Pope exonerated and the case of Grace Budd's disappearance remained open.

It is hard to imagine what a parent would go through in a time like this, holding on to every sliver of hope possible in a world that went from beaming sunshine to gloomy and full of fog. Delia and Albert Budd, as well as their three other children, must have been almost out of their minds before eventually accepting the fact that Grace was really gone. There were glimmers of hope here and there, most notably when a New York newspaper declared that they had found the now-nineteen-year-old Grace Budd alive and well, living under another name. This lead turned into a heartbreaking hoax, but it was nothing compared to the letter

Delia and Albert received nine years after their daughter was abducted in November of 1934.

The letter, which would lead the police to Fish, was a brutal read for the Budd family. Delia was illiterate, so the task of reading the letter fell to Edward, the oldest son and the one who was supposed to have gone off with Fish before he set his watery eyes on little Grace. The letter, in part, read as follows:

> Dear Mrs. Budd. . . On Sunday June the 3, 1928 I called on you at 406 W 15 St. Brought you pot cheese—strawberries. We had lunch. Grace sat in my lap and kissed me. I made up my mind to eat her. On the pretense of taking her to a party. You said yes she could go. I took her to an empty house in Westchester I had already picked out. When we got there, I told her to remain outside. She picked wildflowers. I went upstairs and stripped all my clothes off. I knew if I did not I would get her blood on them. When all was ready I went to the window and called her. Then I hid in a closet until she was in the room. When she saw me all naked she began to cry and tried to run down the stairs. I grabbed her and she said she would tell her mamma. First I stripped her naked. How she did kick—bite and scratch. I choked her to death, then cut her in small pieces so I could take my meat to my rooms. Cook and eat it. How sweet and tender her little ass was roasted in the oven. It took me 9 days to eat her entire body. I did not fuck her tho I could of had I wished. She died a virgin.

Fish would later admit to his attorney that he did in fact rape Grace Budd, but his propensity for telling lies put most of what he would say into question. What got the attention of the police was his intimate knowledge of what happened in the Budd house that day, including the foodstuffs Fish had brought to them as a gift and knowing the complete address of his victim's home.

In addition, Fish had mailed the letter to Albert and Delia Budd using stationary from the New York Private Chauffeur's Benevolent Association. A janitor questioned at the company told detectives that he had taken some of the stationery but left it at his rooming house on East 52nd Street when he moved out.

The current occupant of the room?

Albert Hamilton Fish, who detectives theorized had used the stationery because, for one, it was handy. And two, Fish may have been trying to throw the police off his trail by sending out stationery from a company to which he wasn't employed. It obviously backfired on him and after matching up the boarding house matron's description of Fish with Albert and Delia Budd's description, Detective William F. King was certain that this Fish guy might be their man.

Detective King staked out the boarding house, waiting for Fish to return, and when he did, Fish graciously agreed to go down to police headquarters for questioning. But as soon as Fish got near the door leading outside, he turned and viciously attacked King with a straight razor in each hand. King quickly disarmed him, cuffed him, and took him down to the police station.

Albert Fish

Albert Fish openly confessed to the kidnapping and murder of Grace Budd and he took the opportunity of having a captive audience by relating nearly his entire life story, one that would connect him to yet another murder and the attempted murders of two others.

Fish was born in Washington, DC, in 1870. He'd been named Hamilton, after a distant relative, but preferred to be called Albert, a name he took from his youngest brother who died while still a baby. After the death of his father in 1875, young Albert Fish and his siblings were all shipped off to orphanages as their mother had no skill set and was unable to care for her children.

It was in the orphanage that Albert realized how truly mesmerized he was by pain, both giving it and taking it. Many years later, he would recall seeing many boys spanked with a switch on their bare backsides. Whereas many boys would have been horrified, this visual excited him, even at such a young age. Albert even began to have erections when he would be punished in such a way, something that made him a laughingstock to the other kids in the orphanage.

Fish's mother returned for him and his siblings when he was twelve years old after she'd gotten a fairly nice, steady job working for the government. But the seven years he'd spent in the orphanage had already transformed him into a sadist and masochist, someone who gets a deep sexual thrill out of giving pain and receiving it. In 1882, Fish began an illicit affair with another boy who worked in the local telegraph office. This boy, Fish claimed, introduced him to the vile practice of drinking human urine and eating human excrement, scientifically known as coprophagia. These interests, mixed with Fish's constant visitation of public bath houses, helped to shape Fish into the man he would become.

But the acts of coprophagia and sadomasochistic play don't make one a killer, though the acts themselves are horrific to the layperson. These traits were merely seeds planted in a growing boy's mind and would grow to encompass his every breath, his every motivation. He began working as a male prostitute in order to get his kicks. When he could not have a consensual affair with a young boy, Fish had no problem taking what he wanted by force, something he kept doing even after he'd gotten married. In 1898, Fish married and the two eventually had six children. But he was convicted of embezzlement in 1903 and sentenced to a year in Sing Sing Prison, an institution that he would revisit thirty-three years later.

Getting out of prison, Fish tried to straighten out his life by becoming a house painter, but the draw of children kept bringing him back to the monstrous persona that had grown inside him. He continuously and constantly abducted and molested young boys, most of them under the age of six. During this time, Fish became fascinated by the idea of castration but found it hard to follow through on it. It would take some courage and some time to get it right. In the meantime, he continued to visit the local brothels and whorehouses in town, paying them to beat him with paddles. In "confession letters" Fish would later write after being arrested in 1934, Fish would elaborate on his sexuality in thoroughly graphic detail, revisiting each and every instance of molestation, which often involved acts of sodomy, whipping, and the eating of fecal matter. His love of pain, both taking and giving, would one day become murderous. The pattern was there, and Fish most likely knew it.

In 1917, Fish's wife left him and took their children, marrying a man who had once rented a room in their house. Around this time, Fish claimed to have started hearing voices—voices that would tell him to do mad and inane things, such as wrapping himself up in a carpet because "John the Apostle" had told him to.

Fish had worked his way up to Grace Budd's kidnapping through practice. In 1910, he raped and murdered a young boy by the name of Thomas Bedden. Afterward, he claims to have stabbed, but not killed, two other boys. In July of 1924, in a frightening precede to Grace Budd's kidnapping, Fish came across eight-year-old Beatrice Kiel playing alone in the yard of her home. Fish apparently offered her money to help him harvest rhubarb. Beatrice was about to leave with Fish when her mother chased him away. He would be found later sleeping in their barn when the girl's father told him to leave.

He never returned for Beatrice, but Fish's plan, had it not been for the eagle-eyed mother, would have worked. He fine tuned it and was able to use the new, better lies to his advantage with the Budd family. This time, it worked.

It was Detective King who took Fish's confession and even he must have been horrified at the repugnance coming from the old man's mouth. After Fish had left the Budd house the first time, he purchased what he would call his "Implements Of Destruction": a cleaver, a saw, and a butcher's knife. Initially, as mentioned, Fish had planned to lure Edward Budd to a remote location, restrain him, and cut off his penis so he could bleed to death. But upon seeing Grace, Fish changed his mind and he realized that he *had* to have this girl. It was her that he wanted so desperately to kill and consume.

Albert Fish's first police mugshot, taken after his arrest for embezzling. By this point in his sick life, Fish was fully immersed in sado-masochistic sex and beheld a bizarre and repulsive array of fetishes, unbeknownst to his wife and six children.

Returning to the Budd's house, Fish was able to finagle Grace from the clutches of her parents before disappearing without a trace. He retrieved his bag of knives and took Grace with him to the train station where he purchased a round-trip ticket for himself, and a one-way ticket for Grace to the city of Westchester. He was so caught up in the excitement of what he was going to do to this little girl that he actually forgot his bag of knives on the train. But Grace, having no idea what was in the bag, noticed he'd left it and retrieved it for him.

Fish took Grace to an abandoned house, an old cottage that had been named "Wisteria." Once there, Fish told Grace to play outside as he went into the old house. He went up to the second floor, stripped off his clothes, then called to Grace, telling her to come upstairs. Grace, who had been collecting wildflowers, did as she was told, carrying the bundle of flowers with her.

As she entered the upstairs room, she was horrified to see Fish completely nude. Just the anticipation of Grace seeing him had made him sexually aroused. She turned to run, telling Fish, "I'll tell my mama!" But Fish tore after her savagely, grasping her up into his arms and strangling her with his bare hands. He felt her struggle, listened to her last breaths, and absorbed it all. When he was certain that Grace was gone, Fish propped her head up onto an empty paint can and proceeded to saw it off, using the can to capture as much of the blood as he could. After tossing the blood out into the yard, Fish returned to Grace's body and quickly began to dismember the rest of her. He took parts of her with him, wrapped in newspapers. Later that month, Fish would return to the house and toss away the rest of her body parts, including her head and the tools he'd used to dismember her. Police would find Grace's skull and some of his weapons during a search of the property following Fish's confession.

Detective King was aghast. He couldn't believe that this man had done such an abhorrent thing. "What caused you to do this horrible thing?" he'd asked.

Fish replied, very matter-of-factly, "You know, I never could account for it." He sat in the police station, showing very little emotion, but according to Fish, he felt immediate sorrow for what he'd done. "I would have given my life within a half-hour after I done it to restore it to her."

Oddly enough, neither the detectives or the prosecutors quizzed Fish on his fetish for cannibalism, something he'd written about in his letter to the Budds. Fish, himself, never volunteered any information about it either, though he would later admit he'd gotten the idea as a youngster from a sailor who'd practiced cannibalism with tribes in the South Pacific.

He was also linked to another child murder: that of Billy Gaffney in 1927. Witnesses had identified Albert Fish as the man they saw with Billy on a local trolley car. Fish had stolen Billy from the tenement building he lived in with his parents and took him to an old abandoned house near the junkyards on Riker Avenue. Once there, Fish bound, tortured, mutilated, and eventually killed the young boy over the course of two horrific days. He later claimed to have roasted portions of Billy's body, drank his blood, and ate every piece of flesh he'd cooked.

The issue at hand wasn't whether or not Albert Fish had committed murder. Like Jeffrey Dahmer's trial, Fish's trial would be held to determine if he was sane or not at the time of the murders. And, also like Dahmer's trial, there would be several psychiatric examinations performed that declared him insane. Defense attorneys for Fish reminded the courts that Fish had been held at two different mental hospitals for observation. The last hospital he was incarcerated in, Bellevue, was holding him for tests after he was arrested for sending obscene letters in the mail to a woman who'd placed an ad in the paper. Bellevue Hospital, however, released Fish, declaring him sane.

Fish's court appointed psychiatrist, Dr. Fredric Wertham, was a German-born physician who was renowned in his field of neuropathology. His assessment of Fish's case was new to him. Never before had he known of a man filled with such unparalleled perversity, a man who lusted for pain and constantly pushed the so-called sadomasochistic envelope. "There was no known perversion that he did not practice and practice frequently."

"I always had a desire to inflict pain on others and to have others inflict pain on me," Fish had told Wertham. "I always seemed to enjoy everything that hurt. The desire to inflict pain, that is always uppermost."

Fish's lawyer, James Dempsey, however, focused his attention on Fish's alleged cannibalism, hoping that it might sway the jury into finding his client insane. But Fish had only mentioned devouring Grace Budd and Billy Gaffney in letters to the victims' families. The admissions were *not* part of his statements to police. Furthermore, there was no proof, outside Fish's word, that he had eaten human flesh at all. Dempsey's case for insanity, while inspired, fell flat.

Dr. Wertham found him to be clearly insane, but the opinion of a well-respected psychiatrist and neuropathologist, while valuable in the psychiatric field, was most definitely in the minority inside the court room. The jury were forced to see the Budd family sitting in the courtroom. They were subjected to hearing the most gruesome accounts some of them had ever heard, or ever will hear. Fish's own children, led by Albert Jr., his eldest son, testified against their own father, relating tales of brutality that they were forced to endure to appease their father's sick perversions. The infamous "Crotch X-Rays" were shown in court, showing a multitude of needles that Fish had inserted into his groin to achieve painful bliss. All of the testimonies proved that Fish loved pain, loved doling out pain, but was completely in control of his mental faculties at the time. He knew what he was doing, he knew how to do it, and he went to great lengths to do it without getting caught. It was only his need to revisit Grace Budd's murder in a letter to her parents that became his undoing.

The trial itself lasted ten days, with the verdict coming back in less than an hour: guilty as charged. The judge, in response, wasted no time and ordered the death penalty for Albert Fish. Several appeals failed to change the verdict and he was sent to Sing Sing Prison to die in 1935. Fish welcomed the verdict and the sentence, almost too gleefully. He once referred to his date with the electric chair as the one adventure he hadn't taken yet. A *New York Daily News* reporter wrote, "His watery eyes gleamed at the thought of being burned by a heat more intense than the flames with which he often seared his flesh to gratify his lust."

The electric chair at Sing Sing Prison, the very one that finally took the life of Albert Hamilton Fish in 1936. (*Photo by Fred T. Robbins, courtesy of The Library Of Congress.*)

Fish's last days on Earth consisted mostly of writing, a hobby he enjoyed and one of the few ways he could relive his crimes while still in prison. Like the letters to the Budds and the Gaffneys before, confessing his crimes in intimate detail gave him a chance to rekindle his love of them. Before being taken to the electric chair, Fish passed on a large stack of final papers he'd written to Dr. Wertham, who vowed never to release the contents of the papers in any capacity.

On January 16, 1936, Albert Hamilton Fish became the oldest man ever to be executed at Sing Sing Prison. There was talk that the electric chair might short circuit when the switch was thrown on Fish, due to all of the needles still embedded in his groin. But the needles had little effect on the overall execution, which went flawlessly. "I don't even know what I'm doing here," he'd said before the black hood was brought down over his face.

Following the death of Dr. Wertham, his papers on Fish were donated to the Library of Congress, which in 2010 released every single page Fish had handed to Wertham. These papers, which included Fish's handwritten and typed confessions of nearly every crime he'd committed in disturbingly intimate detail, also included a good number of Dr. Wertham's own analyses of Fish. Collected and edited by serial killer specialist and renowned author John Borowski, the book *Albert Fish: In His Own Words* was finally unleashed upon the public in 2014 by Waterfront

Productions, and the details Wertham had tried to suppress became part of the serial killer lexicon. Albert Fish would no longer be able to hide behind the grandfatherly image he so convincingly projected, for his vile words and deviant nature now betray him at every step.

The Vile Files

Gilles de Rais

(1405-1440)

Gilles de Montmorency-Laval, also known as Baron de Rais, was a leader in the French army and fought alongside Joan of Arc at the Battle of Orleans. However, his best-known reputation is as a child killer and occultist, though many historians believe that writers of the time took great lengths to slander him and distorted many truths. Historically recorded, his confession was graphic and appalling, even by today's standards; judges listened to Gilles confess to raping, sodomizing, mutilating, dismembering, and oftentimes cannibalizing forty boys and girls while being assisted by a number of henchmen and hand servants on staff at his castle in Machecoul, France. Their bodies would be found by authorities following his elaborate confession. On October 25, 1440, Gilles de Rais was sentenced to die first by hanging, followed by his body being burned at the stake. Because he was still technically a nobleman, he was afforded the luxury of being buried in the church of the monastery of Notre-Dame des Carmes in Nantes.

CHAPTER 2

ROBERT PICKTON

"THE PIG FARMER KILLER"

Port Coquitlam, British Columbia

"I'm a legend already."
–Robert Pickton, Speaking to his cellmate, who was also an undercover cop

I knew writing a chapter on Robert Pickton was going to be difficult. It wasn't because of all the details of the murders themselves, but because of the total and complete ban on publicity by the Canadian courts, a move that would have bankrupted American newspapers and magazines. The trial of pig farmer-turned-serial killer Robert Pickton found Pickton himself under a gag order that prevents him, even now, from giving interviews to the media in all its forms. In addition, Pickton never confessed or discussed his crimes with police. His early life, and the events that shaped his genesis into a killer, is vague and shadowy. Instead, what we are left with are the cold, hard facts of the case itself, and we are spared Robert Pickton's narcissistic repartee. We will hear his story from those who knew him well, as opposed to hearing it from Pickton, who would most likely shape the story into a tapestry of half truths to suit his own needs and wrest as much sympathy from a curious crowd as possible. The one drawback is that we may find it difficult to identify with him, much like being kept at arm's length and seeing what happened as if we were watching a TV program. Sometimes, just sometimes, it's better that we see it that way...

It started out as one thing and quickly turned into another. Police were at the Pickton Pig Farm serving a warrant for a cache of illegal firearms that Robert Pickton and his brother David were rumored to have had in their possession. It was during this search that a lone Royal Canadian Mounted Police officer found a strange object lying on the ground: a prescription asthma inhaler. It was labeled with the name Sereena Abotsway. The officer recognized the name almost immediately: it was one of over a hundred names on a list of women who had gone missing over a four-year period in the Downtown Eastside section of Vancouver, commonly referred to as Low Track. Full of filth and a magnet for drug addicts and hookers, Low Track boasted a junkie population from 5–10,000 men, women, and children at any given moment. Johns crept around on the streets, hiding their dark intentions behind tinted windows and shifty eyes, seeking out cheap thrills, whether it came from a needle or a woman. For the most part, what went on in Low Track stayed in Low Track. But when prostitutes began to disappear at an alarming rate, police had to look into it. The prostitutes weren't merely being killed or dropping over dead in the streets. They weren't leaving the life and turning up in a halfway house or mission across town. They were simply disappearing without a trace. And now, in the muddy cleft of a dirt road cutting through the Pickton Pig Farm was something that Sereena Abotsway should not, and would not, have gone without.

The farm was sealed off to the public immediately as a second search warrant was rushed to the location, this time for anything related to or connected to the disappearance of Sereena Abotsway. While Robert Pickton was in jail on the weapons charge, police and forensic teams began the arduous task of combing over the fourteen acres of farmland, searching for any evidence linking Pickton to the numerous disappearances of Vancouver's sex trade workers.

They would not have to search long before finding their first clues, beginning with the discovery of several different body parts in Robert Pickton's freezers. A chilling collection of identification cards and driver's licenses were found strewn across the junk- and garbage-laden farmland. Bits of teeth and bones were also found among the debris. Within two weeks, a simple weapons charge ballooned into murder charges against Robert William Pickton when two sets of remains were identified as being that of Sereena Abotsway and Mona Wilson, two local prostitutes who disappeared in July and November of 2001, respectively. But before long, there would be more charges, and soon, Robert William Pickton would have some explaining to do.

The story of the Pickton Pig Farm began in 1905 when William Pickton, Robert's grandfather, bought up a large chunk of land near an old mental hospital. A second generation hog farmer, William Pickton began what would become his legacy for his children and his grandchildren: raising, slaughtering, and processing pigs. It was dirty, bloody work, a job that afforded Robert an education in killing and disposing of living things. It was a lifestyle that was slowly and methodically becoming ingrained within him, a trait that no doubt made his grandfather proud. But developing roads forced the Picktons to sell their farm and move elsewhere, buying up forty acres of swampland for $18,000. There, in Port Coquitlam, they resumed the family tradition of being pig farmers. By now, Robert and David had a sister as well, Linda, who was brought up in boarding schools in the city; she never did spend much time on the farm. Just as well, as it turns out. She would go on to marry a businessman and live a fairly affluent life near downtown Vancouver.

But for Robert and David, farming was in their blood. They loved every bit of it. "Robert and David remained on the farm, with its shit, its smells, its blood, and butchery," says Charles Mudede, a Seattle journalist who covered the Pickton case for TheStranger.com. "The boys' father died in 1978 and their mother followed him to the grave in 1979. The brothers, then in their late twenties, inherited the farm with their sister."

By 1994, what had once been near worthless swampland in the 1960s was now valued at over $7 million, making the Pickton children millionaires. Portions of the land were sold off to real estate developers and the city of Port Coquitlam, who built not only a park but an elementary school on the newly acquired land as well.

Now wealthy landowners, the Pickton brothers seemed to lose interest in being reputable pig farmers, allowing their farmlands to deteriorate and overflow with garbage. While they still raised pigs, it wasn't really Robert's main focus. With cash flow no longer an issue, his rationality began to lapse. He developed eccentric behavior that seemed to emulate drug use, but others would later testify that he never once did a drug other than aspirin. The "watchdog" on their farm was a 600-pound boar that only seemed to like Robert and David, who allowed it to roam freely across the farm grounds. Bill Hiscox, who worked the farm for the Picktons recalled that, "I never saw a pig like that, who would chase and bite at you. It was running out with the dogs around the property." He recalled the farm as a genuinely "creepy-looking place" and Robert Pickton as a man who was a "pretty quiet guy, hard to strike up a conversation with." Other than the 600-pound watch pig, there were several remaining hogs left on the farm, but business had slowed, probably deliberately, to almost a crawl.

Truth is, Robert William Pickton had other business he wanted to attend to and it dealt with the slaughter and processing of a whole other kind of animal. Robert, and to as lesser extent, his brother David, had an affinity for sex workers, women they could pay to play with every night of the week. In 1996, in an effort to legitimize his fetishes, Robert and David registered a nonprofit charity they called the Piggy Palace Good Times Society, coupled with the Canadian government in an effort to, in their words "organize, manage, and operate special events, functions, dances, shows, and exhibitions on behalf of service organizations, sports organizations, and other worthy groups." But in reality, it was just an excuse for them to stage raves and wild parties, all sporting Vancouver prostitutes in a converted slaughterhouse. Charming, to the last, though, these events tended to pull in as many as 2,000 people, depending upon the function. Still, behind the veneer of this nonprofit costume, Robert Pickton's mind was swirling with ideas and images that haunted him, tugged at him. He found himself cruising the Low Track, picking up prostitutes in his beloved converted bus with the groovy tinted windows. Eventually, he became so well known that all he had to do was make a phone call and the prostitute would come to him. While much of his private sexual life is shrouded in mystery, it can be surmised that he was most likely into the bondage scene, doling out sexual punishment to the women he paid and reveling in being dominant over them. His tastes would have begun with perhaps a few light slaps to the woman, but would definitely have escalated into full-blown torture near the very end. Being a pig farmer, he would know how to quickly hogtie someone into submission, leaving them helpless to defend themselves and allowing Robert to do anything he wanted.

The first time his lusts for sex and blood got out of hand was on March 23, 1997, when he was charged with the attempted murder of Wendy Lynn Eistetter, a local prostitute. She had called the police out to the Pickton Farm, alleging that Robert Pickton had handcuffed her. As she was trying to escape her bonds, he began slashing at her with a knife. When she finally got an upper hand on Robert, she managed to not only disarm him, but also was able to stab him with his own weapon. Both she and Robert maintained that they were only trying to defend themselves from each other and the charge was eventually dismissed in January 1998.

But the incident with Wendy Lynn was only the beginning of Robert Pickton's troubles and just a glimpse into his true intentions with women of the night. After all the years they spent enjoying their wealth and ignoring the purpose of their farm, Port Coquitlam officials sued the Picktons for violation of the local zoning regulations, which basically meant that the land was meant to be a farm, was zoned to be used as a farm, and wasn't being used as a farm. In addition, they were fined for turning the slaughterhouse into a concert and dance hall. These were simple violations of the zoning ordinances that could have been avoided had they had the property rezoned. But rezoning would mean higher taxes and more interest from Port Coquitlam officials. So the Picktons did what most would do in that situation. They ignored the charges and the lawsuit and staged an enormous New Year's Eve party in 1998, which was very quickly followed by an injunction prohibiting them holding any other events in the future. As a result, their nonprofit status was revoked and the Piggy Palace Good Times Society was disbanded.

But Robert Pickton, again, was undeterred. He continued to skulk around Low Track, picking up prostitutes and junkies and bringing them back to the farm. Girls on the street referred to him simply as "Farmer Willy." But instead of paying them well before turning them loose, Robert Pickton chose to keep them. Authorities believed that he would rape, torture, and murder close to fifty of Vancouver's prostitutes. His escapades with them would usually take place in his motor home, or in one of the barns. Chained and helpless, they would be brutally beaten, raped, and stabbed before being gruesomely dismembered. Such was the fate of Sereena Abotsway, the woman who had gone to Pickton's farm and never left, but still managed to leave a clue behind that would seal Robert William Pickton's fate as one of the most prolific serial killers in history.

Her asthma inhaler had brought literally thousands of policemen, forensic anthropologists, and archaeologists were sifting through every bit of Pickton's fourteen acres, looking for something, anything, that could connect him to the disappearances of the Low Track prostitutes. With over fifty disappearances over a four-year period, finding physical evidence should have been easy, but it wasn't. With the exception of Sereena Abotsway's remains that had been found in Pickton's freezer and the partial remains of Mona Wilson found in a fifty-five-gallon drum, very little evidence was being recovered and it gnawed at the Canadian police to no end. If Pickton was guilty, where were all the bodies? And if he wasn't guilty, why were two of the women found brutally murdered and dismembered on his property?

The answer came to most when they stopped sifting through dirt and mud and turned their attention to the few remaining hogs milling about their troughs and pens. Chills ran down their spines when they considered the horrible idea that Pickton may have fed the dismembered remains to his legion of hungry pigs, animals that were notorious for eating everything put into their troughs. Animals whose jaws could easily crush and grind flesh and bone into oblivion.

Such assumptions were greeted with a chill down the spine and a hearty shudder and weren't taken seriously until bits of flesh and blood were recovered from the teeth of a wood chipper on the farm grounds. As the mode of operation came to light, it was apparent that Pickton would first rape and murder his prey, usually through strangulation or stabbing, dismember them, toss their parts into the wood chipper, and feed the shredded remains to their pigs.

Evidence collected amounted to twenty-seven charges of first-degree murder against Robert Pickton, and when he went to trial on January 30, 2006, he pleaded not guilty to each one of them. As mentioned, up until this point, the Canadian Supreme Court had imposed a gag order on information regarding the case. Newspapers, television shows, or magazines were prohibited from sharing information about the murders. Period. But once the trial began and all of the gory details of Pickton's undertakings were revealed, the public was immediately shocked into silence and horror as prosecutors laid out their case against Robert William Pickton.

Police had recovered bisected skulls, with hands and feet stuffed inside. The decomposing remains of one of the victims had been found stuffed in a large, thick garbage bag. Blood-stained women's clothing were found lying among the debris in Pickton's trailer. Jawbones and teeth were recovered near the old slaughterhouse. Perhaps most chilling was the recovery of Pickton's .22-caliber revolver, complete with a large dildo mounted to the barrel. Pickton claimed to have attached the dildo to use as a silencer, but the presence of one of the victim's DNA on the dildo refuted Pickton's claim and gave everyone else a newer, more grotesque idea of what it had actually been used for all along. Numerous handguns, handcuffs, syringes filled with windshield washer fluid, and Spanish fly aphrodisiac were all seized from Pickton's trailer on the farm. Excavating the land took twenty months and yielded 600,000 pieces of evidence. Over 200,000 DNA samples were identified, which had been used to identify thirty of the missing women.

Experts in the field of forensic science testified that they saw marks on many of the skulls indicating that the same saw had been used on a number of the bodies. That same saw, matching the marks on the skulls, was found in Robert Pickton's possession. Fertilizer that was tested on the farm tested positive for human DNA, meaning that Pickton had gone to great lengths to turn his victims into mulch, then mixed it with pig excrement that would be sold later to neighboring farmers.

Testimony from some of Pickton's friends and farm employees related a story of how Pickton had told them his way of disposing of a junkie prostitute was by injecting them with windshield washer fluid, which explained the presence of the needles filled with blue liquid found in his trailer. Another associate named Andrew Bellwood claimed that Pickton had mentioned killing prostitutes by handcuffing and strangling them before gutting them and feeding their remains to his pigs.

Lynne Ellingsen, a former prostitute who offered to clean for Pickton in exchange for a place to stay, testified that she witnessed Robert Pickton butchering a woman, her body hanging from chains in the shed. Pickton was soaked in the woman's blood and when he saw her, he pulled her inside, telling her that if she talked about what she'd seen, she would "be right beside her." Pickton paid her off with a cache of drugs and sent her off in a taxi. Terrified of what he would do to her, Ellingsen had kept her mouth shut.

It was a long, complex, and somewhat convoluted trial. Pickton showed little to no interest in the proceedings except when graphic depictions of how the women were murdered were brought up and explained by the prosecutors. Hearing the gory details, Pickton no doubt was probably elated at being able to relive his "masterworks."

Pickton's defense attorneys attempted to exonerate their client by saying he wasn't smart enough to plan and execute what police were claiming to be close to fifty murders. With an IQ of eighty-six, Pickton wasn't the brightest crayon in the box, but in no way was he mentally handicapped. He used his knowledge of pig processing to get rid of much of the hard physical evidence, and his knowledge of the nature of pigs to help get rid of the rest. What he did was commit the easiest murders possible and nearly got away with it merely by doing what he had learned since he'd been a child. He shaped his murders *around* his intelligence level, not above it.

The trial came to a close on December 9, 2007. The jury had found Pickton guilty of six counts of second-degree murder, a judgment that carried a mandatory life sentence without parole for at least ten years. A severe lack of tangible evidence prevented the jury from convicting Pickton on all counts, but it hardly mattered now. Pickton would spend the remaining days of his life behind bars. In handing down the sentence to Pickton, Supreme Court Justice James Williams said, "Mr. Pickton's conduct was murderous and repeatedly so. I cannot know the details but I know this: What happened to them was senseless and despicable."

The Vile Files

Mohammed Bijeh

(February 7, 1975-March 16, 2005)

Known as "The Desert Vampire," Iranian serial killer Mohammed Bijeh confessed in a Tehran court to raping and murdering sixteen young boys in the spring and summer of 2004 with the aid of an accomplice, Ali Baghi. His sentence was twofold: ordered to take 100 lashes from a whip, he would be brutally hanged immediately after. The execution was carried out in Pakdasht, a town close to his old hunting grounds. Once he'd received his 100 lashes, the mother of one of his victims placed a thick nylon rope around Bijeh's neck. A crane was used to hoist the murderer into the air, strangling him to death 100 feet in the air. His accomplice, Ali Baghi, received only fifteen years in an Iranian prison.

CHAPTER 3

RICHARD RAMIREZ

"THE NIGHT STALKER"

Los Angeles, California

"We've all got the power in our hands to kill,
but most people are afraid to use it.
The ones who aren't afraid control life itself."
—**Richard Ramirez**

Miguel Ramirez was a god to his little cousin, Ricardo. Ricardo looked up to Miguel in the way a son would look up to a father, and while Ricardo did indeed have a father, it was Miguel who'd taken Ricardo under his wing, bonded with him, and showed him pictures of severed heads he'd taken while on tour in Vietnam. While Ricardo Ramirez's father was an abusive alcoholic, it was Miguel who many believe twisted Ricardo's young mind into that of Richard Ramirez, the Night Stalker.

—

Ricardo Leyva "Richard" Munoz Ramirez was born to Julian and Mercedes Ramirez in El Paso, Texas, during the leap year, February 29, 1960. His father had been a policeman in Juarez, Mexico, but became a laborer for the Santa Fe Railroad when he moved to Texas. Julian Ramirez was a die-hard alcoholic, brought about in part by his own father's alcoholism and his job policing the drug and crime riddled borderland of Juarez. Every day, Julian Ramirez would come across headless bodies, mutilated corpses, and the burnt remains of prostitutes, snitches, and cartel associates who'd outlived their usefulness. And every night, Julian would return to his home, drink to forget what he'd seen, and lash out at his family when it wouldn't work. Richard, the youngest, was often a target for his father's wrath and he found himself steering clear of him altogether. By the time he was twelve, Richard was sleeping in graveyards at night, just so he wouldn't have to go home.

So, given the rueful nature of Richard's home life, it isn't much of a surprise that he fell in with his cousin Miguel, who never talked down to him, never beat him, and always seemed to want him around. Together, Richard and Miguel bonded over numerous marijuana joints and stories of Miguel's hard-spent time in Vietnam. Miguel would boast of raping and murdering Vietnamese women in the villages his platoon would encounter on patrol. When Richard told Miguel that he didn't believe him, Miguel provided proof in the form of photographs he'd taken of their severed heads or bullet-riddled bodies. Ironically, it was as if Richard were seeing the demons of Juarez that his father was battling, seeing what made his father drink, seeing what made his father beat him. The viciousness of the crimes were softened by the constant haze of marijuana smoke and the coziness he felt with his beloved cousin. In essence, bonding with Miguel over murder would be something he would try to re-create later in life.

But it was one night, in 1973, that brought all of the horrible pictures Richard had seen and treasured to life. On May 4, Richard was with his cousin when Miguel's wife Jessie engaged Miguel in an argument, a domestic squabble that ended with a .38 revolver being shot off into Jessie's face. Watching Miguel murder his wife, Richard's aunt, cemented the idea in Richard's head that the fantasy that once existed only in pictures could become reality with the simple squeeze of a trigger. Richard's fascination with death and murder, nurtured by his obviously psychotic cousin, began to germinate and blossom.

"It wasn't traumatic . . . but the shock value," confessed Ramirez much later. "I went back into the apartment to collect some things with my dad, because my cousin was in jail. The bed was all bloody. It was there where she had landed after the bullet. She got a .38 to the face. At the same time it was very . . . uh . . . The stillness of the room, the eeriness, you know. We had to open the windows to ventilate the room and it was something. It was . . . it was death. I had known the woman. I had known her very well. I went into the living room and saw her purse. I looked through her purse, saw her ID cards and her things. It was a strange feeling. That was the first time I ever ran across death. Ever since, I was intrigued."

Though Miguel was charged with Jessie's murder, he was found not guilty by reason of insanity, and sentenced to time at the Texas State Mental Hospital. Within four years, Miguel was released and he continued his dark guidance of Richard's dangerous downward spiral into murder and madness.

But while Miguel languished in a mental hospital, Richard moved in with his older sister, Ruth, and her husband Roberto. In Roberto, Richard cultivated the secondary trait that would become part of his Modus Operandi: voyeurism. Roberto was keen on including Richard on his nightly trips around different neighborhoods, creeping through dimly lit or darkened yards and peeping in the open windows of unsuspecting homeowners. Richard learned how to stalk through yards and property without being noticed, wearing dark clothing to camouflage himself in the dark. During a trip to Los Angeles, his brother Ruben, a fairly successful petty thief and burglar, taught young Richard how to properly burglarize a home without getting caught.

By the time he was fourteen, Richard had quit school, was smoking pot everyday, and was now resorting to burglarizing homes in order to feed his habit. Smoking weed evolved into dropping acid and Richard began to nurture his interest in Satanism. He became drawn to heavy metal bands that used a Satanic theme to promote themselves. AC/DC's *Highway To Hell* became his favorite album, a record that contained a song called "Night Prowler," which foreshadowed his media-born nickname and career as the Night Stalker killer.

If you were to take the highly suggestible Richard, show him how easy it was to kill, show him how cheap human life was, and school him on how to get close to people without being seen, it is little wonder that Richard became what he became. He was being educated on how to be a killer by his own family, and yet, to this day, his family looks back on him as "a good kid" and they seem to take little to no responsibility for the dysfunction. In addition, adolescent Richard's idea of sexuality quickly became torture, blood, and death. Rape went hand in hand with murder and it would become as normal to Richard as love making would be to most married couples. Sexual violence was foreplay. Climax was achieved with a thick spray of blood. But at this point in Richard's life, it was all still fantasy. No one, sadly, could see what Richard was thinking of when he saw a pretty girl, for if they had, they would most likely recommend that he be given a room in the Texas State Mental Hospital next to his cousin Miguel. Richard, truly, was in desperate need of help.

Richard Ramirez attended Jefferson High School in El Paso, but dropped out when he was in the ninth grade. He puttered back and forth between menial jobs, finally finding one that would provide him a proving ground for all he'd learned. Hired on as a custodian at a local Holiday Inn, Richard soon discovered that he could use his passkey to rob tenants as they slept. This was a tactic he used often and to great success, but it would be short-lived.

Upon returning from a business meeting, an older man entered his hotel room at the Holiday Inn and was horrified to find the tall, lanky Ramirez attempting to rape his wife. The older man promptly beat Richard within an inch of his life. He was quickly arrested and charged, but the charges were dropped when the couple—who lived out of state—refused to return to El Paso to testify against him. He was still learning the trade and now he knew for sure: kill the man quickly, have uninterrupted fun with the woman.

Soon, Richard's schooling would be over and it would be time to show the world what he had learned. At age twenty-two, Richard Ramirez moved to California. Though living primarily in the Los Angeles area, he was also known to frequent low-income sections of San Francisco as well. The year was 1982, and Richard began settling into life on the West Coast. His interest in Satanism soared and he found that he had many different outlets for that interest in California, most notably Anton LeVey's Church of Satan, as well as many other splinter Satanist and fringe groups. But Richard was never a member of those groups and it is far more likely that he took on the persona of a Satanist in order to instill fear in those around him. The 1980s were known for what was referred to as "Satanic Panic," in much the same way the people of Salem went on a witch hunt in the 1600s. Anyone could be accused of being a Satanist. Daycare workers, doctors, politicians, garbagemen. Anyone who yelled "Satan" was listened to, and lives and careers were destroyed over malicious and often false rumors. Killers like Carl Drew, Robin Gecht, and Sean Sellers were infamous for killing in the name of Satan. Satan was fear. Satan was power. Richard believed that, and he used the Satanic image to spread fear in an already edgy and nervous world. In time, he would be the most famous Satanic serial killer alive and the most feared man on the planet.

It wouldn't be confirmed until DNA evidence was tested in 2009, but the killing of nine-year-old Mei Lung is widely regarded as Richard's first murder. She had been raped, beaten, and stabbed to death, her body found hanging from a steam pipe in the basement of a hotel in San Francisco on April 10, 1984. Her death would soon be followed in June of that year with the murder of seventy-nine-year-old Jennie Vincow, who had been stabbed repeatedly in her sleep. Her throat had been cut so deeply that her head had almost been severed.

The beast was loose, and he enjoyed it. Like most serial killers, Richard felt godlike and omnipotent when causing pain and terror. It would soon begin to spiral out of control as the violence became much more brutal and the need to swim in the gore of his victims became more intense.

It was on March 17, 1985, that Richard Ramirez officially cemented his name as one of the world's most vicious and audacious serial killers, as he attacked not once, but twice in the same day. He struck out at twenty-two-year-old Maria Hernandez in Rosemead, wounding her with a gunshot before killing her roommate, thirty-four-year-old Dayle Okazaki. Less than an hour later, he attacked and killed thirty-year-old Tsai-Lian Yu as she sat in her car.

Maria Hernandez survived the attack by Ramirez and provided police with an incredibly accurate description of her attacker, whom she described as having bulging, wide-spaced eyes, rotting teeth, and long curly hair. Just ten days later, he would strike again, this time shooting sixty-four-year old Vincent Zazzarra as he slept and stabbing Vincent's forty-four-year-old wife Maxine to death. After she was dead, Richard cut out her eyes and placed them in her jewelry box, which he took with him. Police matched up the bullets used at the Zazzarra murder scene to those found in the Okazaki and Lian Yu murder scenes and came to a conclusion that struck fear throughout them: they were officially dealing with a serial killer, but it would be a long time before the deaths would end and an arrest would be made.

From May to August of 1985, Richard went on a burglary and killing spree that earned him his now-famous moniker as the "Night Stalker." In total, he murdered, raped, and burglarized his way through Los Angeles, claiming six lives and massively altering countless others. His madness was at an epoch at this time, his victims random and unconnected. He didn't seem to care if they lived or died. Richard took what he wanted, made his victims swear their allegiance to Satan, and disappeared into the night. Sometimes, those nights were filled with horrific death, other nights were brimming with ruthless sexual assaults, bondage, beatings, and torture. He began scrawling pentagrams in lipstick and blood on the walls of the homes he'd invade. Richard even began introducing himself to his victims as the "Night Stalker," proud of his new moniker and the fright it produced.

But as crazed as Richard was, he was also keenly aware that the media and law enforcement's attention were focused directly on this brazen serial killer; many survivors provided very accurate descriptions of the Night Stalker, and Richard felt a change in location for a little bit might help bring the attention down a bit. He left Los Angeles and returned to the San Francisco Bay area, where he continued his campaign of terror in the name of Satan.

But police did have one very important piece of evidence, one they hoped to keep quiet for as long as possible in the hopes that the killer might repeat his mistake. They had found a shoe print in the flower beds of one of the Night Stalker's victims. Forensics determined that it was a size 11½ Avia sneaker. Given that the crime scenes were downright immaculate when it came to evidence of who the killer was, police knew that, should that shoe print show up again, it would be easier to connect the murders.

But police would be dealt a crushing blow, not from their nemesis, but from one of their own. San Francisco Mayor Dianne Feinstein chose to divulge the information about the Night Stalker's shoes, effectively destroying any leverage the police may have had against their culprit. That night, Richard Ramirez dropped his 11½ Avia sneakers over the side of the Golden Gate Bridge, eliminating the one thing connecting him to any of the murders.

A few days later, on August 24, 1985, he returned to Los Angeles, stole an orange Toyota car, then drove almost eighty miles away to a town called Mission Viejo, where he burglarized the home of Bill Carns and his bride-to-be, Inez Erickson. Shooting Carns three times in the head, he turned to Inez, introduced himself as the Night Stalker, and made her swear to Satan as he bound, gagged, and beat her. After ransacking the house and pocketing money and jewelry, Richard returned to Inez and raped and sodomized her repeatedly. Before he left the house he said, "Tell them the Night Stalker was here."

One thing about smaller communities is the number of nosy neighbors per capita. The town of Mission Viejo was no different, and as Richard left the Carns's house, a particularly eagle-eyed thirteen-year-old boy took down as much of Ramirez's license plate as he could as the car sped away. The boy had seen the man and the car earlier in the day and found both to be very suspicious; the man and the car were both strangers to the neighborhood and strangers in that part of town were rare.

After hearing about what had happened to Bill and Inez, the boy's concerned parents reported their son's findings to the police. The partial plate number, combined with the make and model of the orange Toyota, made it exceptionally easy for police to identify the stolen car. It would be found just four days later, abandoned in Wilshire, California. Knowing that it was more than likely driven by the one calling himself the Night Stalker, forensic teams descended upon the car, dusting it voraciously for fingerprints. But as careful as Richard had been up to that point about wiping away his fingerprints, this time, he missed a spot.

Police were able to obtain and lift one single fingerprint from the rear view mirror of the Toyota. From there, they were able to determine that the fingerprint belonged to a man named Richard Munoz Ramirez, a drifter from Texas with quite an impressive rap sheet of drug and traffic violations. They even had a photo of him, taken as a mugshot when he was booked for auto theft in Los Angeles. When compared to the police artist sketches, there was no longer any doubt. Richard Ramirez was the Night Stalker.

"We know who you are now, and soon everyone else will," detectives announced at a press conference just moments after revealing Richard's mugshot to the world. "There will be no place you can hide."

But this time, Richard—surprisingly—wasn't paying attention to the media. He was trying to lie low and wait for much of it to blow over. In fact, at the time of the press conference when his picture was shown to the entire world, Richard was in Tucson, Arizona, hoping to visit with his brother. When his brother was a no-show at the bus station, Richard took a bus back to Los Angeles, completely unaware that, essentially, the entire city was looking for him. His face was on every television channel, every newspaper, and every telephone pole in the city. Once in East Los Angeles, he stopped at a convenience store, where a group of elderly Mexican women recognized him. They called him *El Matador* (The Killer) and Richard saw his face on the front page of the newspaper on sale inside the store. In a panic, Richard attempted to carjack three different motorists in an effort to escape a growing mob of Hispanic citizens who recognized him. Cornering Richard in an alley, he was beaten unconscious and held down as they waited for police to arrive. When he was finally rescued by police, Ramirez, still in a haze from the beatdown he'd received, reportedly begged them in Spanish, "Please leave me in peace... it's me. It's me."

Charged with numerous murders and a multitude of sexual assaults, Richard sat in jail for three years awaiting his trial and building up what little defense he could. Prosecutors thought for sure that Ramirez would try for an insanity defense, claiming that he was controlled by Satan and forced to kill, rape, and rob his victims. Upon his arrest, Ramirez had remarked to detectives, "You think I'm crazy. But you don't know Satan." He then began banging his head on the table. Detectives even claimed that Richard had confessed to them that he was the Night Stalker, but his attorneys would later deny their client had said anything at all and pushed for an all-out trial. His defense team both knew that there was scant physical evidence of Richard's presence at the crime scenes (barring witnesses identifying him as their attacker) and DNA testing had not yet come fully into the mainstream as a tool for identifying assailants.

Finally, on July 22, 1988, jury selection for the People vs. Richard Munoz Ramirez began. California Attorney General Margaret Maxwell was heading up the prosecution, representing the people of Los Angeles. For a man known to be a violent misogynist, it must have really perturbed Ramirez to be prosecuted by a woman, and later acts during the trial would draw attention to that animosity.

At his first court appearance, Ramirez raised his hand to the prospective jurors, revealing a pentagram drawn onto his palm, and said loudly, "Hail Satan." Most see this as a scare tactic, and it was, but even more than that, it was Richard's way of introducing himself to a room full of judges. He'd used the fear of Satan as a tool for control and this time was no different. His proclamation for Satanism immediately set just about everyone in the courtroom on edge, which was exactly what he wanted.

But his love of Satan wasn't the only tool for terror Richard would utilize. Using the very quick rumormill of the county jail, he spread a rumor that he planned to have a gun smuggled into the courtroom so that he could shoot the prosecuting attorney. Metal detectors were immediately installed and extensive searches were conducted on those coming and going from the courtroom.

Perhaps one of the more bizarre things that occurred during the trial was the appearance of numerous women, dolled up and making goo-goo eyes at the accused murderer. Richard Ramirez would turn in his seat on occasion to view the sea of women who found his smile engaging. He was, after all, a very handsome young man. Girls skipped classes at high school to be at his trial. Housewives were found primping themselves before entering the courtroom. It was a bizarre turn in the story of Richard Ramirez, and Richard certainly seemed to be amused by it all. In an interview given in 1994, Ramirez reflected on the situation:

> I think the girls are attracted to me because they can relate to me. The girls are nice when you're in my situation, but since I'm in here I spend more time writing to them about the relationship, rather than living it, but there are good friendships formed never-the-less. A couple of them are religious, they come into my life to try and help me.

Richard Munoz Ramirez, The Night Stalker in one of his final mugshots at San Quentin Prison. (Public Domain.)

But to the families of the victims, it did nothing but turn their hunt for justice into a disjointed mockery. Luckily, the jurors were unimpressed with Richard's prowess and were hardly swayed by the circus-like atmosphere.

But the one time the Ramirez jury flinched was on August 14, 1988, when Phyllis Singletary, one of the jurors, failed to arrive at the courtroom. While an alternate juror took Phyllis' place, sheriff's deputies tried to find her. Phyllis Singletary was found later that day, shot to death in her apartment. Though it was eventually proven that she had been killed by her boyfriend (who later committed suicide), it still rattled the jurors, who initially believed that Ramirez had been the one responsible. The general feeling was if he could get to one of them, he could get to all of them. That sudden fear revealed for a moment just how terrified the jury was of Richard Ramirez, the demonic Night Stalker.

A month later, Ramirez was found guilty of all charges, including thirteen counts of murder, five counts of attempted murder, eleven rapes, and fourteen burglaries. The sentence? Death.

"Big deal, death always went with the territory," Richard told reporters after being sentenced. "See you in Disneyland."

Incidentally, with his capture, Richard attained everything he wanted. People feared him, he was considered an icon in the California prison system, and he had the love and adoration of numerous women who visited and wrote to him in prison. One woman in particular, a pretty magazine editor named Doreen Lioy, wrote him over seventy-five letters. Their bond was fairly tight, so much so that when Richard proposed to her, she immediately accepted. Married on October 3, 1996, in San Quentin Prison, their marriage went unconsummated; conjugal visits were forbidden for Death Row inmates. But it barely mattered to either of them. Richard knew that sex always ended in violence, and most likely, Doreen knew that as well. For both of them, it was enough knowing that, when Richard was executed, Doreen would commit suicide. Or so they thought. The two eventually separated. Perhaps Doreen came to her senses and realized what she had married.

On June 7, 2013, with all of his appeals exhausted, Richard Munoz Ramirez found death waiting for him, not in the gas chamber, but in a California hospital. Suffering from B-cell lymphoma and hepatitis C, Ramirez died in relative peace at 9:10 a.m. He was fifty-three years old.

The Vile Files

Luis Alfredo Garavito Cubillos

(1957-)

Luis Alfredo Garavito Cubillosis is a Colombian rapist and child killer who openly admitted to the rape, torture, and murder of nearly 150 young boys. But by his own count, the number could be close to 300. All of his victims were peasant children or street kids, unfortunates that Garavito would lure off the streets with money or gifts. Once he got them alone, he would molest and rape them, cut their throats, and dismembered their bodies. Visible signs of protracted torture were evident on the remains that were recovered. When he was captured in 1999, he confessed gladly and was convicted of 139 murders. His sentence? Thirty years in prison. This obscenely short incarceration is due to the constraints of Colombian law, which limits imprisonment to only thirty years no matter the charge. Due to his cooperation in the investigation, his sentence was reduced to only twenty-two years. Today, Garavito claims to be a changed man, one interested in politics and looking to aid mistreated children. With time off for good behavior, Garavito could see freedom by 2017.

CHAPTER 4

DENNIS NILSEN

"THE KINDLY KILLER"

North London, England

"I did it all for me. Purely selfish. . . .There was no sadistic pleasure in the killing. I killed them as I would like to be killed myself, enjoying the extremity of the death act itself. If I did it to myself I could only experience it once. If I did it to others, I could experience the death act over and over again."

–Dennis Nilsen

It is probably very likely that there were many who quietly questioned why Dennis Nilsen didn't shower with the rest of the men at St. Omer Army Barracks and Training Center in Aldershot, Scotland. The quiet, gentlemanly Army recruit was unusually shy but hardly seemed dangerous. Still, while all the other men showered, Dennis Nilsen waited patiently outside, waiting for the shower room to empty so that he could wash the grime and grit of the day's training off him.

–

But for Dennis, it wasn't a matter of shyness. It was 1961. It was the British Army. Dennis Nilsen was a closeted homosexual. He showered alone so that he would not raise the homophobic ire of his bunk-mates when he would get an erection among them. It was a defense mechanism that Dennis used to preserve not only his life, but also the life he wanted to project toward others. Going to such vigorous lengths to conceal his sexual identity began when he was a young child and ended after it was discovered that he had murdered and dismembered as many as fifteen young men. A depraved and lonely necrophile, and suspected cannibal, Dennis Andrew Nilsen would soon go down in history as one of Britain's most prolific and unusual serial killers.

Like so many of our other cases, Dennis Nilsen's troubles began with his family life. He had been born the second of three children in 1945 to Scottish-born Elizabeth Duthie Whyte and Norwegian infantryman Olav Magnus Moksheim,who had married young while Olav was stationed in Scotland. While Elizabeth seemed ready and fit to be a wife and mother to their kids, Olav was not, choosing to spend his days and many of his nights with his friends and comrades in the Free Norwegian Forces. Unfortunately, it could be honestly said that Olav most likely visited his wife at her parent's home only three times during their six year marriage, producing three children: Olav Jr., Dennis, and Sylvia. By 1948, Elizabeth had reached her breaking point with the absentee father of her children and divorced him.

While Olav was no longer in Dennis' life, his mother's father, Andrew Whyte, was, and he provided a fairly sturdy father figure for Dennis, Olav Jr., and Sylvia. Dennis found himself to be particularly close to his grandfather, more so than the others. A lifelong deep sea fisherman, Andrew Whyte often took young Dennis on long walks along the beaches and harbors of Scotland. When Andrew would be off at sea for months at a time, Dennis would begin to feel a depression come over him that would not abate until his grandfather's return.

But contentment would not stay with Dennis. In fact, all forms of contentment were about to go straight out the window. In 1951, when Dennis was only six years old, he lost his grandfather to a massive heart attack. The resulting funeral would be the one clear memory Dennis Nilsen had of his childhood. He remembered standing by his grandfather's coffin, his own heart beating loudly in his chest as his mother said softly, "See Dennis. There's your grandfather. He's sleeping."

The loss of Dennis's grandfather signaled the slow descent into quiet, antisocial behavior. He would perch himself out by the harbors, watching the herring boats arrive and leave, much like he had done with his grandfather. He pushed aside his family, retreating into his own little world and shunning the affections showered upon him by his mother and her family. This behavior was often attributed to his jealousy of Olav Jr., who always seemed to get the most attention from his mother and stepfather. Olav's popularity didn't make it any easier either. While Olav was fun loving, popular, and outgoing, Dennis was not, and rather than strive to be more like Olav, Dennis instead retracted any and all affection for his family. If they weren't going to give him equal affection, he was going to give them none. But on the rare occasions that Dennis sought out attention, he found that he could talk or play with Sylvia, his younger sister, much better than he could anyone else. For many years, she was his only lifeline to the world outside his own.

In an event that would at length mirror his own murderous methodology, Dennis found himself drowning after he'd been swept out to sea while swimming. Initially panicking, Dennis relaxed, somehow knowing that his grandfather would save him before it was too late. As the saltwater filled his lungs, he began to experience a deep tranquility, a tranquility that was broken when another youth dragged him ashore and saved his life.

By the time he was in the throes of puberty, Dennis had become aware that he was sexually attracted to men, a secret he kept close for most of his life. Even more devastating, yet not wholly surprising, was the fact that the boys Dennis was attracted to bore a resemblance to his sister Sylvia. Being that his sister was his most loved family member, it is hardly surprising that he would seek out someone who resembled the one who had made him feel most content or happy with his life. Dennis Nilsen bottled up all of these feelings and hid them away, ashamed of them, though occasionally those feelings of arousal did come out at possibly the worst times imaginable, most notably when he could no longer resist fondling his older brother Olav and his sister Sylvia as they slept. Though he didn't come right out and say it, Olav seemed to know that his brother was a homosexual; Olav would belittle and demean his younger brother in public and with his friends, referring to Dennis as a "hen." In an outward effort to toughen up, but more likely as an effort to be close to a lot of men, Dennis eventually joined the British Army in 1961. Surprisingly, Dennis flourished, calling those years in the Army some of the best in his life. He was a part of the Catering Corps, where he learned the art of butchering meat, a skill he would use later on in his civilian life for a decidedly other use. Though he still felt the need to shower privately so that his arousal would not elicit suspicion, he did tend to masturbate frequently in the bathroom stalls, allowing himself to indulge any manner of fantasy he chose.

Once Dennis had graduated from training, he found himself stationed in Osnabruck, West Germany, assigned to the 1st Battalion of the Royal Fusiliers as a private. It was here in West Germany that Dennis discovered the powers of alcohol, drinking to excess in order to more easily shuck away his shyness. He would occasionally refer to himself and his colleagues as a "hard working, boozy lot," though in fairness, many of his friends would later say that Dennis consumed the most alcohol of any of them. One of the strangest habits Nilsen had was his conversational skills. Those who hung out with him would later comment that he didn't seem to be talking to them, but rather, to himself. Opinionated, controlling, and exhaustively unusual, Dennis found long-term companionship to be a rare commodity in his life.

During one particular bout with the sauce, Dennis found himself getting overly intoxicated with a young German man. After returning to the man's flat, Dennis soon found himself looking over the passed-out body of the drunken man. His head began to swirl with ideas and fantasies of how he could have total sexual control over a man who was thoroughly and completely supine. If they were asleep or unconscious, they couldn't refuse him. If they were unable to fight, he could finally express his inner lust. It wouldn't be long before those thoughts of a placid, willing partner would become fantasies of dead lovers. He would masturbate constantly, fantasizing about performing sexual acts with the fresh corpses of men, though interestingly enough, Dennis often played both parts in his fantasies: that of the dominant, and that of the submissive (or dead) one. He seemed to be at ease with being in either position.

In 1972, after eleven years in the British Army, Corporal Dennis Nilsen retired from military life and attempted to return to a normal life with his mother and siblings as he considered his next move. Though Dennis had designs on joining the police force, his mother Elizabeth voiced her concern for Dennis' lack of interest in other women, that he should consider marrying and having children. But Dennis' older brother Olav told their mother that Dennis was a homosexual, essentially outing his younger brother with a sneering derision. Dennis could no longer deny it, and he was so traumatized and angered by Olav that the two brothers never again spoke to each other.

Had Dennis not moved to London, the chances of him being ostracized and shunned by his family were virtually irrefutable. In 1973, he began training with the Metropolitan Police, but the stress of trying to balance his personal life with his professional life was too much to bear. Here was a guy who was hardly the perfect masculine specimen clotted into a profession rife with masculine posturing. It was hardly a surprise when Dennis suddenly resigned from the police in December of that same year.

Drifting from one casual encounter to another, Dennis found within him a fondness for auto-erotic asphyxiation, wherein sexual climax is achieved through manual or mutual strangulation to the point of passing out. Dennis was willing to be the choker and the choked, playing both parts with fervent ardor. But this practice, which can lead to death if not practiced responsibly, awakened that old feeling in Dennis of having a completely submissive lover. On numerous occasions, he would choke out his lovers to the point where they would actually pass out cold, leaving Dennis to plunder their bodies as they slept.

Dennis found his niche in social work, taking work at JobCentre, a governmental office that would counsel unemployed men and women and help them find work. He was stationed at a branch on Denmark Street, retaining the same quiet, reserved attitude. Dennis would work for JobCentre until his arrest in 1982, so this was more naturally a fit for his eccentric personality.

One of the only smidgens of normalcy for Dennis Nilsen came in 1975 when he met twenty-year-old David Gallichan, a homeless British man he'd met outside a pub. At the time, Gallichan was being roughed up by a couple of hoods, but Dennis, seeing so much of himself in David, stepped in to defend the young man. As it turns out, David was unemployed, was currently residing in a hostel for homeless youths, and was a homosexual. Dennis must have felt an overwhelming relief when he met David Gallichan. Finally, he was able to be himself around a man, to express his homosexuality. After spending an evening together, the two agreed to live together and, with Dennis employed by JobCentre, employment for David was virtually assured.

Using a good portion of his father's inheritance, Dennis and David moved into a small vacant apartment at 195 Melrose Avenue, located in the village of Cricklewood. Chillingly, Nilsen would broker a deal with the landlord, granting him exclusive use of the garden in the backyard. Fully fenced with a six foot tall dog-eared privacy fence, it was only accessible from Dennis' flat. This garden would come in handy for Dennis later on when he would finally snap.

But much to Dennis' chagrin, the relationship between he and Gallichan began to sour. Within a year, they were sleeping in separate rooms and both were taking lovers on the side. Arguments began to overtake casual conversations and David moved out, leaving Dennis alone, who now believed that he was thoroughly unfit to live with.

David Gallichan was the last lucky man in Dennis Nilsen's life. The majority of those who came after him would never survive the night with Dennis. Beginning in 1978, Dennis Nilsen began to lure men home to his apartment. He would ply them with liquor, offering them a room to sleep in, and wait for them to drink themselves into oblivion. Once they had passed out, Dennis would either strangle them, or hold their unconscious heads below the water in his bathtub.

Once dead, Dennis would bathe the corpse, dress them in fresh, clean clothes, and stage them about his apartment. Nilsen was adamant that he had never had sex with any of the corpses, though he did admit to performing sexual acts upon them. The bodies of the dead would be there for weeks, sometimes months, before Dennis dismembered them and burned their remains in a bonfire in the small private garden. When Dennis moved to a more suburban flat on Melrose Avenue, he would dispose of their flesh and smaller bones down the toilet.

Nilsen's first victim was a fourteen-year-old boy named Stephen Holmes. It was December 30, 1978. Nilsen found Holmes in a nearby pub trying to buy alcohol and he took advantage of the young boy's temptation, luring him back to his apartment with the promise of limitless beer and scotch. After passing out in a drunken stupor, Nilsen had already decided the young boy's fate.

"He was going to stay with me over the New Year whether he wanted to or not," Nilsen later told police.

Strangling Holmes into unconsciousness, Nilsen then drowned the boy in a large bucket filled with water. After masturbating twice over the body of his victim, Dennis Nilsen stowed the corpse beneath the floor boards of his apartment, where it stayed for almost eight months.

"I eased him into his new bed beneath the floorboards," Nilsen once wrote. "A week later, I wondered whether his body had changed at all or had started to decompose. I disinterred him and pulled the dirt-stained youth up onto the floor. His skin was very dirty. I stripped myself naked and carried him into the bathroom and washed the body. There was practically no discoloration and his skin was pale white. His limbs were more relaxed than when I had put him down there."

During that time, Dennis would visit and revisit his dead lover, fawning over him, reliving the moments that had led to this point in time. When the remains became too decomposed to be recognized, Dennis Nilsen took the body to his garden and burned it over a bonfire.

Dennis Nilsen now found purpose in his life, the means to end the loneliness in his life. Most of the men he lured back to his apartment found nothing but death and immortality in the body count of a serial killer. But there were some who survived, escaped, and even contacted police. In each instance, Nilsen would be questioned, but his victims would either opt to not press charges, or Nilsen's charm would send the cops away happy.

But these instances were very few and far between as Dennis Nilsen perfected his methods of stalking, hunting, and killing his prey. He even began to photograph his kills, a new idea brought about by the purchase of a new Polaroid instant camera. In this way, he could hold on to his lovers forever in the form of a photograph even after the body had been disposed of in the gardens. He would stage the corpses in provocative and suggestive poses, masturbate over them, kiss and caress their cold flesh, and keep their bodies clean with ritualistic baths. When the bodies began to bloat and decompose, into the floorboards they would go. The foulness of decay and the onset of insects signaled their removal to the bonfires out back.

It was the overpowering stench, not only from the apartment but also from the frequent bonfires, that riled his neighbors into badgering the landlord to evict Nilsen, which he did, yet no one seemed to question why such a stench was emanating from the apartment. Forced to move, Nilsen's new apartment in Muswell Hill had no sub-floor covered by floorboards, nor did he have a private garden in which to burn his victims. He was forced to change his methods, opting to store body parts in plastic bags, lined steamer trunks, and various drawers. He began to use acid baths and cooking pots to break down flesh into a soupy mixture that could be flushed down the toilet. The remaining bones would be broken down into smaller parts and put out into the trash for pickup by garbagemen.

"I could only relate to a dead image of the person I could love. The image of my dead grandfather would be the model of him at his most striking in my mind," Nilsen later explained. "It seems necessary for them to have been dead in order that I could express those feelings which were the feelings I held sacred for my grandfather . . . it was a pseudo-sexual, infantile love which had not yet developed and matured. The sight of them brought me a bitter sweetness and a temporary peace and fulfillment."

Dennis Nilsen's murder spree came to an end in February of 1983, when complaints of a clogged drain drew the attention of the apartment building's landlord, who dispatched a plumber named Michael Cattran. Opening a drain cover on the side of the house, Cattran discovered that the drain was packed with soft, flesh-like material with small fragments of bone dotted throughout. The police were contacted and samples of the material were sent to a pathologist for analysis. The results were bone-chilling: it was indeed human flesh and the bones looked to be from a human hand. While examining the pipe, it was determined by police that the matter had been flushed down the toilet by the resident on the top floor apartment.

Police detectives immediately confronted Nilsen and were surprised by his willingness to confess.

"It's a long story; it goes back a long time," Nilsen told the detectives. "I'll tell you everything. I want to get it off my chest. Not here. . . at the police station."

On the drive to the police station, the detectives asked Dennis Nilsen if the remains in his apartment belonged to one person or two. Without batting an eye and without a nick of inflection in his voice, he calmly replied, "Neither. Maybe fifteen or sixteen, since 1978."

Indeed, forensic crews found bags filled with body parts stuffed into cabinets and cupboards. Human bones and flesh were found hidden in drawers in the bathroom. A tea chest in the living room turned up hidden remains as well. Altogether, forensic crews found the remains of what looked to be three men, men Nilsen would identify later as an anonymous hook-up, a man he knew only as John the Guardsman (later identified as John Howlett) and a man named Stephen Sinclair.

But the forensic team's work was hardly finished. Excavations at Nilsen's former residences yielded the fragments of eight more bodies in the gardens. Dennis Nilsen's confession to police would span sixteen separate interviews and last a total of thirty hours. He was indicted for the murders of six men and the attempted murders of two others who came forward with their claims after Nilsen was arrested. As in his normal life, Nilsen was certain that no one could defend him but himself. No one would—or could—understand. He fought vehemently to defend himself, but eventually relented, allowing a public defender to argue his interests before the Crown and the court of British public opinion.

On November 3, 1983, less than twenty-four hours after closing arguments had concluded, the jury returned to the courts and pronounced Dennis Nilsen guilty. The judge handed down a life sentence to Nilsen, with a recommendation that he serve at least twenty-five years before he could be considered for parole. This stipulation would be knocked down and replaced with what was called a "whole life tariff," which essentially meant that Dennis Nilsen would never again see the outside a prison. This didn't affect Dennis much; he resisted any appeals for freedom and insisted on seeing his punishment through to the end. He would eventually pen an autobiography, which many saw as Nilsen justifying the senseless murders of innocent men. Certainly, this was not a trait held by Dennis alone. Most serial killers find scapegoats to justify their murderous impulses, blaming their mother or their father, the way of the world, or the way the wind blew.

Today, Dennis Nilsen sits in HMP Full Sutton Prison, reading, painting, and writing letters to those who write to him. In the years since his conviction, his mother seems to have embraced him more than she had before his incarceration.

Interviews she gave before her death reveal an unwavering love for her son, despite the horrific acts he committed in her absence.

The Vile Files

Roberto Succo

(April 3, 1962-May 23, 1988)

Italian serial killer Roberto Succo was a deviant, paranoid schizophrenic who began his career in murder by killing his parents in 1981. After a brief incarceration, he went on a killing spree, killing five policemen in cold blood. He escaped prison in 1988, and went off on another bloody killing spree, raping and murdering his way across four countries before finally being caught in Northern Italy, just a few miles from his old hometown. Returned to a mental hospital in Toulon, Italy, he would eventually commit suicide in his cell by suffocating himself with a plastic bag.

CHAPTER 5

TSUMOTO MIYAZAKI

"THE OTAKU KILLER"

Otaku, Japan

"There are devils about."
—**Tsumoto Miyazaki**

He kept hiding his hands. The quiet man from Itsukachi sat there before the policemen, constantly drawing his hands up into his sleeves. But the presence of the handcuffs kept him from concealing them completely and it was hard not to notice the deformities. The fingers were constantly gnarled and drawn in, looking clawlike. Doctors would later testify that the man's wrists had also been permanently fused to those hands. When he wanted to move his hands, he would need to move his entire arm, creating an odd jerking motion that stood out whenever he attempted it. All of this was due to his premature birth, he would tell them, almost as if he'd been cursed at birth.

Tsumoto Miyazaki was cursed, but it was a curse he'd wrought, in part, upon himself. By the time police had caught up to him, he'd allowed his curse to proliferate and swallow up the lives of four young girls, all under the age of eight years. But their deaths were nothing compared to what happened to them afterward.

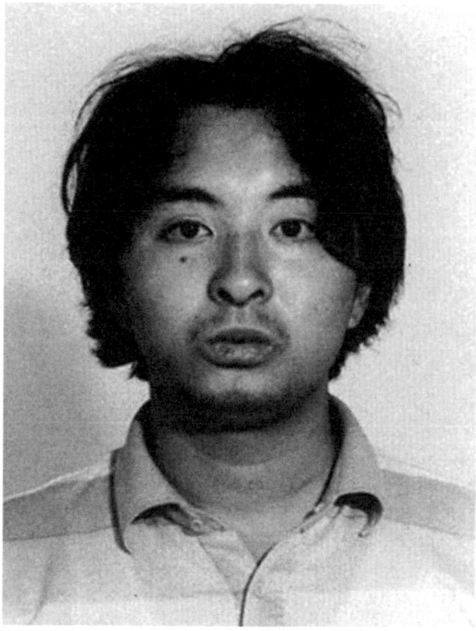

The Otaku Killer, Tstumo Miyazaki, shortly after his arrest for the rape and murder of four little girls.

Born on August 21, 1962, Tsumoto Miyazaki arrived in the world in a less than spectacular manner. Not only was he two months premature, but he was the only child of his parents to be deformed. As Miyazaki grew, he became more and more aware of his handicap. His peers at school ostracized and bullied him because of it, and he was convinced that his parents were ashamed of him. As a result, Miyazaki became withdrawn and quiet, finding solace in the sex-and-violence choked pages of Japanese manga comics and the ultraviolent horror films of Japan, Hong Kong, and the United States.

Miyazaki's grades plummeted, landing him at the bottom of his class, yet another disappointment for his perfectionist parents. Once he graduated from Medei Nakano High School, he'd dropped yet another disappointment in their laps: Tsumoto Miyazaki refused to follow his father's wish and become an English teacher. Instead, he chose to forgo college and attend only junior college, majoring in photo technology.

Myriad personal problems began to plague Miyazaki. His constant diet of pornographic films and books had, at such a young age, desensitized him from even the most sincere and ordinary relationship. Hardcore pornography and sexual conduct were no longer stimulating and he sought out more perverse forms of pornography and horror films. He soon found himself frequenting underground adult bookstores in Japan's seedier neighborhoods, finding himself drawn to snuff films and child pornography. His bookshelves would soon became monstrous, with illegal pornographic films mingling freely with classic gore films by George A. Romero and Lucio Fulci, as well as the notorious Guinea Pig films, well known for depicting brutal and hyper-realistic murders and mutilations. In fact, it was the Guinea Pig episode entitled "Flowers of Blood and Flesh" that provided Miyazaki with his method of butchering his victims; he used the film more as a guide for dissection than for any kind of entertainment value. He would also begin to employ illicit voyeurism into his cadre of perversity; well versed in how to use a camera, Miyazaki began attending women's college tennis matches in order to photograph the players, using the photos as an aid for masturbation.

Sometime in the mid-1980s, Miyazaki moved back to Itsukachi and lived with his parents once more, sharing a small room with his one of his sisters. He was already in the midst of a deep depression and most everyone in his family seemed to reject him except for his grandfather. The only reason he was allowed back in the house was because his parents felt it was their duty to house him. The shunning of Tsumoto affected him more than he had anticipated; during his confession to police, he commented, "If I tried to talk to my parents about my problems, they'd just brush me off. I even thought about suicide."

Rejection from his two sisters, Setsuko and Haruko, came first, most likely caused by his disturbing sense of morbid sexuality. It would not surprise anyone if he had tried to rape or molest them during the time he spent at his parent's home. Whether or not this actually happened is entirely up for debate, but his sisters would have in the very least noticed his perversities and kept their distances from him.

Miyazaki found solace in the relationship he had with his grandfather, who seemed to blindly support his grandson despite any abnormal tendencies. But his grandfather's death in May of 1988 crippled him even more emotionally, casting him further into a wellspring of dark depression. Confused, hurt, and suffering deep loss, Miyazaki attempted to retain part of his grandfather by eating some of his ashes. Something in Miyazaki snapped to the point where he no longer cared what anyone thought and any tolerance for rules went screaming out the window. He constantly spied on his sisters, attacking them when they protested. He even attacked his own mother when she called him out on his disturbing behavior. Before he struck and tried to strangle her, Reiki Miyazaki ordered him to get a job and work more and spend less time with his videos and comic books. Reined in by his father, Miyazaki soon moved out and found an apartment of his own.

Between the month of May and August, Miyazaki's mind continued to warp, his private life of debauchery and violence moving to the forefront of his daily life. The so-called normal people moving about their lives drew more attention to his own deformed life, both physically and mentally. He wasn't like anyone else, that was for certain, and now he no longer cared. Like most classic serial killers, Miyazaki would soon find that part of himself that he no longer wanted to see. "I felt all alone," Miyazaki explained later. "And whenever I saw a little girl playing on her own, it was almost like seeing myself."

Miyazaki's descent into violent and criminal madness was quick and terrifying. Almost as soon as he had finally cut ties with his family for good, Miyazaki began seeking out victims. But it is entirely possible that the murder of children came about accidentally, almost as a spontaneous act following the molestation and rape of them. It would be an effort to quiet a witness, but it would be an act he would find himself enjoying.

His first victim was four-year-old Mari Konno. Miyazaki stole her as she played in the front yard of a friend's house. Driving Mari to a secluded location in the woods near his new home, Miyazaki sat alongside her silently for almost thirty minutes as he mustered the courage to kill the girl. Eventually gaining the courage, he ruthlessly strangled her with both of his gnarled hands and no doubt relished the ferocity with which Mari kicked. He raped her corpse when he was finished, leaving her stripped and abused little body on the hillside near his home. Miyazaki returned home to clean himself up and a few days later, returned to the scene and removed her hands and feet, keeping them as trophies of his kill. He would cremate the remaining parts of her body in his furnace.

A few days later, Mari's family would receive a mysterious box of finely burnt ashes. Among the ashes were photos of Mari's clothes, several of her teeth, and a postcard that read: "Mari. Cremated. Bones. Investigate. Prove." Over the course of several days, he would phone Mari's home and maintain silence when her parents would answer. It was reported that sometimes the phone would ring for up to twenty minutes before they finally either answered the phone or unhooked it.

This was to become Miyazaki's trademark, which he employed three more times before he would be caught. On October 3, 1988, Miyazaki abducted, murdered, and raped seven-year-old Masami Yoshizawa. The following December, he kidnapped four-year-old Erika Namba as she walked home. Miyazaki drove to an isolated parking lot where he forced her to strip in the back seat. As she did, Miyazaki began to take pictures of her, barking orders at her as he snapped picture after picture after picture. With his roll of film depleted, Miyazaki strangled the girl and left her to decay in the parking lot. A note, similar to one he sent to Mari's parents, would arrive at Erika's home a few days later.

"Erika. Cold. Cough. Throat. Rest. Death" it read.

And again, he would crank-call Erika's family home, remaining eerily quiet as he listened to her mother and father repeatedly ask who was calling.

Miyazaki's final murder victim would also be his favorite. On June 6, 1989, Miyazaki approached five-year-old Ayako Nomoto on a playground. Using clever tactics he'd honed over the last few kills, he was able to charm his way into her good graces, and she agreed to let Miyazaki photograph her. But once inside the car, like all of his other victims, Ayako soon found only horrific death between his two gnarled and deformed hands. But in the case of Ayako, her killer chose not to leave her, but take her home with him. Once there, Miyazaki spent the next two days raping and molesting her corpse. He drank her blood and ate parts of her body. He even photographed and took videos of her in different poses. When Ayako began to decompose, he dismembered her, leaving her torso in a graveyard and her head in the nearby hills. Some say he couldn't bear to be away from her, others believe he was afraid of the encroaching police investigations. Whatever the case, he returned two weeks later to retrieve the remains, which he hid in his closet.

Brazen and full of self-serving courage from the murders he'd been committing, Miyazaki made his first and last mistake. This was an error many serial murderers would make in their evolution from mere mortal to a god of death and destruction. There would simply be no conscience left in them and all that would remain would be an overwhelming feeling of elated indestructibility, a feeling of pure superiority over their prey. Thankfully, this conceit would often lead to their downfall, and Miyazaki was no exception.

On July 23, 1989, he'd talked a ten-year-old girl into getting into the backseat of his car. The girl was shocked to find Miyazaki naked alongside her and her fear kept her from screaming out in terror. As he began to molest the girl with the telephoto lens of his camera, he was surprised and terrified when he was suddenly pulled from his car by the girl's father.

Miyazaki fled, naked, on foot, but returned to pick up his car later that night. Naturally, he was arrested by police, who had been waiting patiently for him to return. To the police, he was just another pervert. They had no idea that they had just captured the most wanted villain in Otaku. As Tsumoto Miyazaki sat handcuffed in a police station, his calm demeanor clashed with the brutality of the accusations leveled at him. To the police, he was eerily calm and indifferent to the interrogation he was being run through. But as he waded through questions from police, detectives were raiding and looting his apartment, searching for evidence of his crimes. While the police were hoping to find evidence of his rampant pedophilia, they were absolutely shocked to find child-size hands and feet, nearly mummified by now, in his closet. In addition, a number of video tapes and photographs of his victims were found amongst his collection of over 5,000 anime and horror film VHS tapes. Not only was this man a pedophile and a child pornographer, but he was also the horrific child killer they'd been searching for all along.

Miyazaki was all too happy to confess, enrapturing the police with a cruel story of pedophilia, murder, and cannibalism. He left no story untold and once the story leaked out to the Japanese media, he became christened "The Otaku Killer" and newspapers referred to him as "Dracula." Tsumoto Miyazaki seemed amused by it but dared not show it. He was constantly in the newspapers, usually photographed as he returned to crime scenes with police and homicide detectives as a part of his confession. Miyazaki's father, thoroughly embarrassed and dishonored by his son's actions, refused to pay for his son's legal defense. The senior Miyazaki would disown Tsumoto and finally commit suicide in 1994, unable to bear living with the horror his son had wrought upon his victims, their families, and his own family.

Tsumoto Miyazaki suffered from many different emotional maladies in his life, all of which contributed to his murderous behavior, of that there is little doubt. But it was one of the most human of emotions that triggered the carnage, one nearly every human on Earth has struggled with at one time or another.

Miyazaki's deformity, in a world already pressing for perfection, was a source of constant disgrace for his parents and no matter what he did, he would still be the one with deformed hands, a curse visited upon the living by the vengeful gods. His envy stemmed from the beauty he beheld in the hands of children, specifically young girls who he believed mirrored his own quiet, demure soul. Miyazaki started out coveting their perfect hands, embracing them with his own twisted vision of love. But seeing his gnarled hands on their perfect flesh turned his envy into contempt and he was reminded of his ghastly imperfections.

In the wake of Miyazaki's crimes, a number of copycat murderers came out of the woodwork. One even claimed to be the next Tsumoto Miyazaki, a demand met with scorn by the original killer himself. "I won't allow him to call himself 'the second Tsumoto Miyazaki' when he hasn't even undergone a psychiatric examination," was Miyazaki's reported response.

At his trial, Tsutumo Miyazaki naturally attempted to plead not guilty by reason of insanity, but his seemingly formidable defense almost immediately hit a brick wall when it met up with the prosecution's case, which successfully proved that, while Tsumoto Miyazaki was suffering paranoid schizophrenia, he was in complete control of his faculties at the time of the murders. He was convicted and sentenced to die by hanging on April 14, 1997.

But it wasn't as easy as it may seem. Mental health advocates argued for a retrial, stating that Miyazaki's mental health had essentially forced his hand and that he didn't receive a fair trial from a prosecutor who was determined to exact revenge for the four little girls slain by Miyazaki. Though the mental health advocates made some headway, their cause was eventually shot down by the Tokyo District Court, which argued otherwise. In a statement following their judgment, the courts stated that Miyazaki was "still aware of the magnitude and consequences of his crimes and therefore accountable."

But even though the Tokyo District Court, and subsequently the Japanese Supreme Court, had ruled Miyazaki should die, the killer himself still held out an obscene hope that he would see daylight once more, writing in a letter, "I think I will be acquitted. I don't intend to apologize to the bereaved families." Even before his death, he was courting pen-pals into sending him ultra-violent comic books, complaining that the prison he was in didn't have any available.

Finally, in what seemed to be the culmination of a brazen lifetime of contempt for humanity, Miyazaki was hanged on June 17, 2008, putting an end to the boogeyman that had been haunting the small, troubled town of Otaku, Japan. Eventually, though, like all boogeymen, he would return to Japan and the world in another, more terrifying form, capable of even more horrors than the one who came before him.

The Vile Files

Yang Xinhai

(July 29, 1968-February 14, 2004)

Demented killer Yang Xinhai, China's "Monster Killer," confessed to murdering sixty-five people and raping twenty-three women across the Henan, Anhui, Hebei, and Shandong provinces of China. From 1999 to 2003, Xinhai burglarized, raped, and murdered entire families, often improvising his weapons with materials found on the scene. He was captured purely by accident when he was detained and questioned by police outside a nightclub in Hebei for appearing too suspicious. He was tried and convicted February 1, 2004, and executed only two weeks later.

CHAPTER 6

HENRY LEE LUCAS

"THE CONFESSION KILLER"

Ringgold, Texas

"Killing someone is just like walking outdoors. If I wanted a victim, I'd just go and get one."
—**Henry Lee Lucas**

The two had been fighting vehemently the night of Kate Rich's murder. Becky was absolutely tired of the constant wandering and she was demanding that she and Henry settle down. She demanded that he give up his life of crime and earn an honest living like a real man. She was an angry young woman and was saying what most women on the edge would say. But for Henry, Becky Powell now sounded—and acted—just like his mother. Later, he would lead investigators to two shallow graves, graves which held the remains of Kate Rich and his once-beloved, Frieda "Becky" Powell.

—

With his shiftless, glass eye and standoffish demeanor, Henry Lee Lucas just seemed to naturally emote a dark, James Dean attitude. But once you got past his shifty appearance, his smooth, red-neckish charm would pull you in. It was hard not to be charmed by him to some degree, whether you were a guy talking shop with him at a diner, or a naive young girl who thought he was just the nicest guy. But what hid behind Henry's eyes was nothing short of pure evil.

Or so he would have you believe. Truth be told, most people have only a passing knowledge of Henry's exploits and they see him as a brutal, prolific killer who had confessed to nearly 600 murders of prostitutes, hitchhikers, housewives, and just about every other kind of person in America. But was he really as prolific as he made himself out to be?

Born on August 23, 1936, in the deep rural town of Blacksburg, Virginia, Henry had it rough from the start. His mother Viola was a known prostitute, and his father was an alcoholic railroad worker. According to Henry, his mother routinely forced him to watch her have sex with her clients, dressed him in girl's clothing, and verbally and physically abused him in front of friends and family. Adding to this constant state of humiliation was the horrifying loss of his right eye, which he lost after being stabbed by his older brother. Henry's parents allowed the injury to go untreated for days until the eye finally began to wither away. By the time someone finally got young Henry to a doctor, there was no other recourse but to remove the dead eye and replace it with a glass one.

Most times of the day and night, Henry was an odd and fairly sad sight: dressed like a little girl with a wandering glass eye. He was prone to telling outlandish stories to his classmates, complete with equally outlandish claims, all for the sake of gaining some kind of attention. The attention he received, however, was more or less the kind a circus sideshow performer would garner. But his stories got attention nonetheless, and it was a habit he would carry on well into adulthood.

The only person who really had any inkling of an idea of what young Henry was enduring was his father, Anderson Lucas. Anderson had lost both of his legs while working on the railroad, and Viola Lucas would continually make fun of her husband, knowing that he could never chase her and, as the sole breadwinner of the house, she had carte blanche to do anything she pleased. Anderson's alcoholism escalated to the point where he no longer was Anderson, but a shade. Eventually, in 1949 when Henry was only thirteen years old, Anderson Lucas died of hypothermia, having passed out in the middle of a blizzard. He was found frozen to death, leaning up against the side of the house, crutches at his side. The death of his father left a traumatic and enduring scar on Henry; he'd loved his dad so much and saw him as his only friend and ally in the house. But now, there was only his mother and it was all about to get worse.

As Henry endured his painful life at home, he found an outlet for his rage fairly easily: the killing of small animals and the act of bestial necrophilia. It would be easy to say that Henry started these acts in an effort to control something, that the visage of his mother was on the face of every animal that he squeezed the life out of. That is the pattern of the majority of the world's serial killers. But realistically, Henry most likely just enjoyed it, remarking, "Having sex with a dead animal was better than having sex with a live woman."

Henry quit school at age fifteen while he was in the sixth grade, adding an exclamation point to this act by running away from home. This would have been around 1951. Not surprisingly, no one came to look for him and young Henry Lee Lucas found himself drifting from town to town all over the state of Virginia. He later claimed to have committed his first murder shortly thereafter, killing a seventeen-year-old girl named Laura Burnsley when she spurned his sexual advances. But like most of his later, and more horrific confessions, he would backslide on this admission and claim that Laura had been killed by someone else; he just took credit for it. Indeed, no evidence existed that proved he had killed her. In fact, no one placed Henry Lee Lucas anywhere near Laura Burnsley prior to her murder. But the law did catch up to Henry in one way: in 1954, he was arrested, tried, convicted, and sentenced to four years in prison on over a dozen counts of burglary in the Richmond, Virginia area. At just eighteen years of age, Henry began his first stint in prison, but certainly not his last.

Prison life was torturous for Henry and he continually sought out ways to escape. He succeeded in 1957, spending three days on the lam until he was recaptured. Henry never tried to escape again after that, opting to do his time honestly so that no further time would be added to what already felt like a tremendously long sentence.

Released back into society in 1959, Henry went to Tecumseh, Michigan, to live with his half-sister Opal and her family. Lucas later claimed that, once he'd been released, he was angry, frightened, and mean. He also became quite fond of liquor and he was seldom sober. "I'd drink seven days a week, if I was able," he later said.

But Henry had more to live for now that he was out of prison. While in the joint, he'd struck up a relationship with a woman named Stella. Their pen-pal correspondence was, until that point, possibly the healthiest relationship Henry had ever been in and he desired, loved, and respected Stella more than he had any other woman. She had even begun to erase the bad feelings he'd had toward his mother, and when he proposed to her, Stella eagerly said yes.

But things changed quickly when Viola Lucas came to visit her daughter and Henry in Michigan in 1960. Older, meaner, and quite a bit crazier, Viola wanted Henry to come back to Virginia to take care of her and her home. Of course, Henry refused and stormed off.

Viola found Henry and Stella in a bar, celebrating their engagement and planning their wedding. Crashing the small party, Viola started an argument with them both. Realizing Henry wouldn't be swayed, she turned her wrath upon Stella, berating and swearing at the helpless woman. Exasperated, Stella left both of them in the bar, all the while announcing that the marriage was off. Henry was done with his mother. Again, she had taken something from him that he loved and tossed it away. Henry was done cowering in the corner from his mother.

The both of them returned to Opal's house, albeit separately. But once both were back in the house, the argument picked up where they had left off. Viola was adamant that her son return to Virginia to care for her and the house, and Henry wanted nothing to do with it. But the argument wasn't clean, and Viola stooped to many lows, even accusing Henry of having an incestuous affair with Opal. The argument took a dark turn when Viola picked up a broom stick and wailed it upon Henry, much like she had when he was a child.

It was all the years of abusive behavior. The arduous prison time he'd served. The years of humiliation aimed at him by his domineering and downright mean mother. According to Henry, when he felt the broomstick make contact with his skull, he turned and smacked Viola Lucas alongside the neck. As she fell, he tried to catch her, but realized that he couldn't because there was a knife in his hand and she was bleeding.

Henry couldn't recall how the knife got into his hand and the wound on his mother's neck wasn't life threatening. But the fall resulted in Viola splitting her head open. As she lay motionless in a growing pool of blood, Henry fled back to Virginia. In reality, Viola wasn't dead at the time, but she would soon suffer a massive heart attack as a result of blood loss. Henry was picked up by police a few days later and he was given twenty years in prison. As a resident of the prison's psychiatric ward, Henry was the subject of meticulous psychological tests and intensive psychotherapeutic procedures, all designed to make him more adaptable to the outside rather than heal the emotional wounds he'd suffered for most of his life. In some ways Henry came to terms with his mother's actions. "She done pushed me beyond the limit of my caring. I don't say it's her fault. It's her life. I was just stretched to a point where I wasn't going to be pushed no further."

In 1970, ten years into his sentence, Henry was granted parole. But the convicted killer protested. He wasn't ready. "When they put me out on parole, I said I'm not ready to go. I told them all, the warden, the psychologist, everyone that I was going to kill."

The death of Viola Lucas seemed to trigger an undying madness in Henry that would never be squelched. While doing time for his mother's murder, he began hearing voices in his head, voices that continually taunted and teased him day and night. His mother's voice was strongest, but there were others there as well, voices that haunted him, telling him he was nothing, telling him he would die in prison, telling him that he was good for nothing but being a lying, murdering bastard. They were voices Henry was eventually able to quiet somewhat and once he was released, they seemed to stay away altogether.

In 1975, he married a woman named Betty Crawford to whom he had been writing while in prison, not unlike how he'd met Stella, but he abandoned her when her young daughters, ages six and nine, both accused Henry of sexual abusing them. Drifting around and about, calling in favors from various relatives who hadn't shunned him for murdering his mother and, sleeping in flophouses and abandoned homes, Henry soon found himself in Jacksonville, Florida, living with an old friend named Ottis Toole, Ottis's parents, and Frieda Powell, Ottis's fifteen year-old niece. At the time, Ottis Toole was well on his way to becoming

Florida's most hardworking serial killer, leaving a trail of bodies all over Florida. He was a man to whom Henry could definitely relate.

Henry and Ottis had met at a local soup kitchen in Jacksonville. Going back to Ottis's home, he and Henry had sex, eventually becoming regular lovers, traveling the country together as they committed murder after murder. But Ottis was the jealous type. Whenever Henry would pick up a female hitchhiker or a prostitute, kill her, then have sex with her, Ottis would almost always go crazy, lashing out at the dead woman's body, mutilating and desecrating her even more than Henry had, all because she took Henry's attention away from him.

"Ottis was a sick person. He was a homosexual. I'm not saying all homosexuals are sick, ya know," Henry said in a prison interview. "But *he* was. Mentally sick."

For the most part, life was stable for Henry at this time and he finally set about getting his life right. He found steady work as a roofer and mechanic. Frieda, who frequently went by her middle name "Becky," had taken quite a shine to Henry, despite his somewhat frightening, sleazy image. Henry would later claim that Becky would constantly come on to him, asking for sex whenever she could, advances that Henry always rebuffed. In Becky Powell, Henry found an angel, someone who genuinely cared for him. But Henry Lee Lucas also knew what he was: a monster who equated sex with death, and vice versa. Rebuffing Becky Powell's advances was Henry's way of keeping the young girl alive, for to him, she was an angel, not a filthy whore like the others.

But things were different with Ottis. Henry took it upon himself to re-educate Toole in how to properly murder someone without leaving trace evidence or patterns behind for police to use. Toole, himself already a degenerate arsonist, rapist, and murderer, took to the schooling happily. Henry advised him to vary his methods of murder so that a pattern couldn't be established linking them to any one crime. The two never stayed in one place after committing the murder. Constantly on the move, they eluded both capture and suspicion. By the time the corpses were found, Henry and Ottis were two states away with absolutely nothing to connect them to the deceased.

"He was doing his crimes all one way," Lucas said. "I started to correct him in his ways, in doing the crime where he wouldn't leave information."

The year 1980 found Henry's most famous murder, that of a still unidentified female hitchhiker nicknamed "Orange Socks," for that was the only article of clothing she was wearing when her body was found in a culvert on Interstate 35 near Georgetown, Texas. She had been strangled, raped, then unceremoniously dumped over the guardrail. She was believed to be a destitute hitchhiker heading west; authorities didn't recognize her as a known prostitute in the area. Female hitchhikers like "Orange Socks" were a favorite target for Lucas, who would murder them coldly before raping their corpses. Toole would do the same, though he always opted for male hitchhikers instead. The two would murder anyone they robbed or carjacked. No one would be left alive who would be able to somehow tell another what they looked like or what their names were.

It was during their cross-country trek that Ottis Toole supposedly introduced Henry Lee Lucas to the Hand of Death cult, a Satanic sect that practiced child sacrifice and used rape as a tool of punishment. Members of the cult allegedly trained Toole and Lucas to be professional killers, whose job it was to eradicate any of the sect's enemies or turncoats. However, while Blood Cults are a very real institution, particularly in Texas and towns close to the Mexican border, no such cult is known to have ever existed as relating to this trek. Police agencies eventually blew off Lucas and Toole's stories as the nonsensical ramblings of men who thought they were more important than they actually were.

But Henry and Ottis' lives of murder and terror came to a pause in 1982, when they found out that Becky Powell had been placed in a state shelter following the tragic deaths of her mother and grandmother. It wasn't difficult for Henry to convince Becky to escape the state shelter, and together they fled to California. Once there, they drifted from motel to motel, finding odd jobs here and there. All the while, Henry continued to turn away Becky's sexual advances—she saw them not so much as runaway lovers but as husband and wife. Henry adored Becky and he loved caring for her and providing for her. But sexual relations were a trigger for Henry's murderous libido. It was a demon in him, nestled and curled up comfortably just under the skin. Those who saw the demon erupt never lived to describe it. This was also the reason why Henry could function better in a homosexual relationship, namely with Ottis Toole, who was almost a mirror of Henry himself. Henry could—in his own narcissistic way, which is a trait shared by all serial killers—have sex with himself, the only person he trusted in the world. But somewhere along the way, Ottis and Henry had a massive falling out, whereupon Ottis returned to Florida, leaving Henry and Becky out on the road together.

Henry's employers noticed how close he and Becky were, and they were impressed at how seriously Henry took his job at the roofing company. The boss offered Henry and Becky a job in his old hometown of Ringgold, Texas, with Henry continuing his roofing jobs through another office, and Becky caring for his ailing mother, eighty-two-year-old Kate Rich. They took him up on the offer, but found themselves homeless and jobless by month's end. Turns out, Henry and Becky had been slacking off on their jobs and stealing money from Kate Rich's checking account.

Having to start all over again was taking its toll on Henry and Becky. They'd hooked up with a religious commune near Kate Rich's place, and Henry was offered a job doing maintenance in exchange for an apartment. Becky, meanwhile, became homesick for Florida and demanded to be taken back. She must have also grown tired of constantly being sexually rejected by Henry, though that was most definitely for her own good.

It all came crashing down for all of them late in 1982 when Henry and Becky allegedly murdered Kate Rich, took a substantial amount of cash, and began a trek back toward Florida. However, it didn't take long before police, tipped off by Kate Rich's suspicious family, pulled over a car owned by Kate Rich. They found

Henry Lee Lucas behind the driver's wheel and immediately took him into custody. But according to Kate Rich's family, Henry had had an accomplice, Becky Powell. Eerily, Henry was alone when he was found. Where was Becky Powell? According to Henry, she'd ditched him in Bowie, Texas. But his charade didn't last long. Henry knew he was caught. Not only did he confess to the murder of Kate Rich, he told the truth about what happened to Becky Powell.

While hitchhiking on a deserted back road, an argument between Henry and Becky turned physical as Becky slapped Henry violently. Henry retaliated by stabbing her deep in the chest with his knife, a tool he'd stolen from one of his jobs as a meatcutter at a butcher's shop. Horrified by what he had done, Henry watched the only woman who ever truly loved him die quickly in front of him. "She was gone before I knew it," he later recalled. But the moment of regret faded quickly, for he laid out Becky's corpse on the ground and raped her lifeless body, referring to the sex as being the best he'd ever had. Once he had finished, he dismembered her corpse into nine pieces and spread them about a nearby field. He truly seemed to regret Becky's murder, but knew he could do little to rectify it. Instead, he returned to the scene, collected as many body parts as he could find, and buried them next to Kate Rich. Henry would eventually return to the site one last time when he led police to the graves. But while the police and Henry both knew he had committed those murders, forensic analysis could not determine if Henry had actually been the one to kill them. No evidence was ever found corroborating his story. No bite marks, no hairs, no semen. Nothing. The only thing police detectives had was Henry's word and his knowledge of their burial site. It was a loophole the size of Texas and one that they were all afraid Henry's defense team would utilize.

When Henry was returned to the jail in Williamson County, Texas, detectives from all over the state descended upon him with their cold case files, hoping that this man might be able to end speculation over who killed these massive numbers of men and women. Henry didn't disappoint. In fact, he was able to clear up 219 unsolved murders from all over the state of Texas.

Forensic analysis of the victims, much like the analysis of Kate Rich and Becky Powell, proved inconclusive. Bite marks didn't match Henry's bite radius. It wasn't until forensic psychologists ran an exhausting battery of tests on Henry that they uncovered what may have led to Henry's constant confessing. From a very early age all the way up until he was in the jail cell, Henry Lee Lucas liked to tell tales. The more outlandish and horrific, the better. It was a way for a hopelessly banal little boy to garner amazing attention and it hardly seemed to matter what attention he received, be it good or bad. It was a pattern of behavior that he carried with him every day of his life. But by now, Henry Lee Lucas didn't even know if he was telling the truth or not.

Although Henry eventually confessed to almost 600 murders, he was convicted of only ten in 1985, including Kate Rich, Becky Powell, and "Orange Socks." He'd received nine life sentences, plus one death penalty conviction for the rape and murder of Orange Socks.

Most of those convictions were based solely on Henry's elaborate and oftentimes confusing confessions, which were most often contradicted by forensic evidence. Incredibly, police and Texas Rangers had also allowed Henry to peruse open cold case files, essentially allowing Henry to fabricate very detailed confessions. Time sheets and eyewitness testimony from Henry's employers from various jobs around Texas, Florida, and California placed him away from many of the crime scenes before, during, and after the murders themselves. A report on the guilt or innocence of Henry Lee Lucas was published by Texas State Attorney General Jim Mattox, who wrote:

> Lucas was confessing to hundreds of murders. . . those with custody of Lucas did nothing to bring an end to this hoax . . . We have found information that would lead us to believe that some officials 'cleared cases' just to get them off the books.

It was this evidence alone that got his death sentence commuted to life imprisonment in 1998 by then Governor George W. Bush. Governor Bush pointed out the inaccuracies of Henry's involvement in the "Orange Socks" murder in particular, the one conviction that had gotten him his death penalty.

> "Henry Lee Lucas is unquestionably guilty of other despicable crimes which he has been sentenced to spend the rest of his life in prison," said Bush. "However, I believe there is enough doubt about this particular crime that the state of Texas should not impose its ultimate penalty by executing him."

After that, Henry completely changed his tune once more, declaring that he wasn't a serial killer, that he hadn't killed all those people and that he was guilty only of killing his mother, a crime for which he'd already done time. But his late protestations were all for naught. Henry Lee Lucas died in prison on March 13, 2001, from a massive heart attack at the age of sixty-four. Interred at Captain Joe Byrd Cemetery in Huntsville, Alabama, he was buried without a headstone to prevent the cemetery from becoming a ghoulish tourist destination.

Thus ends the long, strange tale of Henry Lee Lucas, but his legacy lived on, most notably in Ottis Toole, who found himself on Death Row in Florida for his part in a multitude of grisly sex-related murders. And, like Henry, he too wavered on his own guilt or innocence, made up stories and retracted them. But in Ottis Toole's case, forensic evidence backed up his initial claims, which kept his demented soul on Death Row.

Shortly before his death on September 15, 1996 of cirrhosis, Toole confessed to the unsolved murder of six year-old Adam Walsh, who had disappeared from a Sears department store in Hollywood, Florida in 1981. While some believe it to be another "Ottis Toole Tale," Adam's father, John (from the acclaimed *America's Most Wanted* television program), adamantly believed that Toole, for once in his life, had told the truth.

The Vile Files

The Bloody Benders

Between 1871 and 1873, John and Kate Bender, along with their adult children John Jr. and Katherine, owned a small boarding house and general store deep in rural Labette County, Kansas. In the tight economical times following the Civil War, the Benders took to mugging, robbing, and murdering visitors to their isolated establishment. Relatives of one of their victims found the Bender store to be empty, but the grounds surrounding the structure yielded the corpses of up to ten men and women, including George Newton Longcor and his eighteen-month-old daughter, Mary Ann, who, incidentally, used to be neighbors of the real life Charles and Caroline Ingalls of *Little House on The Prairie* fame when the Ingalls resided in Independence, Kansas. According to Laura Ingalls Wilder, her father had even joined a posse in a hunt for the now aptly named "Bloody Benders" but soon became resigned to the fact that they would never be found. Several vigilante mobs claimed to have killed the Benders, though no conclusive proof of this exists and no one came forward to claim the reward of $3,000.

CHAPTER 7

ROBERT HANSEN

"THE BUTCHER BAKER"

Anchorage, Alaska

"I'm not saying that I hate all women, I don't. Quite to the contrary, if, I guess in my own mind what I'm classifying is a good woman, not a prostitute. I'd do everything in my power, any way, shape or form to do anything for her and to see that no harm ever came to her, but I guess prostitutes are women I'm putting down as lower than myself."

—**Robert Hansen**

She watched him as she ran, stealing glances over her shoulder as she tried to disappear into the snowy landscape. He'd stayed behind by the small single engine plane, the one that had brought her to this vast, lonely wilderness, high-powered rifle leaning anxiously at his side. The dark eyes behind those horn-rimmed glasses seemed to dance with the anticipation of the hunt and she hadn't even realized that she was naked in an unforgiving Alaskan wilderness. She would never realize the futility of her trek to find help. Her feet would soon become so rough and bloody from the brambles and briers that she would unknowingly leave behind streaks of blood in a trail of gore that would lead her hunter to her. The adrenaline that coursed through her kept her warm now, but when it gave out, hypothermia would set in. But the woman didn't realize this, didn't want to realize it. She believed that she had been given a chance at freedom from the sadistic rapist who now hunted her like wild game. Behind her, Robert Hansen was following her every footstep, and soon, this master hunter would claim yet another trophy.

Robert Christian Hansen was one of those guys who everybody knew in school. He was the one with terminal shyness, hiding behind thick, horn-rimmed glasses. He had an uncontrollable stutter when he tried to speak and devastating acne had claimed much of his face. His tall, yet slight, build made him the butt of most everyone's jokes. Even to the school misfits, Robert was an outcast, a nerd, one who was easy to tease and taunt because they knew he wouldn't fight back.

It's no real secret that even the most standoffish misfit of a man pines for the attractive and popular girls in school, and Robert was no exception. But his attempts to woo them were met with barbed insults and brazen cruelties. Very soon, Robert found himself courting thoughts of revenge upon them for this mercilessness. It was a hatred that would stay with him for the rest of his days and was a turning point in his transformation from quiet oddball to sadistic killer.

He never tried to fit or blend into the crowd; rather, he just wanted to be left alone and be allowed to disappear into the woodwork. Even the idea of the safety of home was a myth to Robert; his domineering father, Christian, usually picked up where his brutal classmates left off. Harsh and critical, Christian Hansen belittled Robert daily, even when Robert would help out in the family bakery. It was obvious that nothing right could ever be done by Robert's hands in the eyes of his father. But it was Robert's mother, Edna, that ultimately shaped how he classified women. Like Ed Gein before him, he looked upon his mother as a saint, the epitome of woman. All others had to match up to his mother or they were seen as lower than the low, true scum that deserved to be wiped away.

Deep inside his mind, Robert's anger at society was brewing, and it was beginning to seep out in all directions. His thoughts and sexual fantasies of women were fraught with scenarios of how he would kill his female conquests after he'd raped and tortured them. But like most sexual psychopaths, Robert tried valiantly —and vainly—to keep that horribleness inside of him, hidden from an unforgiving society that could not, or would not, understand why. The mask of sanity had to be in place at all times and for a long time, Robert Hansen succeeded.

Once he'd graduated high school, Robert enlisted in the Army Reserves, possibly hoping that in doing so, he might be given a chance to act on his murderous impulses in the heat of government sanctioned war. But after a year, he was discharged from his post and became an assistant drill instructor for the Pocahontas, Iowa, police academy. It was also around this time that eighteen-year-old Robert met a seventeen-year-old girl. After dating for a year, they married. Life took a downward spin when he was arrested for burning down a school bus garage in December of 1960, a malicious act that Robert eventually called an instrument of revenge for the myriad amounts of abuse and torment he'd received from Pocahontas citizens over the years. For his young bride, the embarrassment of Robert's jailing was too much: she quickly and quietly divorced him and relocated away from Pocahontas.

Over the next few years, Robert would find himself in and out of jail on numerous occasions, usually for petty thefts or shoplifting. He remarried in 1963 and decided to leave Iowa for good in 1967, opting for the last wild frontier of Alaska. It was a good decision for Robert and his second wife. He felt as if he could start fresh in a new state around people who didn't know about how he used to stutter, or how he looked behind a mask of acne. Nor would these new people know about his numerous run-ins with the law. He was allowing himself to start over.

Living in Anchorage, he was well-liked by his neighbors, was close to being a true pillar of the community, and became known as quite a masterful hunter. His exploits in the wilds of Alaska with his hunting rifle and bow and arrow were on the verge of legendary as he set and broke numerous local and national records. His home quickly filled up with moose, ram, and bear trophies. He was frequently photographed for the local newspapers following successful hunts in the wild. He even bought himself a small plane so that he could more easily travel to the more remote areas of Alaska to hunt.

But in 1972, Robert was arrested both for the attempted rape of an Anchorage housewife as well as the rape of a local prostitute, two charges that netted him only six months in prison. It was obvious that Robert's internal struggles hadn't been left behind in Pocahontas, Iowa. They had followed him to Anchorage. In 1977, Robert was picked up for the theft of a chain saw from a hardware store. He was sentenced to five years in prison, but the sentence was reduced on appeal. However, it was during this stint in prison that he was officially diagnosed with bipolar disorder, a condition marked by periods of both errant rage and excitability and downright hopelessness. In extreme cases, bipolar disorder can also trigger psychotic episodes, such as hyper-realistic hallucinations or delusional thoughts. If left untreated, the bipolar disorder could transform into a near constant psychotic state as those who suffer from it try vainly to stave off the depression by feeding the manic portion. In Robert Hansen's case, he needed to feed the manic portion by continually showing dominance over women, those members of the human race who had emasculated him the most and were the cause of much of his depression.

Robert was prescribed lithium, a powerful anti-depressant that seemed to control his violent mood swings fairly well. But he was never officially court-ordered to take the drug regularly, and once he was released in 1978, Robert ceased taking the drug altogether.

Returning to Anchorage, Robert continued to express his love for hunting, and he even opened a small but very popular bakery, continuing on with his family tradition. He was the father of two and the loyal husband he needed to be to his wife. While he loved, honored, and defended his wife, he absolutely hated and despised exotic dancers, prostitutes, and drug addicts. Like the girls in Pocahontas, they were the bottom of the barrel, the scum of the earth, the lowest of the low. No decency, no pride, and no shame for what they did or how they acted. While in prison, Robert Hansen had undoubtedly met and befriended fellow rapists, murderers, and other lowly misogynists, people who he liked and felt a kinship to, people who had similar troubles with women, people who most likely inspired him to stop worrying about getting caught and do what must be done to satisfy the demon within.

Once on the outside, Robert began to slowly and methodically plot his hunts, coming up with an ingenious plan to satisfy his cravings for rape and his burgeoning thirst for murder. He would set out onto the streets of downtown Anchorage and the surrounding cities, kidnapping prostitutes and dancers. Hansen would repeatedly rape and torture the women, forcing them to act out his sick fantasies, before flying them out into the wilds of Alaska in his own personal plane.

"If they came across with what I wanted, we'd come back to town," Hansen later recalled during his confession. "I'd tell them if they made any trouble for me, I had connections and would have them put in jail for being prostitutes." That fear of being blackmailed into jail helped save the lives of thirty women. But seventeen women weren't so lucky. Those seventeen women, who either protested or demanded money for their services, were usually stripped naked and sent off into the Alaskan

The Alaskan Wilderness, America's final untouched frontier and playground for notorious hunter and serial killer, Robert Hansen. *(Photo by Carol Highsmith, courtesy of The Library Of Congress.)*

wilderness, with Hansen behind them in frenzied pursuit, stalking them with his favorite high-powered rifle. This was a giddy excursion for Hansen, who knew that these women would never be able to survive their flight to freedom. If the hypothermia or the bears didn't get them, Robert Hansen would. It was all just a matter of who got to them first. Didn't matter to him anyway. As long as they were dead.

Soon, bodies began popping up all over the Alaskan landscape. Construction workers would inadvertently unearth the shallow grave of a young woman in 1980. Later, another turned up in a gravel pit near Seward, Alaska. Yet another body was found in a shallow grave near the Knik River. It was very evident that a killer was at work and a task force was organized to track down this vicious butcher.

But Hansen's plot was constantly evolving and his needs were becoming more urgent. He was looking to save himself both time and energy, a problem that he solved by deciding to bring his victims back to his home. Referring to it as his "Summer Project," Hansen first sent his wife and children on a summer-long European vacation. With his family out of the way, he then began placing personal ads in the local newspapers. Those who responded were met at Robert's home with a vicious and brutal assault before being shot or stabbed to death in the wild. Over the course of the summer, Robert Hansen raped, hunted, and murdered eleven women before finally being brought down by a seventeen-year-old girl who escaped as she was about to board his plane.

On the evening of June 13, 1983, a trucker was passing through when he noticed a young woman flagging him down on the side of the road, a pair of handcuffs still dangling from her wrist. Giving her a ride, he eventually dropped her off at the Big Timber Motel, where she apparently called her pimp to come pick her up. While she never called police, the trucker himself drove on to nearby Anchorage and alerted police himself.

Officer Gregg Baker was dispatched to the Big Timber, where he found the girl outside the motel office, alone and still in handcuffs. She gave her name as Cindy Paulson, and she had been approached on the street by a man in his forties who offered her a stalwart $200 for oral sex. She agreed on the price, but halfway through the act, the man locked a handcuff around her wrist and pulled a handgun, telling her he would not kill her as long as she did what she was told. Reluctantly and fearfully, she had agreed. The man drove Cindy to his house in Muldoon, a fairly affluent suburb of Anchorage, where he viciously raped her, bit her nipples, and performed a sex act upon her with a hammer. She was able to rest for a few hours before the man packed her into his car and drove her to the remote airport where his small plane was housed. Once there, the man shoved her inside the plane, but once his back was turned, Cindy pushed open the door and ran. The man chased after her at first, but backed off when she was able to flag down the truck driver.

It was now only a matter of time. Robert knew it was all over. He was barely surprised when task force detectives knocked on his door and took him in for questioning. Though he at first denied it, the growing mountain of evidence against Robert was becoming an overwhelming obstacle that he could no longer avoid. With the help of his attorney, Robert Hansen agreed to plead guilty to four of the murders task force detectives were investigating. He also agreed to lead them to the rest of the women he'd murdered and buried in the wilderness. Ultimately, he confessed to a total of seventeen murders over the course of his lifetime and he had very little trouble pointing out the graves of his victims. He'd even marked their graves on one of his aviation charts, making it very easy for investigators to locate each and every victim. Most of the bodies would remain unidentified, lost forever to the ages. However, there were six who were: Rox Easland, Lisa Futrell, Andrea Altiery, Angela Fetter, Teresa Watson, and Delynn Frey. These were women who were all reported missing during Robert's killing spree of 1983, and all were found buried in the Alaskan wild where Robert Hansen said they were. But although seventeen graves were uncovered, as part of his plea agreement, he would only be charged with the first four bodies investigators found.

On February 18, 1984, Robert Hansen pleaded guilty to four counts of first-degree murder, receiving a sentence of life in prison, plus 461 years. He started his sentence at the United States Penitentiary in Lewisburg, Pennsylvania, but was eventually returned to Alaska in 1988.

FBI profilers flocked to Hansen, eager to interview him about his methods in an effort to more accurately profile possible serial killers at large. Hansen wasn't eager to speak, but he did so voluntarily; perhaps he couldn't help but feel a bit proud of how well he'd done. So proud that, like many serial killers, he wanted to brag a little about how he acted during each kidnapping.

> I pull out the gun—I think the standard speech was, "Look you're a professional. You don't get excited, you know there is some risk to what you've been doing. If you do exactly what I tell you you're not going to get hurt. You're just going to count this off as a bad experience and be a little more careful next time who you are gonna proposition or go out with," you know. I tried to act as tough as I could, to get them as scared as possible. Give that right away, even before I started talking at all.
>
> Reach over, you know, and hold that head back and put a gun in her face and get 'em to feel helpless, scared, right there . . . I'm sure—maybe it's not the same procedure for you—you always try to get control of the situation, so some things don't start going bad . . . maybe I've seen some cop shows on TV, I don't know, OK?

In May of 2014, Hansen's health began to steadily deteriorate, so quickly in fact that it forced his transfer from Spring Creek Correctional to Anchorage Correctional Complex. It was a state of the art prison where Robert could get adequate medical attention to whatever malady he was suffering. To this day, no one knows what was afflicting Hansen, but whatever it was took his life at 2:00 a.m. on August 21, 2014. The medical examiner would later classify the seventy-five-year-old serial killer's death as "natural causes."

The Vile Files

Glen Edward Rogers

(July 15, 1962-)

Dubbed the "Casanova Killer," Glen Rogers was convicted in 1999 of the rape and murder of Tina Marie Cribbs, though he was suspected in the deaths of four others in California, Mississippi, Louisiana, and Florida. His death sentence was commuted to life imprisonment upon appeal, and he serves out his days in a Florida penitentiary. In 2012, his brother produced a documentary about Rogers that aired on *Investigation Discovery* in which Glen Rogers admitted to being the one who had slain Nicole Brown Simpson and her friend Ron Goldman in 1995. Rogers had allegedly worked for Nicole Simpson and it was O. J. Simpson who had hired him to initially steal a pair of expensive earrings from her jewelry box. After Nicole caught him in the act, Rogers allegedly killed her, then killed Ron Goldman when he wandered onto the scene. No proof of Rogers's involvement exists and most people write it off as a tall tale. However, Glen Edward Rogers was living in California at the time of the murders and resided very close to the Brentwood home owned by Nicole Brown Simpson.

CHAPTER 8

GORDON STEWART NORTHCOTT

"THE WINEVILLE CHICKEN COOP AXE MURDERER"

Wineville, California

"A prayer . . . Please say a prayer for me."
–Gordon Stewart Northcott's final words

I'll be the first to admit it. Prior to seeing Clint Eastwood's sublime thriller *Changeling*, I had no idea who Gordon Stewart Northcott was. His name never appeared in books alongside the old classic killers such as Manson and Gacy, and it seems the world was much better for it. Of all of the killers I researched, profiled, and wrote about, Gordon Stewart Northcott was one of the most unrepentant, malicious, and downright evil of them all. His crimes shocked the country in the late 1920s, and the world would soon rally to see him hang.

Gordon Stewart Northcott literally had no excuse. He was simply an evil man who enjoyed what he did. The fact that he did it to children made it all the worse.

Born in 1906, in Saskatchewan, Canada, Northcott emigrated to Los Angeles, California, with his father and nephew in 1924. While not much is known about his early, formative years, one can easily guess that—given the known patterns of a sexual serial killer—Gordon was an odd young man, perhaps quiet and reserved as his brain attempted to rationalize his inner thoughts of destruction and murder. Chances are very good, as well, that he had been repeatedly molested as a child, perhaps by an uncle or even his own father, though no evidence exists that this was the case. Like Dahmer and Nilsen, Gordon would have been fascinated by death for most of his life, even killing small animals sporadically over the years in an effort to exert control over a victim. As he grew older, and no doubt bolder, he would become a full-fledged pedophile, targeting young boys, then shaming or threatening them into secrecy until he and his family left Canada and settled in California.

When nineteen-year-old Gordon, his father, and his thirteen-year-old nephew Sanford Clark arrived in California, they settled in the small burg of Wineville about fifty-five miles east of Los Angeles. Gordon's father was in the construction business and together they built the home in which Gordon, his parents, and Sanford would live. Gordon paid particular attention to the family chicken coops in the back of the house, designing and building them virtually on his own.

Once the home was finished and his father returned to Canada, Gordon systematically terrorized and sexually molested his young nephew. He was so good at manipulating Sanford that the young boy became a blind participant in what was to happen.

On February 2, 1928, Los Angeles County sheriff's deputies pulled alongside the road in La Puente. Both men in the car had noticed the large burlap sack lying haphazardly in the ditch. They were horrified to find the headless body of a Mexican teenage boy stuffed inside. An autopsy would later reveal that a .22-caliber bullet to the heart, fired by a rifle, was the primary cause of death. It was a disturbing find, but one that seemed random until more boys began to disappear across Los Angeles County. Walter Collins, nine, vanished in March without a trace on his way to the movies, and brothers Nelson and Louis Winslow, ten and twelve, went missing that May while walking home from a model yacht club meeting.

A severe lack of communication and imagination prevented the Los Angeles Police from seeing the connections until it was too late. Their bungling of these disappearances resulted in a scandal in which the LAPD would try to pass off another child as Walter Collins in an attempt to cover-up said bungling. They even went so far as to incarcerate Walter's frantic mother, Christine, in an insane asylum to keep her quiet about the whole affair.

All three disappearances and the mystery of the headless boy found in the La Puente ditch would come together and make sense to the police following a mysterious phone call. Federal immigration authorities received the phone call

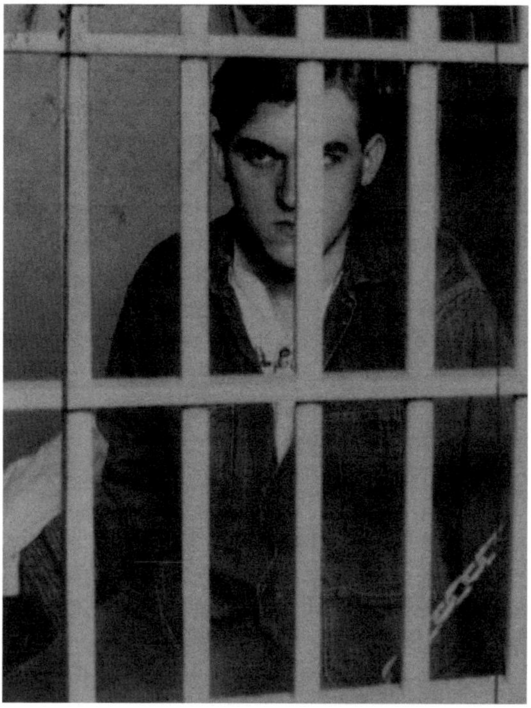

Sadistic ax murderer and pedophile Gordon Stewart Northcott.

from a Canadian woman who told them how her nephew had kidnapped her son and held him against his will at a chicken ranch in Wineville in Riverside County.

Police arrived at the ranch in Wineville and found Sanford Clark, now fifteen, and his sister Jessie, age seventeen.

It was Jessie who had contacted their mother in Canada, who in turn notified the federal authorities about her son's dire situation. Northcott and his mother, Sarah, had already fled the scene. What Sanford Clark told the police both horrified and baffled them.

According to Sanford, he was forced to help Northcott kidnap little boys, rape and molest them, and then kill them with an axe. Using quicklime, Northcott would dissolve much of the corpse before they were buried in the earthen floor of the chicken coop. Sanford said that there were three boys who were killed at the ranch and one Mexican ranch hand who had been shot, beheaded, and dumped somewhere in a burlap sack.

Clothes belonging to the Winslow boys were found in the house, as well as several personal articles that belonged to them, including a letter they had written to their parents reassuring them that they were fine. When police investigators began to excavate the chicken coop, they found clumps of flesh, large amounts of quicklime, bits of a bloodstained mattress, and a .22-caliber rifle. A pair of axes were also found, stained with blood and human hair. Sanford Clark eventually admitted to killing one of the Winslow boys, though he asserted that Northcott had forced him to participate. What was odd was that, while there was human flesh discovered, no bones were recovered. Again, police looked to Sanford, who said that the whole bodies had been there before, but may have been moved the night before by Gordon and his mother, taken to the surrounding desert, and either burned or buried in several different locations.

All of the pieces were coming together and police realized that they had a true monster on the loose. Police began to scour the area looking for Northcott and his mother.

Federal authorities eventually found Northcott and his mother hiding out in Canada. Both Gordon and his mother Sarah were summarily extradited back to Los Angeles, where Gordon led police on a tour of the property in Wineville. Initially, he confessed to murdering nine boys on the ranch, then to only five. At the end of the day, in his written confession to police, he admitted to only one: the murder of the Mexican ranch hand, a teenager named Alvin Gothea, who was the one authorities found in the burlap sack.

The story took a nastier twist when talk turned towards the whereabouts of nine-year-old Walter Collins. According to Sarah Northcott, Walter Collins' murder was the glue that held the three of them together. The boy simply knew too much about Gordon, Sanford, and herself. At her insistence, Gordon, Sanford, and herself would all wield an axe upon young Walter. That way, neither Sanford, Gordon, nor Sarah could go to the police and implicate the others without first placing themselves at risk. An axe was chosen because it made less noise compared to a gun.

The three of them went to the chicken coop and found Walter lying asleep on a filthy cot. Each of them landed a crushing blow to Walter's head as he slept. Thankfully, it is probable that Walter never knew what hit him and his death was most likely instantaneous.

When informed of his mother's vivid confession, Northcott grinned, shook his head, and muttered, "She is crazy."

Sarah Northcott received a life sentence following her confession. Sanford Clark refuted Sarah's confession, reiterating that the only murder he participated in was that of the older Winslow boy, Louis, and that it had been under the threat of his own murder at the hands of Gordon Northcott.

Gordon Stewart Northcott was officially charged with the murders of Walter Collins, Lewis Winslow, Nelson Winslow, and Alvin Gothea. When jury selection began in January of 1929, the presiding judge excluded women from the jury pool, believing the crimes to be far too grisly for a woman to have to experience.

Judge John Gabbert, a retired appellate court judge, was a student at the time, attending Riverside City College. In a 2006 interview with the *Los Angeles Times*, he reflected upon Northcott's trial. "I waited around the courthouse a long time to get a seat. Northcott was a very self-possessed guy, not overawed by the trial at all. During breaks, he kidded around with the prosecutors. He was as much at home in the courtroom as any attorney but didn't know what he was doing [legally]. He was a conniving, smart guy, in a limited way."

Gordon Northcott eventually turned the trial into a maddening circus, firing multiple defense attorneys and even taking over his own defense. His final defense attorney warned him against defending himself. "You'll be hanging yourself!" he is said to have told Northcott.

"It will be worth it," Northcott reportedly replied. "My name will become known all over the world."

He would growl obscenities at the prosecutor, Deputy D. A. Earl Redwine. He even cross-examined himself and ordered D. A. Redwine to take the stand. He accused sheriff's deputies of plotting to kill him. The judge, he said, would not give him "a square deal." He accused family members who testified against him, namely his niece Jessie, her brother Sanford, and their mother, Winifred, of being liars bought out by the prosecution.

But D. A. Redwine was unflappable. He approached Northcott's delusional ravings with the hard facts, the evidence they had collected, and the testimonies of those who were present when Northcott committed murder. Every time Northcott attempted to undermine the prosecution's case, Redwine would fire back with hard facts that Northcott couldn't refute.

In an attempt to elicit sympathy, Northcott had his mother bussed in from Techachapi State Prison to testify on his behalf. That first day of testimony revealed a scandalous bombshell.

According to Sarah Northcott, her husband Cyrus had had sex with their daughter Winifred, an unholy union that produced Gordon Stewart Northcott. Essentially, Northcott was Sanford Clark's half-brother *and* his uncle. It was a shocking admission, but it did nothing to sway the jury. After a twenty-seven-day trial, the jury deliberated for only two hours before finding Northcott guilty of murder and sentenced to hang.

Sanford Clark was sentenced to the Whittier State School for Boys where he stayed until his twenty-first birthday. After that, he returned to Canada. Considering how horrific much of his early life was, it was utterly amazing that Sanford would go on to become a decorated World War II veteran, an employee of the Canadian Postal System, and a loving father and grandfather, living the most ordinary of lives. He died in 1991.

Ironically, Christine Collins, Walter Collins' bereaved mother, was one of the only people to actually lobby for Northcott's death sentence to be either suspended or commuted to life imprisonment. Her stance on the matter was that Northcott—who seemed to enjoy alluding to the truth about Walter's fate—would crack and one day confess truthfully about what had happened to her son.

Northcott toyed with Christine Collins in the same manner he'd toyed with the police: telling her everything and nothing. Sending her on wild goose chases that led to dead ends. By the time his appeals were exhausted and Northcott faced the gallows at San Quentin, Christine Collins was left with as much information about Walter's whereabouts as she had before, which was absolutely nothing. She would spend the rest of her life searching for him.

Even to this very day, the truth about Walter's fate would never conclusively be known.

On October 2, 1930, Northcott's once-beaming bravado and audacious personality that had been so prevalent during his trial suddenly disappeared and was replaced by anxiety, terror, and pure cowardice. He was shaking like a leaf as the guards at San Quentin were prepping him for the gallows, asking them if his execution would hurt. Northcott even requested a blindfold so that he wouldn't have to see the gallows as he entered the room, which was essentially nothing more than a large old warehouse.

Even though he couldn't see the gallows through his blindfold, Northcott still screamed and kicked and dragged his feet. So terrified of walking those steps to his fate was he that the guards literally had to pick him up, flailing and wailing, and carry him up the thirteen steps to the noose.

"Please! Don't make me walk so fast!" he cried out in horror.

It certainly wasn't anything the guards hadn't seen before. Many men had been dragged to their fates like Northcott, some wailing like children and others as stone-faced as a gargoyle. But there had to be some sort of satisfaction in Northcott's unbridled terror, especially to those who came to witness the execution, many of whom were most likely relatives of Northcott's victims.

As he stood on the pedestal, noose secured about his neck, Gordon Stewart Northcott shouted, "A prayer—please say a prayer for me."

The trap door sprang open and Northcott dropped to his death and into the history books as one of the most vile killers to have ever walked the planet. Following the execution, San Quentin's presiding warden, Clinton T. Duffy, would later write that Northcott told him he'd killed "eighteen or nineteen, maybe twenty" young men and boys. While cleaning out Northcott's cell, Duffy also found what appeared to be a crudely drawn map of the so-called "Murder Farm." Off to the side of the page, Gordon Northcott had written, "I am not guilty." But on the map, he'd drawn several coffin-shaped boxes with a cryptic message written above them. "If you look here you will find what you want."

Authorities followed the map to a tee, but found nothing, chalking it up to Northcott's morbid sense of humor and the last in a long line of hoaxes he'd constantly pulled on the police since his arrest.

The macabre story of Gordon Stewart Northcott seemed to fascinate and terrify the world, but it was a source of exhausting anguish for the city of Wineville. Fed up with the publicity, they unanimously decided to change their name. Today, Wineville is known as Mira Loma, a quiet little city that definitely prefers it that way.

The ranch house that Northcott built with his father still stands to this day, though the infamous chicken coops have all been torn down. Tourists still flock to the town, looking for the Northcott's house, which is currently a private residence. Interest in the case rose again in 2008 when Clint Eastwood's sublime crime drama *Changeling* premiered. Focusing on the plight of Christine Collins's futile search for her missing son, the film starred Angelina Jolie as Collins and Jason Butler Harner as Northcott.

The Vile Files

Wayne Williams

(May 27, 1958-)

Wayne Bertram Williams was an Atlanta music promoter and photographer in 1981 when he was arrested and charged in the notorious "Atlanta Child Murders." Williams was stopped near the Chattahoochee River after police heard a loud splash and saw Williams driving away. The body of twenty-eight-year-old Nathanial Carter would be recovered from the river the next day. The Chatahoochee had been a well-known dumping-ground for the murderer, who, by this point had killed close to twenty-four African-American boys across the city. Though Williams denied he was the killer, bloodstains and other forensic evidence that belonged to two of the victims were recovered from his car. He was convicted of the two murders and given two life sentences. Though Atlanta police eventually cleared their books and declared that Wayne Williams was the man responsible for *all* the killings, Williams himself still maintains his innocence. Conspiracies point to Atlanta police cover-ups as well as the involvement of the Ku Klux Klan, and while criminal profiler John Douglas believes that Williams committed many of the murders, he is certain Williams did not commit all of them. "It isn't a single offender and the truth isn't pleasant," he once commented rather enigmatically.

CHAPTER 9

CARL PANZRAM

"THE MEAN MAN"

East Grand Forks, Minnesota

"I have no desire whatever to reform myself.
My only desire is to reform people who try to reform me,
and I believe the only way to reform people is to kill 'em.
My motto is: Rob 'em all, rape 'em all, and kill 'em all."
–**Carl Panzram**

He was writing so hard, the pencil lead kept snapping. Furious strokes and indomitable intensity pushing the pencil across the paper as he punched out his life story. It was the guard's idea, and Panzram still couldn't believe he'd given him a sharpened pencil. Normally, he'd have used it to kill a dozen men by now; but this time, he was using it to let the world know how much he hated them and why they should fear him. When it was all over and the story found its way out of the prison, the whole world would know his rage. He just wished he could see their faces when they realized that yes, real monsters were out there, and this one enjoyed what he did.

There was a true monster inside Carl Panzram, one that seemed to be in him from the very beginning, though I assure you, he wasn't born with it. Rather, it was given to him, like most serial predators, from those who should have loved him most. But while Carl's mother didn't seem to hate him, she certainly showed him no love whatsoever, and his father and older brothers abandoned them both one by one.

He was born Charles Panzram on June 28, 1891, the youngest child of John and Matilda Panzram, joining five older brothers and one older sister. Though he was named Charles, his father would shorten it to Carl most of the time until it stuck. While his siblings remained honest, hardworking, and dependable, young Carl seemed to be listless, rebellious, and insubordinate.

"I have been a human animal ever since I was born. I was a thief and a liar," he would say. "The older I got the meaner I got."

Carl was seven years old when his parents separated. There was no divorce. John Panzram simply left his wife, a decidedly more civil route than today's divorce courts, but one that left his children in the lurch. Carl's older sister, presumably, married and left the family homestead. His brothers, meanwhile, saw the mean streak in Carl and doled out routine beatings upon the boy when he misbehaved or got into trouble with the law. Eventually, the beatings became more random and required less of a reason, but Carl had the last laugh. He'd learned to like them.

"Everybody thought it was all right to deceive me, lie to me and kick me around whenever they felt like it, and they felt like it pretty regular," he later wrote.

Instead of dissuade him from breaking the law, the beatings only hardened him until he no longer feared anything. He was an alcoholic at an early age, making his first appearance in a courtroom for drunkenness at the age of eight. When he was eleven, he broke into a neighboring home, stealing anything that wasn't nailed down, including a pistol. When his brothers found out, Carl was beaten so badly that he lay unconscious for two days before he was arrested by local law enforcement. He was sent to the Minnesota State Training School in 1903 as a result. Located in the town of Red Wing, the Minnesota State Training School boasted a population of 300 boys, aged ten to twenty and it would be the first in a long series of incarcerations for Carl Panzram. The school's admissions log

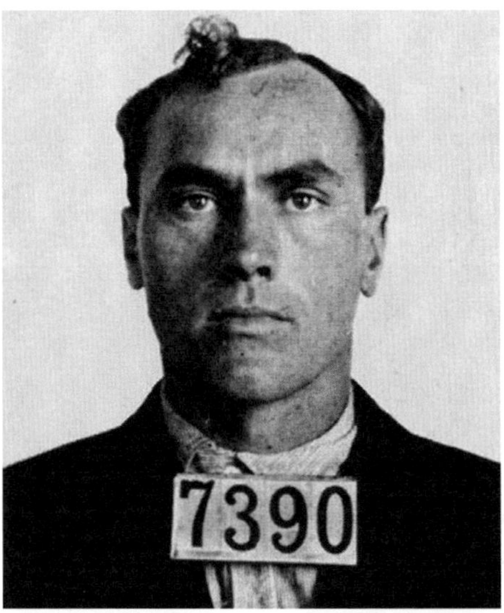

Carl Panzram's 1915 mugshot, going under the alias Jefferson Baldwin, when he was arrested for burglary.

listed Panzram's crime as being "incorrigibility," which is nothing if not a gross understatement if you consider burglary and public drunkenness to be signs of incorrigibility.

Like most reform schools, the inmates were left at the mercy of unsupervised and unscrupulous jailers. Harsh corporal punishments were common for the smallest infractions. "I may not have accomplished much in a scholarly way while there, but I learned how to become a first-class liar and the beginnings of degeneracy," he would write later. "I first began to think that I was being unjustly imposed upon. Then I began to hate those who abused me. Then I began to think that I would have my revenge just as soon and as often as I could injure someone else. Anyone at all would do."

Carl endured as many beatings as one can imagine, taking licks from shaving straps, whips, and boat paddles. At times, he was stripped naked and lashed in front of his cohorts. Little Carl would grit his teeth and take the beating each time and each time he felt the whip, he hated the world that much more. But he would have his revenge. He began by setting fire to the school's industrial complex, burning it to the ground as he giggled in his bunk. That industrial complex, nicknamed "The Paint Shop," was where Carl and numerous other boys were beaten and tortured, all the while being preached to from the Bible. It was a fitting place for him to begin his reign of terror against humanity.

His behavior wouldn't change much as he grew older. In fact, it could be said that, while his body grew up, Carl's way of dealing with a world that he hated did not. It was as if he were stuck in a constant state of childish revenge against some wrong that had been done to him over and over and over again. He loved to burn things, destroy, terrify, and horrify. Punishment had no effect on him. It was an unending cycle of frustration for his guardians, to be sure, for no matter how harsh the punishment, Carl would return to his old ways within seconds, and with a vengeance.

By late 1905, Carl had learned to say what the parole board wanted to hear and he convinced them that he was a changed boy, that the Christian teachings of the school and its masters had done the trick. But "I was reformed all right. I had been taught by Christians how to be a hypocrite and I had learned more about stealing, lying, hating, burning, and killing," he said later. "I had learned that a boy's penis could be used for something besides to urinate with and that a rectum could be used for other purposes."

Taken back home by his mother, Matilda Panzram noticed the changes in Carl. He'd been a withdrawn child before, but he was even more so now, eerily quiet and pensive.

But Matilda Panzram was too caught up in her own troubles to be bothered with Carl's. Her health was failing and work on the farm was doubling up. Instead of reaching out to help her son, she instead ignored him, hoping he might be able to untangle his problems on his own. But her distance from him definitely caused more damage than she thought. A deep resentment began brewing inside Carl toward his mother.

"Mother was too dumb to know anything good to teach me," he would later write. "There was little love lost. I first liked her and respected her. My feelings gradually turned from that to distrust, dislike, disgust, and from there it was very simple for my feelings to turn into positive hatred towards her."

To this point, Carl had led a life filled with beatings, torture, humiliation, and hatred. There was a point in his life where he looked upon himself in the mirror, loathing all that lay behind him, and vowing to burn it all. "I fully decided when I left there just how I would live my life. I made up my mind that I would rob, burn, destroy, and kill everywhere I went and everybody I could as long as I lived."

Carl left home early, probably much to his mother's relief. A boy, so full of rage and hate, out among the world's citizens. He had no interest in work, no interest in anything but exploiting his rage. Finally, he just left home, still quite a young boy at the age of fourteen or fifteen. Carl learned how to ride the rails, stowing away in boxcars to get where he needed. A turning point in his metamorphosis came when he was gang-raped by a crew of hobos in a boxcar.

"What they couldn't get by moral persuasion, they proceeded to take by force."

Carl's embarrassment, humiliation, and grief was so intolerable that he would use that very same tactic to dominate and humiliate his victims. It also fueled his rage and he became uncontrollable, finding peace in violence and harmony in destruction.

Carl even lied about his age and joined the Army at one point, but was jailed and discharged after a month for being a habitual drunk. It also didn't help that he constantly robbed the commissary and his platoon members' foot lockers.

The Army decided to make an example out of Panzram, sentencing him to be dishonorably discharged, with forfeiture of all pay and benefits, and to be confined for three years of hard labor at Fort Leavenworth. His sentence was approved by then-Secretary of War William Howard Taft. Verily, it would not be the last time their paths would cross.

He was released in 1910, and Panzram left prison with another man named Jimmie Benson. The two managed to steal several pistols before heading toward the town of Terry, Minnesota. Panzram's hatred of Christianity reached its epoch at this time, as he taught Jimmie how to burglarize, then burn, churches. By robbing, then burning the Christian churches he happened upon, it was almost as if Carl Panzram were paying back God for all the pain he'd taken in His name.

"Naturally, I now love Jesus very much, " he said, "Yes, I love him so damn much that I would like to crucify him all over again!"

Benson and Panzram eventually split up, going off in different directions. Carl began to move across the United States, becoming a ruthless master thief, committing robberies, muggings, and burglaries with the greatest of ease and the least amount of regret possible. In the summer of 1920, Panzram found himself in the city of New Haven, Connecticut. He would cruise the streets at night, looking for an unsuspecting drunk to mug, or young boy he could rape. Mainly he would look for a house to burglarize. He found the perfect house that summer, located at 113 Whitney Avenue. Entering the house through an open window, he began to rifle through the bedrooms and studies, looking for anything he could fence downtown. He would eventually come across large amounts of jewelry, a thick stack of old war bonds, and a .45-caliber automatic handgun. But it was the name on the war bonds that piqued his interest the most.

It was William H. Taft, the man who had approved his hard-labor sentencing at Leavenworth—the same man who would become president of the United States. The same man who, at this moment, was the current professor of law at Yale University.

Revenge had been served and a bureaucratic "Fat Cat" had been chopped down to size. The only thing missing for Panzram was Taft being raped and murdered by his own hands.

He used the money he'd gotten fencing the stolen goods to buy an old yacht, and while he was ruminating on how to fix it up, he happened upon a plan to keep the supply of men handy. Panzram began to hire a string of laborers to help him out with the boat. When he grew tired of them, he raped, then shot them. When they outgrew their usefulness, he raped and shot them. Then he would hire another. The same cycle would continue until the boat was finished or until Carl got bored, whichever came first.

"Every day or two I would go to New York and hang around 25 South Street and size up the sailors," Panzram said. "We would wine and dine and when they were drunk enough, they would go to bed. When they were asleep I would get my .45 Colt automatic, this I stole from Mr. Taft's home, and blow their brains out."

In late August 1920, a huge storm hit and the yacht was smashed to pieces against the rocks. Panzram barely escaped with his life. A few days later, he stowed away on a ship and landed in Angola, a Portuguese colony on the west coast of Africa.

While working for an oil company in Africa, it is said that he murdered and raped a young boy before murdering six men he hired to help him hunt crocodiles. After he returned to the States, Panzram's newly awakened blood lust sent him on a whirlwind of murder, larceny, and rape. These killings were all random and unmotivated, keeping the police from easily connecting them to one person. He would go by alias after alias, never using the same name twice when he would be arrested. Panzram, no doubt, never wanted to be recognized by this world, a world he despised, a world he wanted to burn to the ground.

It was while Panzram was at Dannemora Prison that he did the unthinkable: he made a friend. Prison guard Henry Lesser would be the only person in the world to gain the trust of Panzram and, as a result, he would be the only one to which Panzram would ever confess. According to Lesser, Panzram admitted not only to committing numerous acts of murder, but also to raping over 1,000 men in his lifetime, an act that he used not for sexual pleasure, but for unmitigated control over his victims by humiliating and degrading them in much the same way the gang of hobos had done to him. To Panzram, raping an innocent man was the same as raping and degrading part of the world that he loathed.

Lesser convinced Panzram to write down his life story, an idea that Panzram resisted at first, mostly because Panzram only had a sixth-grade education and barely knew how to write a full sentence. But once he got started, he found he couldn't stop. The text of the "memoir" betrayed his formal education: it was a well-thought-out, grammatically sound work that would eventually become a celebrated look into the mind and life of a brutal killer. He wrote of every crime: every burglary, every murder, every rape. No punch was pulled and every graphic detail was written down. It was an honest and valid attempt to tell his story in 40,000 words. A small part of the story dealt with Carl's problem with his ears when he was much younger, a problem that may have been one of the roots of Panzram's free-floating hostility. Because his family was so poor, they always took their kids to doctors who barely knew anything about surgery or general health. It was, after all, all they could afford. One of these "doctors" found a large tumor outside young Carl's left ear that seemed to grow into the brain. When it was excised, a small amount of brain came with it. Some doctors today believe that this could have led to an imbalance in the brain. It could also be the reason he had such low impulse control. Henry was both horrified and fascinated with Carl Panzram's life story and he would spend nearly forty years trying to find a publisher courageous enough to print it.

But there was a reason why Carl Panzram was known as "The Houdini of Prisons": he had an uncanny ability of escaping prison. He'd done it before, and he would try it again at Dannemora, climbing up the thirty-foot-high walls. But he misplaced his footing and fell, breaking both ankles and rupturing a testicle.

"I was dumped into a cell without any medical attention or surgical attention whatever," Panzram wrote later on. "My broken bones were not set. My ankles and legs were not put into a cast. The doctor never came near me and no one else was allowed to do anything for me. At the end of fourteen months of constant agony, I was taken to the hospital where I was operated on for my rupture and one of my testicles were cut out. I suffered more agony for many months. Always in pain, never a civil answer from anyone, always a snarl or a curse or a lying, hypocritical promise which was never kept. Crawling around like a snake with a broken back, seething with hatred and a lust for revenge, five years of this kind of life. The last two years and four months confined in isolation with nothing to do except brood upon all the wrongs that had ever been done to me. I hated everybody I saw." He dreamed of bombing train tunnels, robbing millions of dollars from the gimpy trains, and using that money to finance a war between England and the United States. His goal, essentially, was to be the reason millions of people died.

Panzram was left with a pronounced limp that followed him around for the rest of his life. The escape attempt was a failure, and with his new limp, he would never be able to escape police. Now serving a twenty-five-year sentence at Leavenworth for stealing, prison guards took advantage of his new handicap, regularly taking him from his cell down into the prison basement, where he would be routinely beaten and tortured. The first time, Panzram didn't fight. But the second time, and all the times after that when they came for him, Panzram fought like a demon, breaking noses and bones before being subdued enough to be shackled and carried off.

Enraged and frustrated, Panzram vowed to kill the first person who bothered him. That person was the Leavenworth laundry foreman Robert Warnke, who hadn't heard of Panzram's vow and unknowingly irritated the psychotic killer. Warnke was a civilian employed by the prison and by most accounts was a bully who delighted in beating the prisoners in his employ. Panzram, in particular, was a target of Warnke, who used to frequently taunt Panzram about his "moral habits," namely his use of sodomy on other men. Carl Panzram did his best to be good, but found resistance to his old ways to be absolutely futile. This man, a product of the brutal prison system, gave in to what he did best: exploit his rage and hatred. On June 20, 1929, Panzram crushed the man's skull with an iron bar. It was a scene of utter chaos as Panzram's fury became unhinged, loosed upon the world. Other inmates in the laundry room ran for the exits as Panzram chased them with an iron bar, breaking bones when he could. He raged like a madman, screaming and yelling his hate. By the time guards arrived, Panzram was calm and complacent. He was peacefully moved to a segregated cell without any further provocation. Furthermore, in his new surroundings, he was left alone, fed well, and was treated even better. Panzram himself reflected on this change, writing to Henry Lesser, saying, "If, in the beginning I had been treated as I am now, then there wouldn't have been quite so many people in this world that I had robbed, raped, and killed. And perhaps, also very probably, I wouldn't be where I am today."

His trial for the murder of Robert Warnke was a sham, at best. Everyone knew Panzram killed Warnke. There were at least four other men who would testify against him, eyewitnesses to Panzram's furious anger. But Panzram pleaded not guilty, daring the judge to prove his guilt.

It really didn't take that much to prove. It was an open and shut case. The only mystery is why it took the jury only forty-five minutes to come to a verdict in the matter. For the murder of Robert Warnke, Panzram received the death penalty, sentenced to hang before 1930 was over.

Robert Stroud, who would later become known as the Bird-man of Alcatraz, was a neighbor of Panzram's, sitting in his own cell next door. Stroud, who was no slouch in the misogynist/psychotic realm that Panzram seemed to be captain of, would later write that Panzram was restless the night before the execution, but that it was far from a nervous restlessness. "All night long that last night he walked the floor of his cell," he wrote, "singing a pornographic little song that he had composed himself." Stroud also believed that many of the stories Panzram told of murders, rapes, and burglaries were pure fiction, told to gain a fearsome reputation amongst guards and convicts alike.

Stroud, like Panzram, was a sullen, maniacal misanthrope who seldom spoke to anyone. But both Panzram and Stroud would watch their gallows being constructed right outside their cell windows. Stroud would eventually escape the noose by being transferred to Alcatraz, but would remain a prisoner there until his death in 1963.

Panzram was resigned to his fate on the gallows. To be more blunt, it was a fate that he seemed to welcome and embrace. In fact, when a local group opposed to the death penalty asked Panzram if they could intervene on his behalf, Panzram refused, saying, "I choose here and now to be hanged by the neck until I am dead. I look forward to that as a real pleasure, a big relief to me. I prefer death before spending more years in prison... the only things you or your kind will ever get for acting on my behalf is that I wish you all had one neck, and that my hands were on it."

On the morning of Friday, September 5, 1930, Carl Panzram was taken from his cell for the last time at 5:55 a.m. and escorted to the gallows. He was as insubordinate as always, flaunting that rebellious attitude that had gained him so much notoriety. As he passed by his mother, he cursed at her for bringing him into the world. Robert Stroud later described Panzram as a vicious bulldog being led by a leash.

Panzram was escorted up the thirteen steps and US marshals attempted to place a black hood over his head. But before they could, Carl Panzram spat at the executioner, growling, "Hurry up, you Hoosier bastard, I could hang a dozen men while you're fooling around!"

With the hood secured, they wasted no more time and gave Carl Panzram what he asked for; the trap door was sprung and the hall was filled with silence. At 6:18 a.m., he was pronounced dead and cut down from the gallows. Not surprisingly, his body would remain unclaimed and he was buried in the prison graveyard, his marker bearing his prisoner number of 31614. He lies there today in row 6, plot 24.

Today, the majority of Carl Panzram's writings, confession, and diaries lie in the Special Collections department of San Diego State University, donated by Henry Lesser himself. Among writings by Charles Darwin, Mark Twain, and President John F. Kennedy, are words of wisdom such as this:

> I am sorry for only two things. These two things are I am sorry that I have mistreated some few animals in my lifetime and I am sorry that I am unable to murder the whole damned human race... All that I leave behind me is smoke, death, desolation, and damnation.

The Vile Files

Joe Ball
(1896-1938)

Joe Ball, also known as "the Alligator Man," opened a saloon called the Sociable Inn in Elmendorf, Texas, following his service during World War I. The saloon's high point was a large man-made pond that he stocked with five alligators. He would charge people to view them, especially during feeding time when he would serve his gators stray cats and dogs. When a number of women in his life, such as barmaids, girlfriends, and his own wife came up missing, sheriff's deputies paid Joe a visit in 1938, asking him about them. His response? He grabbed a pistol from his cash register and shot himself in the head. A handyman later admitted to helping Joe Ball dispose of the bodies and that Ball had murdered at least twenty other women, their remains destroyed by the alligators. His story became legendary and would go on to inspire the Tobe Hooper cult classic, *Eaten Alive*.

CHAPTER 10

JOSEPH KALLINGER

"THE SHOEMAKER"

Philadelphia, Pennsylvania.

Oh, what ecstasy setting fires brings to my body!
What power I feel at the thought of fire!
Oh, what pleasure, what heavenly pleasure!
—A poem by Joseph Kallinger

The first time I met Joseph Kallinger was in 1988 on the Oprah Winfrey show, back when her program was still a tad more exploitative than it is now. I met Kallinger again around that same year in an interview with journalist Geraldo Rivera. Those television interviews, conducted from his "home" at the State Correctional Institution in Cresson, Pennsylvania, were the most honest I'd seen to ever come from a serial killer as vicious and merciless as he and I was thankful for the distance it put between us.

I honestly don't remember the first time I heard about John Wayne Gacy, Jack the Ripper, or Albert Fish. But I do remember the first time I heard about and met Joseph Kallinger. At the time he was a soft spoken, gentle man with a bushy salt and pepper beard, but when he opened his mouth to speak, it became frighteningly evident how much of a monster this man really was and his ease of speaking about death and madness still makes my skin crawl. His mission, given to him by "God" and supervised by a ghastly severed head with long hair and brown eyes named Charlie, was to kill the entire population of the world, then murder his family, and finally, commit suicide and become God himself.

Beginning in July of 1974, Joseph Kallinger and his thirteen-year-old son Michael would embark on a horrific mission of murder, rape, torture, and mayhem. But as horrific as Kallinger's crimes were, how he became the monstrous creature is perhaps even more unsettling. Joe was a severely disturbed paranoid schizophrenic, possibly from the time of his birth, but never properly diagnosed until he was well into adulthood. There was never a time where his behavior wasn't looked upon as weird or odd, and it is quite possible that he may also have had autistic tendencies as well. Nevertheless, none of these maladies would see treatment until it was much too late.

Joseph Kallinger was born Joseph Lee Brenner III in 1935 to Joseph Lee Brenner Jr. and his wife Judith. From the very beginning of his life, Joseph Kallinger had to deal with the issues of dysfunction within his family. His father abruptly abandoned him and his mother in 1937 and Judith Brenner, unable to care for the child on her own, placed young Joseph in foster care. By 1939, Joseph was adopted by Stephen and Anna Kallinger. Stepping out of foster care and into a more permanent home turned out to be Joseph Kallinger's undoing. His new parents were incredibly strict and their punishments seemed more like bouts of torture than anything else. Joseph was randomly beaten by both his mother and his father, many times for no apparent reason. He was beaten so badly once that he required surgery to repair a hernia brought on by the abusive behavior. It was this hernia surgery that opened the door to Joseph's transformation into a psycho-sexual serial killer. After he was released from the hospital, Stephen and Anna Kallinger sat their son down. Horrified, Joseph listened as his parents told him how his doctor had performed an operation on him to release an evil spirit that was slumbering inside him.

"Where was the demon?" young Joseph asked.

Anna Kallinger glanced, then pointed to Joseph's crotch. "In your bird," she replied in her thick German accent, referring to his penis. This demon "worked for the Devil, not Jesus" and Stephen and Anna Kallinger went out of their way to emasculate and traumatize Joseph into thinking that his "bird" was too small to house a demon and that erections were caused by the Devil. Of course, the doctor hadn't really excised a demon from young Joseph, but the Kallinger's took the ball and ran with it, instilling a sense of paranoia and absolute terror into their son that would stay with him for the rest of his life.

Other times, Joseph faced punishments ranging from eating his own excrement to forced starvation. All of these consequences were for infractions as harmless as bed-wetting and insubordination. Stephen and Anna Kallinger taught their rules with criminal consequences and created one of the most horrific murderers who ever walked the Earth.

To add trauma to his already fractured view of sexuality, nine year-old Joseph was sexually assaulted by a group of teenage boys. A knife was held to his throat as another boy performed oral sex on him. In later years, dogged by puberty, Joseph would discover that he could not gain an erection unless he was holding a knife in his hand. But even the mere presence of the knife would do little to placate his libido. Anger, humiliation, sexual desire, and the need to exert control would all come crashing together inside of Joseph and he would retreat to the darkest recesses of his mind when it came to his sexual fantasies. He would imagine himself awash in the blood of women, women who squirmed under his penknife and left behind great rivers of gore as they relinquished all control to him. Many times, Joseph would pleasure himself to this image of himself as God, finally exerting control over those who controlled him.

But Joseph wore his "mask of sanity" fairly well in those early years of his life. He was able to maintain an aloof quality, but not quite give himself away as a young man with dark intentions. The one thing in Joseph's life that seemed to be his last finger hold on normality was his passion for acting. It was an art he stumbled upon when he was fifteen and had been cast in the middle school production of *A Christmas Carol.* Again, his adoptive parents were less than supportive of their son, telling him he was awful and that he shouldn't consider acting ever again. They instead pushed him back into his work as an apprentice for his father's shoe repair business. It would be, after all, his business when his parent's were gone. But Joseph's tolerance for his parents' rules was beginning to wane, quickly. He began to steal from his parents on a regular basis. To curb his stealing, the Kallingers offered Joseph steady wages for his work in the shoe shop, though in almost the same instance, they began charging him rent for the use of his own bedroom in their house.

But it wasn't just stealing that Joseph dabbled in; he was prone to vandalism and arson as well. And when punishments were dealt to him, he now took them without flinching, as if he were watching television or brushing his teeth. His unsettling gaze would send chills throughout their bodies. Stephen and Anna Kallinger noticed the shifts in his personality immediately. They would hear him in his bedroom having loud conversations with entities that weren't there, laughing heartily at jokes no one else could hear. There was a stoic, threatening feel to their adopted son, one so terrifying that they would eventually install a dead bolt lock on their bedroom door.

"You're not like anyone we know," Stephen would tell his son. "You're cold. It's like we don't know you now. We can't tell what you'll do."

When he was fifteen, Joseph met a young girl by the name of Hilda Bergman at a local movie theater. Hilda was a pretty, fifteen-year-old girl who lived just a few doors down from the Kallingers with her family. It was obvious from the start that Joseph loved and adored the girl, for she was, after all, an attractive, attentive, loving girl, something Joseph had never experienced before. The two young lovers seemed to connect on several different levels and Hilda found Joseph to be a quiet, caring young man. But her angelic comforts did little to influence the savagery raging inside of Joseph Kallinger. When they made love, he thought not of Hilda and her loveliness, but instead fantasizing about murdering and bathing in the blood of other women until he would climax.

Through most of his teenage years, Joseph did fairly well keeping the demon inside. Under his father's instruction, he quickly learned how to repair shoes very well. One might even think that Stephen Kallinger might have actually been proud of Joseph. Shoe repair was a perfect diversion from the flood of voices and hallucinations Joseph had now begun to suffer from. He was regularly visited by visions of God, angels, and demons, and the voices in his head were starting to become louder and more insistent.

Eventually, the Kallingers grew weary of fearing their son and his thoroughly odd behavior. It could be said that Joseph grew tired of his parents as well. He used the wages he earned from his father and found a room in a nearby boarding house, one that was close enough to his father's shoe shop as well as Hilda's house. Joseph seemed more at peace with this arrangement, and his parents were no doubt delighted as well.

In time, Joseph and Hilda married and had two children. But their blissful married life was extremely short lived. Hilda and their children left Joseph after a particularly nasty bout of domestic abuse. It can be said that thankfully, Hilda and her children got out when they did. Things only went downhill for Joseph Kallinger after that.

On September 4, 1957, Joseph admitted himself to St. Mary's hospital suffering from severe headaches and a total loss of appetite. Doctors believed it was stress from his divorce that was causing the headaches, but one can't help but wonder if Joseph knew he was dangerous and was trying to seek help for himself. Surely, if he were under a doctor's care, then they would see the things that were going on with him, right?

Apparently not, as they discharged him the next day. Again, Joseph Kallinger was on his own, dealing with a darkness very few of us could ever understand. Joseph eventually remarried on April 20, 1958. The union with his second wife, Betty Baumgard, produced five children. Though he was outwardly optimistic about this second marriage, inside he was raging and insecure. He often became abusive toward Betty and his children, inflicting the same punishments on them that he had suffered from Stephen and Anna Kallinger.

Joseph's psyche continued to decay during his second marriage, and blackouts became commonplace, which were often precipitated by stammering headaches. On one occasion, Joseph left Betty and the kids, telling them he was going to see his doctor. Two days later, Joseph Kallinger woke up in a hospital nearly seventy miles away from his home. He had been admitted as an amnesiac who apparently had been picked up by police walking along the highway in a semi-catatonic stupor. For several days, Joseph languished in the psychiatric ward of Hazelton Hospital, unable to talk, move, or communicate in a decipherable way. His identity was proven eventually by Stephen Kallinger, who took him back to his home in Philadelphia.

Joseph returned heartbroken, for Betty, fearing that Joseph had walked out on her, had left their home and returned to her mother's house. Joseph, in turn, thought that Betty had walked out on *him*. Being in love with Joseph and perhaps against her own better judgment, Betty reconciled with her husband. But the marriage was very strained after Joseph's time spent in the hospital. His already deranged mental state was becoming more and more pronounced as the illness became harder to contain behind his mask of sanity.

Betty's parents, who'd never cared much for Joseph in the first place, found him to be incredibly odd and they certainly didn't care for his controlling methods toward their daughter and grandchildren. The marriage was strained, and they barely stayed together, with Betty spending much of her time at her parents house with her much younger children. The four oldest children, Michael, Joey, Jimmy, and Mary Jo, all stayed primarily with Joseph, who had now taken up the shoe repair business from his father and became the sole proprietor when Stephen Kallinger retired.

But the hallucinations and eerie voices in Joseph's head continued to badger and torment him, causing him to set neighborhood buildings on fire. The voices urged him to be ultra strict with his kids, even suggesting insane punishments for them when they acted out.

Finally, in 1972, three of Joseph's children reported their father to the police, who arrested him on charges of neglect and child abuse. Bruises and wounds dotted their arms and legs, and they told stories of harsh, ritualistic punishments that involved merciless beatings and humiliation. It was as if Joseph were reenacting his childhood, but now, *he* was the one who was in control.

Joseph was arrested and sent to jail to await trial. While in jail, his IQ tested at eighty-two and staff psychiatrists finally diagnosed him with paranoid schizophrenia, which, to many people in Joseph's life, was explanation enough for his aberrant behavior. But then something odd happened.

His children recanted their stories, telling police that they made it all up because they didn't like his punishments. Much later on, Joseph would confess to his doctors that he had urged them to recant so that he could continue to work as a shoemaker and better provide for them. It could also be said that his children were terrified of him and recanted out of the sheer terror of what he might do to them should he be released from jail. But the police didn't buy it. Joseph was charged for abusing his daughter Mary Jo and his son Joey, both charges bringing a lengthy probation but no jail time. Shockingly, after being convicted of this, he was still allowed to remain in the home with his children.

By 1974, Joseph's children were beginning to mimic their father in his youth. The boys Michael, Joey, and Jimmy Kallinger were often found to be stealing, burglarizing, and setting fires. They were in and out of reformatories, failing multiple subjects in schools, smoking cigarettes, and drinking alcohol. Joseph had even developed an unnatural affection for his teenaged daughter, often coming across more as a jealous boyfriend than as a concerned father when he would spot her on the street holding hands with another boy.

Not only had Joseph lost control of his children, he had also lost his place as their father and king. Joseph saw the strength of his sons and his daughter as so overpowering that he essentially allowed them to run roughshod over him, which hearkens back to Joseph's days as a youth being put in his place by his father, neighborhood bullies, or any number of controlling figures who'd had their way with him. Michael and Joey were calling the shots now, and they insisted that their father join them on burglary outings. The boys were only twelve and eleven, and they were already lost to madness and mayhem.

But the voices were still in Joseph's head, and one day, the voices joined together to become one, that of God Himself. Joseph had a vision of God whereupon God told him that he was to murder 3 billion people on the Earth before then murdering his family and committing suicide. Joseph's act of suicide would culminate in him actually becoming God. This hallucinatory voice would accompany Joseph for the remainder of his life, sometimes appearing as a shriveled head named Charlie, floating above his shoulders.

The sudden loss of his position of power in the household and the appearance of an all-powerful entity aren't coincidental, as Joseph's psyche tried to come up with a way to exert power over his children, children he felt were beneath him, but who had usurped his throne, so to speak. Joseph was reluctant to undertake the mission set forth for him by "God," but he agreed to join Michael and Joey on their burglary trips in an effort to prepare himself for the murder of 3 billion people.

Joseph's newfound mission for committing murder was intoxicating and he set out to test himself. Because he and Michael had become so close during their burglary outings, it was fairly easy for Joseph to convince his son to aid him in his work for "God." Michael was shockingly agreeable to this pact, telling his father, "Glad to do it, Dad." They then set out on a mission to find someone for them both to kill, a murder that would bond them as father and son, as well as prepare them both for the murders to come.

They found eleven-year-old Jose Collazo, a Puerto Rican boy, on the streets of Philadelphia. Luring the young boy to an abandoned factory, Michael and Joseph took turns sexually assaulting, stabbing, and mutilating the boy, the final act being the severing of young Jose's penis, which Joseph took with him as a trophy. Empowered by their acts of bloodshed, Joseph and his son set about the mission given to him by "God," but after numerous episodes of burglarizing, torture, and arson, Joseph was challenged once again by "God." He was told that he must kill his son Joey to further test himself, to see if he were capable now of committing 3 billion acts of murder by killing his own son. In Joseph's mind, this act was no different than Abraham sacrificing Isaac to God in the Bible. It was the final test of his faith in "God."

It was a test he passed. Construction workers found Joey's lifeless corpse in the ruins of an abandoned building in Philadelphia. Oddly enough, Joey had been killed only two weeks after Joseph had taken out a sizable insurance policy on him. Today, it certainly casts doubt upon Joseph's claims of mental illness, looking much more like a premeditated killing than a crime of insanity. Joseph would later admit that he and Michael had tried to first get Joey to fall off a cliff "accidentally." Their next idea was to burn Joey alive. But when neither worked out as planned, they simply drowned him and left his body under piles of rubble in the abandoned building.

Together, Michael and Joseph burglarized numerous homes. They presented themselves as traveling salesmen in order to gain entrance and once inside, they would rob, beat, and rape numerous women, children, and men. For six long weeks in 1974, they forged a trail of blood and terror the likes of which had never been seen in Philadelphia. Police sketches of Joseph and Michael Kallinger made the rounds around town, but nothing ever came of the odd man and his teenage accomplice.

But on January 8, 1975, the Kallingers crime spree came to an abrupt end. Michael and Joseph were holding eight people hostage while they ransacked a home in Leonia, New Jersey. One of the hostages, a twenty-one-year-old nurse named Maria Fasching, was ordered by Joseph Kallinger to bite off the penis of one of the men tied up in the room. When Maria refused, Joseph swiftly cut her throat, her blood gushing onto his once immaculate shirt. During the chaos of Maria's murder, one of the other hostages had managed to flee the house, flagging down neighbors and screaming for help. Panicked, Joseph and Michael fled, using a city bus as their getaway car as they anonymously disappeared into the night.

But they had to get rid of the shirt. There was no way they would have been able to explain the massive bloodstain to Betty, and Joseph couldn't very well walk about the town wearing such a distressed garment. Without thinking, Joseph doffed the shirt and discarded it in a ditch before walking home with Michael.

Later, while attempting to track the movement of the killers using the schedule for the bus they may have taken in their escape, police found the bloody shirt and were elated to find the last name of it's owner handwritten on the tag.

"Kallinger," it read.

It was only a matter of time before the police came for Joseph, arresting him and his son Michael for the robberies, assaults, and murders around New Jersey. In time, the two would be charged for their crimes in Philadelphia and Maryland as well. But Michael, who many believe was just as disjointed mentally as his father, was deemed "under the influence of his father" and not at fault for his portion of the crimes. Psychologists believed that Michael had been taught by his father to do much of the aberrant and vile acts upon their victims simply by coaching him. Michael was therefore sentenced to live in a state reformatory for boys until he turned twenty-one. A period of strict probation followed, which lasted until his twenty-fifth birthday. After that, Michael Kallinger moved out of the state of Pennsylvania and had his name changed. His whereabouts are unknown.

Joseph Kallinger, on the other hand, was convicted of nine felony counts of assault, robbery, and murder. Convicted in 1976, he eventually garnered life in prison, plus thirty to eighty years, which he began serving in Pennsylvania's State Correctional Facility at Huntington. Joseph Kallinger was now Prisoner K-2719, a resident of B Block, the maximum security portion of the prison. He spent his entire day behind a locked cell door.

But he wasn't alone.

Charlie was with him: that demonic severed head that haunted him mercilessly, that evil soul whose long hair hid his dark eyes. Locked in a cage with nothing to calm the demons in him, Joseph Kallinger fell victim to Charlie's antics. When Charlie ordered Joseph to fling his feces or food around the cell, Joseph did as he was told. When Charlie refused to get off Joseph's bed, Joseph slept on the floor. When Charlie told Joseph to kill another inmate, Joseph complied, slashing the inmate's throat with a homemade knife. Eventually, Joseph began to faithfully attempt suicide on a regular basis, a practice that landed him on a continual suicide watch for the remainder of his life. For years and years behind bars, Joseph Kallinger struggled with the need to kill 3 billion people, to fulfill the promise he made to "God." Up until the day he died, in 2006, Kallinger swore that he would pick up where he left off if he were ever released.

Kallinger's lawyer, Paul Giblin, reiterated to the press following Kallinger's death that, "I never wanted him to be acquitted. I wanted him in a mental institution for the rest of his life. He was sick. He was an evil man, and the evilness was a manifestation of the illness."

The Vile Files

Peter Kurten

(May 26, 1883-July 2, 1931)

Known as "the Vampire of Dusseldorf," German serial killer Peter Kurten grew up in an extremely abusive household fraught with physical and sexual abuse, traits he would inherit from his alcoholic father. He claimed his first victim, ten-year-old Christine Klein, in 1913 when he was thirty years old. A prison sentence of eight years kept him from continuing his rampage; but, by 1929, released from prison and newly married, Kurten would resume his murderous path. He was finally caught in 1931 and confessed to over seventy murders, though police

could only prove he was responsible for nine. Kurten's primary focus for murder was sexual gratification, brought on mostly by the sight, smell, feel, and taste of blood. Sentenced to death by guillotine, he asked his executioner, "Tell me, after my head is chopped off, will I still be able to hear, at least for a moment, the sound of my own blood gushing from the stump of my neck? That would be the pleasure to end all pleasures." His mummified head is currently on display at the Ripley's Believe It or Not museum in the Wisconsin Dells, Wisconsin.

CHAPTER 11

LOUIS WAGNER

"THE SMUTTYNOSE BUTCHER"

Smuttynose Island, Maine

"The thought of death on the gallows was painful, yet it was preferable to a lingering, lonesome life within prison walls."
—**Louis Wagner, 1873**

Folklore in general has a way of presenting us with a darkness and foreboding that we very seldom get to see or feel. In a lot of ways, the truths behind some folk tales are rather benign, almost understated. American folklore is chock full of these kinds of tales, those stories of bad endings that come to good people, and they're usually twisted in a way so they present a moral. In almost every way, the story behind the Smuttynose Axe Murders reads like a classic folktale from the turn of the century, teeming with greed, murder, and suspense. But unlike the classic tales where the murderer escapes and you look for him under your bed later, this story's villain was identified and the story was 100 percent true. What happened on that island off the coast of Maine in March of 1873 was gruesome and tragic, and would stain the once-idyllic island with the unshakable stigma of greed and deception.

The story of the Smuttynose Axe Murders began in 1866 for John and Maren Hontvet, who like many immigrants of the time, set out for the promise of a better life in America, leaving their home country of Norway behind them. The two settled initially in Boston, but made their way north once they could afford to leave the city for greener pastures. Finding themselves in Maine, they immediately found and fell in love with a home on Haley's Island, nicknamed Smuttynose Island by some of the raunchier fishermen of the area, some ten miles from the coast of Maine. It was an island that had reminded them both of home, but the promise of better work made this home much more tolerable. Coming from the fishing life in Norway, John Hontvet found it rather easy to set up a fishing boat and ply his fresh seafood on the nearby shore in Portsmouth. Again, once he'd raised enough money, John sent for his brother, Matthew, and Maren's sister, Karen Christensen.

Matthew went to work immediately for John on his fishing schooner, but it was soon evident that, while Matthew was a great help to John, extra hands would definitely be necessary. John found a willing laborer in Louis Wagner, a Prussian immigrant hailing from New Hampshire, who offered to work for John in exchange for room and board. It could be said that Louis was happy to work for the Hontvets but was cagey about not being paid, though he enjoyed the steadiness of the work and the familiarity of family life. He was also happy about having two attractive Norwegian women feeding and caring for him. But rheumatoid arthritis kept Louis from working 100 percent of the time and when more of John and Maren's relatives came to stay with them, he already knew that his time there was drawing short. With the arrival of Maren's brother Even and his wife Anethe, John Hontvet terminated the arrangement with Louis and sent him on his way.

It wasn't until several weeks later that John and his brothers-in-law once again came across Louis Wagner. The four of them had taken the schooner to Portsmouth to procure bait for their next fishing venture. John Hontvet, always one to offer a hand to someone in need, offered a job to Wagner helping to cut the bait. The only hitch was that the ship carrying the fish bait was delayed, having had to navigate around an oppressive storm. All of them were going to be staying the night on the mainland that night, essentially waiting for that ship to come in. Wagner readily took the job and agreed to meet the men at the wharf later that night.

When the ship finally arrived, Wagner was nowhere to be found. John Hontvet and the brothers wrote it off as Wagner having changed his mind. They shrugged it off and got to work. But off the coast of Smuttynose Island, a tiny rowboat cut through the choppy waters, its helmsman aiming for a dark patch of beach close to the only inhabited home on Smuttynose. As he ran the boat aground and stepped out, Louis Wagner looked up at the Hontvet's home and a ghoulish curl ran up and down his stomach. For months, he'd known the ins and outs of the Hontvets. He knew their financial station in life. He knew much of their secrets. He also knew where John Hontvet stashed most of his earnings. This was the reason he

Smuttynose Island.

was here, and as he stood on that beach in the dark, the snow tumbling down around him, he knew this would be the last night that he would have to work for free room and board. With callous purpose, he walked through the snow toward the glowing light of the Hontvet's home.

In the house, the three women had settled in for a long, cold night. They had chosen to all sleep downstairs close to the fireplace to stay warm. Maren and Anethe had chosen the downstairs bedroom, while Karen and Ringe, Maren's dog, slept on a cot in the kitchen close to the warm stove. They knew their husbands were staying the night in Portsmouth, so imagine Karen's surprise when the kitchen door opened slowly with a loud, bone-rattling creak. The sound of the door alarmed Ringe, who immediately began barking, waking Karen.

As she sat up and looked to who she thought was John Hontvet, she was met by the crushing blow of one of the kitchen chairs. Louis Wagner brought the wood down upon her repeatedly. It's unknown what he was thinking as she screamed her last words.

"John is killing me!" she kept screaming, still thinking that it was Maren's husband who was beating her to death. The screams of her sister-in-law woke Maren from her sleep and she opened her bedroom door, seeing only the darkened form of a man standing in the kitchen, holding bloody pieces of kitchen chair in his steady hands. Maren pulled her sister and Ringe away from him and pulled them into the bedroom with her and Anethe. By the time she'd bolted the door, Wagner was banging upon it, pushing and kicking against the wood.

"We have to get out of here," Maren told Anethe. She pushed open the window sash and persuaded Anethe to escape. But once outside, the biting cold and confusion of what was happening forced Anethe to stop in her tracks. She froze, unaware of where she was or what she was doing. By the time she'd regained her bearings, Anethe had turned to find Louis Wagner in front of her, brandishing an axe that had been lain against the house earlier in the day.

From the bedroom window, Maren also, finally, understood who was attacking them.

"Louis! Louis! Louis!" screamed Anethe.

Louis raised the axe and brought it down in one crushing blow against Anethe's skull. She immediately dropped to the white ground, her dark red blood pooling eerily against the melting white snow. Though her skull had been crushed and she made no further movements, Louis continued to bring the axe down upon her, crushing her head completely beyond recognition.

Once he was finished, Louis ran back into the house and continued to pound on the bedroom door. Karen, slowly dying from her wounds, drifted in an out of consciousness as Maren pondered what she should do. No way could she escape and take Karen along with her. It would be the death of both of them. Maren ran back to the window, snatched Ringe the dog into her arms, and began to escape when Louis burst through the door and rushed at her with the axe. He brought the axe down so hard against the sash that it actually snapped in two midway through the handle.

Maren fell to the ground as she listened to Louis Wagner use the axe head to finish off her sister, the sickening crunch of destroyed bone and Karen's terrified screams echoing in her ears. She ran off as quickly as she could, Ringe the dog tucked under her arm. She found a section of rocky beach, cloaked in darkness and far away from the house and hid among the tall stones. With only her sleep wear and Ringe to keep her warm, Maren hid among the rocks until dawn's first light, when she hurried to Malaga, a neighboring island connected to Smuttynose by a rough hewn seawall. She shouted across the jetty to a group of children playing on the beach, who ran to alert their parents. Maren was safe, finally.

Louis Wagner had not spent the night looking for Maren. He'd spent much of the night rowing himself back to shore, where he was seen in an eatery in Portsmouth, partaking in an early breakfast and looking like death warmed over. In short order, he paid the bill and left. Very few people actually noticed that he'd left Portsmouth altogether, taking a train into Boston around 9:00 a.m.

Before he'd even arrived in Boston, word about what Louis Wagner had done to Anethe and Karen had made its way back to the mainland and an official manhunt began. Once in Boston, the once-penniless Wagner somehow now had enough money to buy himself a suit, a new pair of boots, and pay for a shave and a haircut, which radically altered his appearance from the previous night. In fact, most who knew him in Portsmouth would have never recognized him. But once word of his crime made it to Boston, all those who knew him previously knew exactly where to send the police to find him: his old North End neighborhood.

Louis Wagner was arrested that night without incident and promptly shipped back to Portsmouth. Once there, he was greeted by a literal mob of people, carrying torches, cursing his name, and throwing stones packed into snowballs. Escorted by armed guards, he was taken to the police station where he was extradited to Maine and was finally officially booked for the murders of Anethe and Karen.

It didn't take long for the evidence to begin to pile up against Wagner, who maintained his innocence with flimsy stories of having worked for a fisherman he couldn't name, stationed on a boat he couldn't remember on a pier he couldn't point out to authorities. He said he'd worked all night, had a few beers at the local tavern, then fell asleep outside until daybreak when he headed back to Boston.

The case against him was much, much stronger, and Maren's testimony against Wagner made it all the more airtight. Fifteen dollars had been stolen from the Hontvet's house, while Wagner's suit that he'd purchased in Boston cost exactly $15. Among the change found in his pocket was one of Maren's dress buttons, placing him inside the house. In addition, one of his shirts, caked and smeared with blood, had been found tucked and hidden in a nearby outhouse, his name embroidered on the collar. Then witnesses came forward, citizens familiar with the docks and Wagner's near constant presence on them, testifying that they had often heard Wagner offer to commit murder for money.

But it was Anethe's last words, spoken to her killer and related by Maren in her testimony that slammed Wagner's coffin shut for good.

"Louis! Louis! Louis!" she'd screamed just before he brought the axe down, silencing her forever.

Without batting an eye, the jury found Wagner guilty in less than an hour, and he was sentenced to hang.

Most all of the evidence pointed to his guilt and although many different scenarios have been brought up as alternate takes on the crime, many believe that justice was done the day Louis Wagner hung from his neck until he was dead. Wagner is still known as the state of Maine's most notorious killer. His body lies buried at the Old Prison Burial Grounds of the Maine State Prison at Thomaston. His plot is the oldest in the cemetery and is still the most sought after.

The house on Smuttynose, which John and Maren had hoped would be their dream home, is now, sadly long gone. Following the murders, John and Maren refused to return to the house and souvenir hunters and curiosity seekers descended upon the Hontvet house. They made away with bloodstained pieces of floor, walls, and windows. In a matter of months, the house had been completely desiccated and discarded for the sake of a few morbid keepsakes.

The only monument that remains is the large granite stone that Maren slept under. Called Maren's Rock now, it is still sought out to this day. It has become a symbol for Maren's hard-edged determination to survive what must have been the most horrifying night of her life.

Anethe and Karen were laid to rest in the South Cemetery of Portsmouth, New Hampshire. John and Maren Hontvet returned to their homeland seven years after the murders in 1880. It is not known why the couple chose to go back to Norway, but it is very probable that Maren grew ill and wanted to return to her homeland. John traveled back to the United States in 1884, while Maren remained

The graves of Anethe Matea and Karen Christenten, victims of Louis Wagner.

in Norway until her death in 1887 at the age of fifty-two. John, who remarried after Maren's death, died in 1904 in Portsmouth. John and Maren's only daughter, Clara, succumbed to bronchial pneumonia when she was only thirty-six years old.

It is obvious that life became even more difficult for Maren and her family after the horrific murders of Anethe and Karen on Smuttynose Island on that cold March night in the winter of 1873. But the legend of the Smuttynose Axe Murders lives on to this day, for it was a night of unparalleled terror that reaches its gnarled hands across the ages and touches us on the cheek. Were it not for the iconic and uplifting sight of "Maren's Stone," the memories would most certainly be all grim and lacking in real hope.

The Vile Files

The Sawney Bean Gang

The story of the Sawney Bean Gang of Scotland has been the inspiration for countless horror films, notably Wes Craven's *The Hills Have Eyes*, over the years. The validity

of the legend has always been staunchly debated, though most accede that the story of Sawney Bean rose from the ashes of other true stories of vicious highwaymen. The most widely accepted account of the legend has it that the gang was started in the 1500s in Scotland when psychotic couple Alexander "Sawney" Bean and his wife hid out in a massive cave system along the Scottish coast in Bennane Head. They were an all inclusive family, producing eight sons and six daughters, who, through incestuous relations, produced up to thirty-two grandchildren. Over the years, the Gang took to sleeping during the day and kidnapping and murdering passersby at night. They robbed their victims, then cannibalized them, tossing their bones into the sea below. Eventually, after claiming untold numbers of victims, the feral clan was discovered, apprehended, and executed without trial. It was said that the men had their genitalia, hands, and foot cut off, and were allowed to bleed to death. The women and children were all burned alive.

CHAPTER 12

RICHARD KUKLINSKI

"THE ICEMAN"

Jersey City, New Jersey

"I would move Heaven, Hell, and anything in between to get to you. You wouldn't be safe anywhere if I was mad at you. You could pull a gun on me and if I'm mad at you, I'm coming forward. You'd have to shoot me to stop me. And if you don't kill me, you're stupid."
—**Richard Kuklinski**

His claims were outrageous. Not only that, they were also chillingly believable. He would commit or aid in the murder of some of the underworld's most notorious figures, all the while maintaining a slick, glossy family life as a loving husband and father in suburban New Jersey. Normally, one might exclude the world's most prolific Mafia hitman from the lists of notorious serial killers and mass murderers. The code of conduct in the life was that it was business and if you were in the business, you took your life into your own hands. But chances were excellent that if Richard Kuklinski hadn't been paid to kill, he would have ended up doing it for free anyway. It would have only been a matter of time.

Kuklinski wore the same "mask of sanity" that Gacy, Bundy, Kallinger, and a myriad of others wore during the peak of their crimes against humanity—maintaining a smiling outward appearance to those he loved and trusted, while hiding their true intentions, dark as they were. But I don't believe that Kuklinski was insane. He was a killer who liked what he did, refused to kill women or children, and was paid handsomely for his craft. It was the proliferation of his "American Dream." But we mustn't make any mistake about what Kuklinski was: an incredibly cold, merciless killer who could not be reasoned with, nor would a bargain ever be brokered. Chances are, if you ever saw Richard Kuklinski walk up to you, you were already dead.

Kuklinski was born Richard Leonard Kuklinski in 1935 to a Polish immigrant and railway worker named Stanley Kuklinski and his devoutly Catholic wife, Anna. Discipline was the order of the day for Stanley and Anna's children, which also included Richard's older brother Florian, a younger sister named Roberta, and younger brother Joseph. But the disciplinary actions often deviated into full-blown child abuse as both parents took delight in beating their kids with broom handles, lamps, and generally anything else that was within reach. Florian eventually died from injuries sustained in a beating from his father, and the remaining children were ordered to tell authorities that Florian had gotten hurt by falling down the stairs. This was a polarizing incident in Richard's life; it haunted him for decades afterward and contributed to his extreme hatred toward his mother and father. In addition, it taught Richard, as well as his brother Joseph, about the cheap nature of human life.

From the ashes of that severe dysfunction, the world took on two new monsters: Richard and Joseph Kuklinski. Joseph would eventually find himself in prison for the 1970 rape and murder of a twelve-year-old girl. Richard, on the other hand, developed his style of murder through the ritualistic killings of cats and other small animals, carefully and meticulously learning the trade he would come to embrace as an adult.

When asked about his brother Joseph's crimes, Richard simply replied, "We come from the same father."

As Richard grew into manhood, he became a hulking, six-foot-five force to be reckoned with in the shady billiard halls of New Jersey where he would shark his talent at playing pool. Those who rubbed him the wrong way, tried to welch on a bet, or were just plain annoying would often feel a tremendous beatdown at the hands of Richard Kuklinski, if he didn't kill you first.

His even-tempered punishments caught the eyes of the DeCavalcante family out of Newark, New Jersey, and the Gambino family out of New York. It was the Gambinos that tested Richard first, sending Roy DeMeo, a soldato, or soldier, to meet with the icy killer. DeMeo pistol whipped Kuklinski mercilessly. Richard was packing a pistol at the time, but refrained from using it. Truthfully, Kuklinski could have killed DeMeo and his henchmen a hundred times over before any of them could have pulled their own weapons. But Kuklinski knew who DeMeo was, and out of respect, he allowed the beating to continue. His reluctance to pull his gun on DeMeo impressed the Mafia soldier, who immediately retained him as a contract killer for the Gambinos. In addition to staging murders, Kuklinski also assisted in robberies and pirating pornographic video cassettes. Past members of the Gambino family have alleged that Kuklinski would travel from Philadelphia to New Jersey to New York almost constantly, handling everything from debt collections to trafficking of illegal pornography to murder for hire. All of these actions had been ordered by either Roy DeMeo or Robert DiBernardo, an associate from the DeCavalcante family.

Over the course of thirty years, Kuklinski murdered at the behest of the Gambinos or the DeCavalcante families, eluding suspicion by maintaining a perfectly normal family life and by constantly changing his methods of killing. It was a practice that had allowed Henry Lee Lucas to kill so freely without suspicion as well: change up the cause of death, so that the deaths stay unconnected. If the police thought they were looking for fifty different killers, there was little-to-no chance he'd have been suspected at all. He would use guns sometimes, knives another. For those times when he felt a need to get some exercise, he would resort to bare-knuckled beatings.

One pet method he enjoyed using was cyanide poisoning, which was difficult to find in toxicology reports and could be administered using the least amount of physical contact possible. Kuklinski was also extremely careful. He was rarely photographed outside his family at home, and he was a quick and clean murderer. In essence, Kuklinski was a ghost known only to those who paid him and those who died at his hands.

Richard Kuklinski saw himself as a dyed-in-the-wool family man, but when he would get the call from his superiors from the Gambino or DeCavalcante families, he would drop everything and go on the job. This happened often and his children and wife often told of times that he would leave the house in the middle of the night or even in the middle of Sunday dinner, only to return hours later without explanation.

One call he got came from a member of the Genovese family, known only as Tony P. There was a Union worker in Detroit who had been giving the bosses in New York a hard time and the order was put out that this guy was to be taken out. Tony P. had called Richard simply because of Richard's icy reputation and attention to details. He was also one of the most trusted killers anyone from the five families had ever encountered. So Richard and Tony P. and a two-man crew set out for Detroit, driving the whole way. Once in the Motor City, the crew met up with their mark at the Machus Red Fox Restaurant, a rural suburb just outside Detroit. Once he was in the car, Richard cold-cocked the mark and drove a hunting knife through the back of his skull, minimizing the amount of blood and maximizing the chances of sudden death. They then tossed the body into the trunk and drove back to New Jersey. The body was burned, then sealed inside a fifty-gallon drum and buried in a junkyard under the Pulaski Skyway. Richard didn't think anything more about the body in the junkyard until one of the crew got pinched by the FBI. Thinking that he might give up the location of the body, Kuklinski dug up the body in the drum, stuffed it into a junked car, and had it essentially crushed into a four foot cube, which was then sold to Japanese automakers as scrap metal. According to author Philip Carlo in his book *The Ice Man: Confessions of a Mafia Contract Killer*, the mark's name was Jimmy Hoffa.

"He's part of a car somewhere in Japan right now," Kuklinski would say with a grin. He eventually recanted slightly, telling reporters later that he had only heard rumors of what had happened to Hoffa and that he hadn't been involved. But his intricately detailed story of what happened to the Teamsters boss shouldn't be taken lightly. Chances are, by recanting, he was attempting to divert attention away from his bosses, the ones who might have ordered the hit in the first place. Sammy "the Bull" Gravano, an enforcer and right-hand man for the Gambino family, would also tell his own story of how Jimmy Hoffa ended up, only in his story, Hoffa was now a part of the Meadowlands Arena in New Jersey. All six pieces of him.

Eventually, the tides of Mafia life began to turn. A young, idealistic Capo for the Gambino family by the name of John Gotti was rallying his enemies and his supporters in favor of assassinating current Gambino head Paul Castellano and reestablishing new, fairer deals with all of the families of New York and New Jersey. Castellano had long been regarded as an iron-fisted ruler of the underworld, pocketing the majority of cash earned from the toils of his subordinates. Under Gotti, it would be a fairer deal for everyone.

Richard Kuklinski got the call from Sammy Gravano, who offered a substantial sum to Kuklinski if he aided in the design and execution of Paul Castellano's assassination. Kuklinski readily accepted.

The murder of Paul Castellano was a shocking scene. He'd been gunned down in public as he got out of his car in front of the Sparks Steakhouse in New York. Two shooters, presumably Sammy Gravano and Richard Kuklinski, rushed the car and peppered Castellano and his driver with a hail of bullets.

The Gotti era of Mafia life propelled everyone to the top of the food chain. Everyone except Richard. Following Castellano's assassination, Kuklinski slinked back into his life as a family man until the next call came in. To him, Castellano didn't matter any more than some street hood. He simply took his paycheck and went home.

As John Gotti rose to the top of the criminal underworld, Richard Kuklinski himself began his own criminal empire. He was the head of his own crew, one that specialized in burglaries, illegal pornography, and contract murder. It was also around this time that Kuklinski would earn his ominous moniker, the IceMan.

Kuklinski was fascinated by death, and moreover, the concealment of the details of death. He'd experimented with cyanide, which caused a slower, more indeterminate death. And now, he'd happened upon a method that would disguise the time of death. After hooking up with a fellow hit man by the name of Robert Pronge, who went by the nickname "Mister Softee" after the brand of ice cream truck he used to pass seamlessly in and out of neighborhoods before and after a hit. According to Kuklinski, it was Pronge who'd given him the idea of storing the corpses of his marks in an industrial freezer. The rapid freezing of the body would delay the decomposition of the flesh, thereby making a time of death a relative mystery. Kuklinski and Pronge's friendship didn't last long; it all ended when Pronge asked Kuklinski to rub out his wife and child, something Kuklinski always maintained he would never do. Later on, Pronge would be found shot to death in his ice cream truck. His killer was never found, but it is probable that Kuklinski had a hand in it somehow.

Richard Kuklinski's career of murder was now entering its fifteenth year, and like many stone-cold killers who'd grown sure of themselves, he became sloppy in his methods of murder and in the cleanup of his crimes. He would brazenly leave bodies where they lay. Sometimes he would put the bodies in a fifty-gallon drum and leave them on the sidewalk near where they had been killed. One of those victims was thirty-seven-year-old Gary Smith, a collaborator of Kuklinski's in an auto theft scam. He was fed a cyanide-laced hamburger by Kuklinski and Daniel Deppner, another of Kuklinski's associates. But the poison took longer than Kuklinski had hoped and he grew impatient waiting for the man to die. Kuklinski ordered Deppner to strangle Smith, which he did with a torn out electrical cord. The two killers stuffed Smith's body in between the mattress and the box spring and left. The room was rented out twice after that before the body was discovered. Patrons commented on the odd smell, but never once thought to look under the bed.

David Deppner didn't fare any better, though. His body was found on a wooded portion of Clinton Road in West Milford, New Jersey, half frozen and being scavenged by a flock of turkey vultures. Another associate of Kuklinski, videotape broker Louis Musgay, was also found dead near a town park in Orangetown, New York. He had been shot once in the head and was also partially frozen. Kuklinski had broken one of his own rules and established a linking modus operandi.

Authorities now knew they were dealing with one man instead of a trio of different killers. In addition, all three dead men had been under the employ of Kuklinski, who had gained the attention of the Alcohol, Tobacco, and Firearm Bureau when he started his criminal syndicate. In all, five murders were attributed to Kuklinski by the ATF because it had well been established that he was the last man to see each of the victims alive.

In 1985, Kuklinski's reign came to a shattering end as he was arrested for attempting to buy cyanide from an undercover ATF agent posing as a fellow hit man. He would be arrested near his home in New Jersey and it would be the first time his beloved wife would see the Richard Kuklinski the rest of the world knew. As he was arrested, the hulking murderer thrashed and screamed in frustration, knowing his world was coming to an end, and knowing that he would no longer be able to hide his rage from his family.

He was charged with five counts of murder, six weapons violations, and attempted murder, robbery, and attempted robbery. He was convicted in 1988 of committing two of the murders, and orchestrating the other three. He received multiple life sentences and was ordered to serve his time at Trenton State Prison, the same prison where his brother Joseph now laid his head.

Kuklinski found notoriety in his incarceration. Networks and cable outlets, prosecutors, criminologists, and psychiatrists lined up for interviews with the IceMan, and he obliged. Richard Kuklinski, from behind bars and protective custody, spilled his guts to HBO in a series of *America Undercover* documentaries that chillingly recounted Kuklinski's life as a contract killer. His passive, cool demeanor as he rattled off horrific stories of murder by his own hand disturbed and fascinated viewers, who readily turned him into an underworld icon. His face and quotes from the HBO specials would begin to show up on subway walls in New York and New Jersey.

But there were several people who didn't think much of Kuklinski's loose lips and his willingness to talk about his crimes. When Kuklinski died March 5, 2006, his death was ruled a result of natural causes, but author Philip Carlo had spent many weeks with Kuklinski and the former mobster seemed to be in very good shape up until the time of his death.

"He was healthy and robust and he got sick all of a sudden," Carlo maintained. "Family members believe he was poisoned."

Carlo also said that Richard Kuklinski had developed heart, lung, and kidney problems over the course of almost four months, coupled with dementia and the inability to remember the names of his three beloved children. He really did seem to be suffering from a gradual, very slow death brought on by cyanide, his favorite weapon of choice. But hospital officials did confirm that Richard Kuklinski had been treated several times for an "undisclosed medical problem."

Kuklinski was pronounced dead at 1:20 a.m. It seemed to be a rather unfit end for such a monstrous person, but the conspiracy theories leapt up almost immediately. He had been scheduled to testify against Sammy "The Bull" Gravano, who was standing trial in New York for ordering the murder of NYPD detective Peter Calabro. Kuklinski confessed that it was Gravano who had hired him to kill Calabro and theorists suggested that Gravano had Kuklinski silenced before he could testify. Kuklinski's body was quickly cremated and his ashes were remanded to his family. Prosecutors dropped the charges against Gravano, but he was later arrested and imprisoned on drug charges in Arizona.

In the end, Kuklinski was considered by many to be a gentleman killer, a romantic figure. But not much separates Kuklinski from Gacy, Dahmer, or even Jack the Ripper. He was a perfect killing machine, a shark. As he would later recall in an interview from Philip Carlo's book *The Iceman*:

> By now you know what I liked most was the hunt, the challenge of what the thing was. The killing for me was secondary. I got no rise as such out

of it...for the most part. But the figuring it out, the challenge—the stalking and doing it right, successfully—that excited me a lot. The greater the odds against me, the more juice I got out of it.

The Vile Files

Richard Biegenwald

(August 24, 1940-March 10, 2008)

New Jersey serial killer Richard Biegenwald was a high-school dropout and petty criminal before he turned to murder when he was convicted and sentenced to life in prison in 1958 for the murder of a shopkeeper. Released on good behavior seventeen years later, Biegenwald attempted to put his life back together, but struggled as a life of crime called on him to return. Soon, he would become embroiled in bouts of arson and rape before upping the game with the murder of Maria Cialella in 1981. Her murder would be followed by four others before he would be caught and sentenced to death by lethal injection in 1983. In 2008, Biegenwald escaped the needle and perished on his own, dying of respiratory and kidney failure.

CHAPTER 13

JEFFREY DAHMER

"THE MILWAUKEE CANNIBAL"

Milwaukee, Wisconsin

"Go ahead and kill me. I don't care if I live or die."
—**Jeffrey Dahmer's,** last words to his killer

I was working at a Lafayette, Indiana, truck stop in the summer of 1991. I was the midnight-til-7:00 a.m. guy and while it wasn't my proudest moment of employment, it did afford me the opportunity to meet some thoroughly bizarre people—but none of them so bizarre as compared to the plain looking guy I saw in the newspaper early one morning in July 1991. That was the day I met Jeffrey Dahmer for the first time. Initially, his story was really only a single-column, three-paragraph blurb somewhere on the second or third page. But soon, very soon, the details of Jeffrey Dahmer's life and livelihood would become the most talked about, read about, and heard about story of that year. His murderous exploits moved beyond page two and clogged the front pages of thousands of newspapers for the rest of the year.

He was one of the few serial killers who would become a part of the popular culture lexicon while still alive, becoming the punch line to millions of sick jokes, while his boyish face became the visage of evil for those affected by his compulsions. He was seen on T-shirts, dime store biographies were rushed out before he'd even gone on trial, and just about every talk show from Phil Donahue to Geraldo Rivera dedicated at least one episode to his tale. His crimes were a media firestorm.

But what separated Jeffrey from killers such as Bundy and Gacy was his unending sense of remorse for what he'd done. Remorse was a rarity for the serial killer-type. In fact, most all serial killers do what they do because they have to and are arrogant enough to believe that they are in the right. But with Dahmer, there were no taunting letters to newspapers and policemen, no arrogant swagger or "catch me if you can" attitude. There was just Jeffrey, haunted by those he'd killed and forever remorseful to the families left behind.

Jeffrey was born May 21, 1960, in West Allis, Wisconsin, the son of Joyce and Lionel Dahmer, two fairly intellectual parents who had a knack for arguing. The tension between the two of them tended to supersede nearly everything else, including young Jeffrey, who found himself left alone as he listened to his parents argue. This was how it was for much of the time Lionel and Joyce were married. Joyce had a history of depression, even resorting to a suicide attempt, while Lionel immersed himself in his work as a student in chemistry at Marquette University.

In truth, Jeffrey was a boy immersed in sadness, watching the only two people that meant something in his life both physically and emotionally combat each other, while they both forgot that their son was absorbing all of it. Their fighting taught Jeffrey, above all else, to fear the separation that might come as a result. In school, Jeffrey was regarded by teachers and students alike as very quiet and uncommunicative. Teachers thought he might have felt neglected or lonely, while students just simply called him "the quiet kid" and although he was generally left alone, Jeffrey still managed to corral a small group of friends.

Jeffrey's main interests in his youth were animals, namely insects and butterflies when he was young, and larger animals later on. Eventually, his interest turned to the anatomy of animals, and he routinely began collecting roadside carcasses and taking them home with him, where he would dissect and dismember them in an effort to see how they "fitted together." This interest in the bodies of animals actually had its genesis when Jeffrey was four years old. He had observed his father removing old bones from underneath the house and, according to Lionel Dahmer, his young son seemed incredibly excited by the sound the bones made as they jostled together. Now, as Jeffrey neared eight years of age, he was separating different body parts and putting them into separate jars. He even went so far as to impale the skull of a dog on a stick in the woods behind his family's house.

In 1968, after having received his degree in chemical engineering, Lionel and Joyce Dahmer moved their family, which included newborn baby David, to Bath, Ohio. Two years later, over a family meal of fried chicken, Jeffrey calmly asked his father, "what would happen if the bones of the chicken were to be placed in bleach." Jeffrey's calm and introverted manner hadn't been lost on Lionel. Indeed, his father worried about his son's social life, but was delighted when Jeffrey showed an interest in science. So, after dinner, Lionel went about innocently showing his oldest son how to clean and preserve animal bones, a talent he would utilize later in his life as a serial murderer.

But Jeffrey's troubles didn't end because he found a hobby dissecting and preserving dead animals. It only got worse. He became more and more withdrawn, and by the time he was a freshman in high school, he was not only an introvert, but also a confirmed alcoholic. He was constantly smuggling beer and liquor into school by concealing it in the lining of his Army jacket, referring to it as his "medicine" whenever a peer caught him sipping it. But even so, Jeffrey was looked upon as a fairly polite student and regarded as highly intelligent, though he only managed to garner average-to-above average grades.

It was around this time that Jeffrey discovered that he was a homosexual, a fact that he kept secret from his parents, though it was hinted at that he had been in a relationship with another young man from Revere High School. His fantasies were dripping with thoughts of control and dominance over his partner and his main fantasy revolved around making sexual use of an unconscious man, having complete control over someone without protestation. It was a common fantasy for someone who probably had no such control in real life, but it became problematic when Jeffrey began to incorporate dissection into that fantasy. He even began to imagine and plan scenarios where he would attack other men he found attractive and have his way with them as they lay unconscious, a scenario he almost pulled on a local jogger in Dahmer's neighborhood.

By 1978, Jeffrey's grades had declined, his alcoholism continued to rise dramatically, and both of his parents were quarreling constantly. Eventually, Lionel Dahmer moved out of the house and into a local motel, leaving Jeffrey and his younger brother David alone with their mother. Joyce, in turn, was awarded primary custody of David, but because Jeffrey was now eighteen, he was not part of that custody arrangement. Joyce Dahmer took David to live with her parents in Chippewa Falls and she left the family home.

Jeffrey Dahmer was now totally and utterly alone. His greatest fear had come true. Everyone had abandoned him. Lionel Dahmer wouldn't realize that Jeffrey was home by himself until a few months later. But by then it would be too late. Lionel's eldest son had already started down a dark path that he would never stray from no matter how hard he tried.

Dahmer committed his first murder that summer of 1978, an eighteen-year-old hitchhiker named Steven Hicks. Lured back to Dahmer's empty house with the promise of beer and rock music, Jeffrey beat Hicks with a ten-pound dumbbell, then strangled the youth with the bar of the same dumbbell. Completely isolated and having a chance to act out his fantasy, Jeffrey stripped Steven's body of clothing and masturbated as he stood above the corpse. In the following days, Dahmer methodically dissected and dismembered Hicks' body. Jeffrey initially buried the pieces of the body in a shallow grave behind the house, but opted to return a few weeks later. He disinterred the body parts, separating flesh from bone. He dissolved the flesh in acid, which he then flushed down the toilet, and crushed the bones with a sledgehammer, scattering the pieces across the forest floor.

A month and a half later, Jeffrey's father returned to the house with his new fiancee and was shocked to find his son living there alone. Lionel was, perhaps, more shocked that his ex-wife had abandoned Jeffrey so quickly and he tried to get his eldest son back on track. Jeffrey tried his hand at college, enrolling at Ohio State University. But his incessant alcoholism rendered his education completely moot. He dropped out after three months.

After doing a stint in the Army and floating around the beaches of Miami, Florida, for a time, Jeffrey Dahmer finally gave in, called his father, and returned to Ohio. But Jeffrey's alcoholism followed him everywhere and Lionel did his best to try and break his son of the habit. In December of 1981, Lionel sent Jeffrey to live with his grandmother in West Allis, Wisconsin, hoping her influence and a change of scenery might help wean Jeffrey off the drink. It seemed to do the trick at first. He started going to church, he helped out around the house, and he actively sought out a job. In early 1982, his hard work paid off and, due to medical training he received in the Army, was employed as a phlebotomist at the Milwaukee Blood Plasma Center. He worked hard and stayed at it, but after ten months, he was laid off. He would remain unemployed for two years.

Jeffrey's demons just wouldn't stay down, beginning with an arrest and conviction for indecent exposure on August 7, 1982, while visiting Wisconsin State Fair Park. The arrest brought back to life his need for alcohol and for an additional three years, Jeffrey remained unemployed.

But again, his life began to turn for the better, thankfully. In January of 1985, Jeffrey took a job at the Milwaukee Ambrosia Chocolate Factory, working the 11:00-7:00 a.m. shift as a chocolate mixer. Working six nights a week left Jeffrey with little time to consider alcohol or any other kind of social life, which seemed to suit him and his family just fine. It had been seven years since his first murder in Bath, Ohio, and he was hoping that his life had turned around for the better. He'd been able to pack away his homosexuality to the point where it became a non-issue. Not only was there the shame of it, but he also most certainly must have seen the correlation between sex and his fascination with violence and control.

But an incident at a Milwaukee library reopened old wounds and got Jeffrey's wheels turning once more. A stranger, just some random guy, passed Jeffrey a note asking to perform oral sex on him. While Jeffrey politely declined, the incident reanimated old feelings and his once shackled fantasies of controlling other men through force came roaring back to life. Jeffrey sought out Milwaukee's gay bars, adult bookstores, and gay bathhouses, and by 1985, Jeffrey Dahmer was a regular visitor to all three types of places. He found being in those places "relaxing" but became unnerved when his partners insisted on moving during a sexual encounter. They had to be completely subservient, almost like corpses, or the fantasy in Jeffrey's mind wouldn't work. To that end, he began to employ sleeping pills into his sexual regimen, dropping them into his partners' drinks. When they would finally fall into sleep and pass out, Jeffrey would take every sexual advantage with them that he could until, eventually, his deceptions were discovered and his memberships at the bathhouses revoked. Without the bathhouses, Jeffrey resorted to using hotel rooms, which afforded him quite a bit more privacy, but it would be more difficult to get his prey into the room.

A favorite haunt of his, the Ambassador Hotel, became the scene of what would become the turning point in Dahmer's career as a sexual serial killer, where fantasy became reality and his fascination with death took ultimate control over him. Jeffrey had brought a young man named Steven Tuomi back to his room at the Ambassador. According to Dahmer himself, he had no intention of hurting Steven, but woke the next morning to find Steven lying beneath him, his chest crushed and blood seeping from his mouth. There were bruises tattooing Jeffrey's forearms and his fists were bloody and raw. Sometime during their encounter, Jeffrey beat Steven Tuomi to death with his hands and arms and still, Jeffrey had no recollection of it happening at all. After purchasing a large suitcase, Dahmer then dismembered Steven's body and filleted the meat from the bones. Like he had done with Steven Hicks in 1978, Dahmer shattered the bones into pieces and discarded them. The meat he simply tossed into heavy duty garbage bags and tossed into the trash. It was only a two-hour process and Dahmer was back at his grandmother's home before lunch. Still, he kept one trophy for two weeks, a prize that he treasured on a nightly basis: Steven Tuomi's head, wrapped in a blanket. Eventually, he would bleach the flesh from it and retain the pearly white skull until it became too brittle to keep.

The murder of Steven Tuomi turned Dahmer's interest in violent dominance into a brutal compulsion, a compulsion that sent him out into the Milwaukee gay scene night after night, seeking out new additions for his trophy room. But according to Dahmer, his mission wasn't to kill but to create a subservient, almost zombie-like slave that would do his bidding without reproach or hesitation. But the compulsion to kill was far stronger than the compulsion to control, and Dahmer found himself drugging, then strangling nearly all of his lovers, almost always saving the skulls as a memento.

As Jeffrey was perfecting his methods of destruction, he was also exercising another demented facet to his sexuality: exposing himself to children in public. One such occurrence happened when he propositioned a thirteen year-old boy into posing for nude photographs. Another instance found Jeffrey being arrested for masturbating in public in front of two children. These two charges netted him a year in jail and a spot on the Sex Offender Registry.

Once he got out of jail, Jeffrey moved back in with his grandmother and continued his killing spree, barely switching up his style at all. In time, he would move into Apartment 213 at the Oxford Apartments across town in a fairly shady part of Milwaukee. This would be Jeffrey's final place of residence before he was caught and where a majority of the most aberrant and unnatural activities would take place. Being in his own home, knowing he would not be disturbed, granted

Jeffrey a complacency and a comfort level that allowed him to fully surrender to the beckoning darkness within him. His murder spree continued, of course, but now he had taken lengths to better dispose of the bodies and preserve the parts he wanted to keep. He began using acid and an industrial barrel to turn body parts into a grotesque sludge that he could flush down the toilet or empty into the bathtub. Body parts, mostly hands, heads, and genitalia, would be found in the refrigerator. Skulls, neatly cleaned, would be found all over his apartment.

Perhaps more alarming than his macabre collection of body parts was his newfound habit of eating the more edible portions of his victims. In this way, they would become a part of Jeffrey forever. No matter how quickly their bodies dissolved in acid, or how brittle their bones would become, his dead lovers would always be with him in this way. Jeffrey was grieving the loss, memorializing them in his own sick way by ingesting them. Unlike Albert Fish, who practiced cannibalism to gain a sexual thrill, Dahmer viewed cannibalism as paying homage to the victim who fell by his own hands.

His neighbors at the Oxford Apartments began to complain of foul odors coming from apartment 213, which Dahmer explained away as spoiling meat from a broken refrigerator, an excuse that seemed to hold them off, at least for a time.

In the early morning hours of May 27, 1991, three women on their way to work found a young boy, naked and noticeably distraught, standing on a street corner near the Oxford Apartments. He was a fourteen-year-old Laotian boy, spoke no English, and was quite obviously agitated. As one of the women left to call 911, the remaining two were approached by Jeffrey Dahmer, who told them that the boy was actually his nineteen-year-old lover before attempting to lead the boy back to his apartment. But the women remained steadfast, keeping Dahmer from taking the boy until police arrived. When officers arrived, Dahmer politely explained that the boy, Konerak Sinthasomphone, was actually his nineteen-year-old lover who had gotten way too drunk the night before and had tried to start yet another fight with Dahmer. But Konerak was bleeding profusely from his buttocks and he'd shown great resistance to being returned to Dahmer's apartment, two observations that the women on the scene brought up to the police. They were told, in no uncertain terms, to "butt out," that the incident was merely a domestic squabble and none of their concern. Had the police actually asked for Dahmer's name and ran it through their database, they would have found that Dahmer was a convicted sex offender. Truly, the tide would have turned in Konerak's favor that day had they followed procedure. Instead, Konerak was returned to Dahmer, who killed the boy by injecting muriatic acid into his brain before dismembering him. Ironically, Konerak was the younger brother of the boy Dahmer had exposed himself to who had earned him his first stretch in prison.

By 1991, Dahmer had seventeen murders under his belt. His confidence level was high and his motivations were still as keen as they ever were. He'd gotten a thirty-two-year-old man named Tracy Edwards to come back to his apartment on the pretext of just keeping Dahmer company, to which Edwards would receive $100. But once in the apartment, Dahmer made his intentions clear, slapping a handcuff onto Tracy's wrist. When he found he couldn't get the other handcuff onto Tracy's other wrist, Dahmer used it to drag his latest catch first toward the bedroom, then back to the living room. For over five hours, Edwards talked Dahmer down, trying to get the killer to relax. He kept asserting to Dahmer that he was his friend and wasn't going to run away, which eased Dahmer's mind a bit, but didn't fully sway him from letting go of the other handcuff. It was only when Dahmer seemed to suffer a momentary lapse of concentration that Edwards punched Dahmer directly in the face and ran out the front door, where he flagged down a passing police car.

Initially, it seemed as if it would go the same way it had gone for Konerak. Dahmer tried to explain that Edwards was a willing participant but had merely freaked out once the handcuffs were on. When asked about the key to the handcuffs, Dahmer simply replied that it was "in the bedroom." But when one of the officers stepped into the bedroom and found the key, he also found several Polaroid pictures of various bodies in different stages of decay.

When Dahmer saw that they had uncovered his Polaroids, he went ballistic, charging the officers, who quickly overpowered him, handcuffed him, and called for backup. As Dahmer lay on the floor beneath the two officers, he muttered the words: "For what I did I should be dead."

Milwaukee police and crime scene technicians were horrified by what they found in Dahmer's apartment. Four severed heads were found in Dahmer's refrigerator, plus two human hearts and a portion of arm muscle wrapped inside plastic bags. Investigators discovered an entire torso, plus a bag of human organs and flesh stuck to the ice at the bottom of the freezer. Seven skulls were found in Dahmer's bedroom. Two entire skeletons, a pair of severed hands, two severed and preserved penises, a mummified scalp and, in the fifty-seven-gallon drum, three dismembered torsos dissolving in acid.

Dahmer had also been in the process of constructing an elaborate, private altar from the skulls of his victims. This display of skulls was to be adorned at each side with the complete skeletons of victims Ernest Miller and Oliver Lacy. The chief medical examiner would later state that, "It was more like dismantling someone's museum than an actual crime scene."

Dahmer would eventually confess all to police and would be indicted on fifteen counts of murder. The State of Ohio would eventually indict Dahmer for the murder of Steven Hicks, whose scattered remains had been collected following Dahmer's confession. Dahmer pleaded guilty but insane on all counts. The trial lasted two weeks and centered around whether or not Dahmer had been insane or not during the killings. In the end, he was found to be completely in control of all of his faculties during, and after, the murders. He received fifteen life sentences in an Ohio court for his crimes, and a sixteenth when he was convicted of murdering Steven Hicks.

Upon sentencing, Dahmer was transferred to the Columbia Correctional Institution in Portage, Wisconsin, spending the first year of his incarceration in solitary confinement. Once he was released into a less secure portion of the general population, he was given jobs cleaning the toilets and showers for two hours a day. He also became a born-again Christian in 1994. Dahmer and his minister at the prison regularly discussed the prospect of death and Dahmer constantly questioned whether he was sinning against God by continuing to live. The entire time Dahmer was in custody he'd shown a remarkable streak of genuine remorse for his actions, and while he languished in prison, he felt complacent and comfortable with the idea of being dead. It was almost as if Dahmer were either expecting it or hoping for it.

On the morning of November 28, 1994, Dahmer left his cell to conduct his assigned work detail, accompanied by fellow inmates Jesse Anderson and Christopher Scarver. The three were unsupervised in the showers for approximately twenty minutes. At approximately 8:10 a.m. Dahmer was discovered on the floor of the bathroom in the gym suffering from extreme head and facial wounds; he had been severely bludgeoned about the head and face with a twenty-inch metal bar. His head had also been repeatedly struck against the wall in the assault. He was pronounced dead one hour later at the hospital. Jesse Anderson had also been savagely attacked with the same instrument and died two days later from his wounds. Christopher Scarver, a twenty-five-year-old man serving a life sentence for murder, had attacked Dahmer with the metal bar. According to Scarver, Dahmer did not yell or make any noise as he was attacked. Scarver then turned his attention to Anderson, who received the same deadly treatment.

"Now is everybody happy? Now that he's bludgeoned to death, is that good enough for everyone?" was the response from Joyce Dahmer-Flint, Jeffrey's mother, when she received word of her son's murder in prison. In September 1995, Dahmer's body was cremated, and his ashes divided between his parents.

Upon his death, the results of multiple psychiatric examinations on Dahmer were released to the public, painting a picture of a desperately lonely man who tended to display a tendency to experience recurrent depressive affect, feelings of worthlessness, low self-esteem, suicidal tendencies, and a strong fear of abandonment. Most agreed that Dahmer suffered from major depressive disorder, generalized anxiety disorder, substance use disorder, sexual paraphilias, and borderline personality disorder.

The Oxford Apartments at 924 North 25th Street, where Dahmer had killed twelve of his victims, were demolished in November 1992. The site is now a vacant lot, though some had thought the idea of a community playground or recreational center would be a good monument to the lives lost in apartment 213.

The Vile Files

Leonard Lake

(1945-1985)

Charles Ng

(1960-)

Charles Ng was a Hong Kong serial killer who teamed up with American murderer Leonard Lake, using Lake's cabin in remote Wilseyville, California, to stage their hideous crimes. Utilizing a specially built dungeon, it is believed that Lake and Ng kidnapped, raped, and murdered as many as twenty-five men, women, and children, often videotaping their exploits. The two were so good at what they did that they may have gotten away with it indefinitely if it weren't for Charles Ng's propensity for shoplifting. He'd been caught stealing a vise from a San Francisco hardware store. Ng fled the scene, but Leonard Lake, wanting to do some damage control for his partner, arrived to pay for the vise and was summarily questioned by police. After finding a silencer-equipped gun in his car, Lake was taken into custody. Ng, meanwhile, escaped to Canada. Lake attempted suicide while at the police station by swallowing cyanide pills he'd sewn into his clothes. Over the course of four days, he confessed all to the police and implicated himself and Ng in the murders before succumbing to the poison. A search of the lakeside cabin uncovered all the evidence police would need to convict Charles Ng, including the identification cards of all of their victims and the cache of videotapes documenting their murders. After a lengthy extradition process, Ng was finally returned to the United States. In 1999, he was convicted of the murders of eleven men, women, and children, receiving a well-deserved death sentence. As of 2015, he still sits on San Quentin's death row.

CHAPTER 14

FRED & ROSEMARY WEST

"THE KILLER COUPLE"

Gloucester, United Kingdom

"It's only a mystery because you want it to be a mystery."
—**Rosemary West**

Some people don't always take into account the emotional toll a jury endures when hearing about the lives and crimes of some of the worst, most severely damaged people in the world. One can picture the images in their minds as they listen to the charges and opening statements. It is hard not to picture it as they tell you tales of incest, familial sexual abuse, and cold-blooded murder. Such was the case of Fred and Rosemary West, two of the most damaged, most depraved sexual serial killers in the history of crime. What were the jurors thinking as Rosemary West sat in the courtroom? Were they trying to picture this seemingly idyllic couple committing these atrocities, trying vainly to imagine these two doing what everyone was saying they were doing?

As with most stories of serial killers, it all began with the fracturing of a family and, in particular, the deviant conduct of a father. Rosemary Pauline Letts was born in Barnstaple, Devon, in the United Kingdom to Willia and Daisy Letts, the product of a turbulent and difficult pregnancy. Daisy Letts suffered from deep bouts of depression for which she received regular treatments of electro-shock therapy. She received numerous treatments while she was pregnant and it is thought that it may have altered Rosemary's brain chemistry in the womb. She grew to be a moody, sullen teenager and her marks in school left much to be desired. Her father, meanwhile, was a paranoid schizophrenic, whose outbursts and episodes often resulted in fits of terrifying violence in the household. Indeed, if there were any people in the world less suited for being parents, it would be William and Daisy Letts.

Rosemary first chose to live with her mother when the two divorced in 1969. Rosemary was only sixteen years old at the time and found life with mother to be somewhat strict. She decided to try living with her father in Bishop's Cleeve near Cheltenham. But life for Rosemary didn't get any easier. She was frequently sexually abused by her father. This, in and of itself, is a true horror, yet she continued to stay at her father's house, all the while knowing that she could return to the relative safety of her mother's home at any time. Why Rosemary stayed with her father is somewhat of a mystery, but one could surmise that she began to enjoy playing the role of her father's wife. Whether she was brainwashed into living this role or she stepped into it willingly is unclear.

Rosemary took a job at a cafe near her father's home where she soon met twenty-seven-year-old Fred West, a construction worker who lived with his young daughters Anne-Marie and Charmaine in Bishop's Cleeve. The twelve year age difference didn't seem to matter much to Fred and Rosemary, but it did to her father, William, who forbade his daughter from having anything to do with Fred West. He even threatened to call Social Services on him, though he must have known that by doing so, he risked exposing his own incestuous affair with Rosemary.

Fred West had grown up in much the same way Rosemary had. His father, Walter West, had routinely abused his daughters sexually on numerous occasions. Walter West's motto? "Do what you want. Just don't get caught doing it." Supposedly, Walter also introduced his son to bestiality, and Fred's own mother began to have sex with him when he was just twelve.

Fred quit school in 1956 at age fifteen and suffered a life-altering motorcycle accident when he was seventeen, which landed him in an eight-day coma. Upon awaking from this coma, his family reported that he had suddenly become prone to fits of unadulterated rage, a condition that definitely points to an imbalance in the brain that may have been a root cause for his deviant and murderous behavior later on in his life.

At age twenty, he was arrested for molesting a thirteen-year-old girl and, while he was convicted, he somehow got out of serving any prison time. Ironically, as messed up as his family was, his conviction for raping a thirteen year old was too much for them to bear, and they disowned him. Though not conventionally attractive in the physical sense, Fred displayed a charm and a confidence that always seemed to get him the woman he was pursuing at the time, though they would rarely stay with him once his penchant for children and rape came to light. He'd married former girlfriend and prostitute Rena Costello in 1962, becoming stepfather to her daughter, Charmaine. They would also have their own daughter, Anna-Marie, in 1964. West's sadistic nature took its toll on Rena, who left him in 1966 and moved to Scotland, leaving the children in Fred's less than capable hands. Ann McFall, a good friend of Rena's, fell in love with Fred and moved into Rena's vacated position in his life.

Rena returned from Scotland occasionally to see her children and found that McFall, who had been eight months pregnant with West's child, had disappeared. According to Fred, Rena returned to live with him for a year before finally leaving for good. Fred wandered about, parlaying his talent for woodworking into construction jobs around Gloucester to support his daughters, which is how he came to know Rosemary.

Fred hired Rosemary to care for his daughter Anne-Marie and his stepdaughter Charmaine. Shortly after Rosemary moved in with Fred West, however, she became pregnant and the new blended family moved to Midland Road, Gloucester. Fred was subsequently arrested shortly thereafter for theft, a crime which netted him six months in prison. While he was in prison, his stepdaughter Charmaine mysteriously disappeared while under Rosemary's care. Being that the girl had no other relatives other than Fred and Rosemary, no one seemed to pay attention or inquire about her whereabouts until years later during the subsequent trial.

Over the years, the West Family grew to include a whopping eight daughters, filling every inch of 25 Cromwell Street to the brim. Sadly, only five of these children were Fred's. The remaining three children were biracial daughters fathered by Pakistani customers of Rosemary's, who was being pimped out by Fred. Shortly after they'd married, Fred had convinced Rosemary to work as a prostitute, entertaining clients at all hours of the day and night in the family home. They even remodeled the upstairs to make it more accommodating for Rosemary and her clients. Peepholes and listening devices were installed so that Fred could watch his wife frolic with her clients. Her most frequent client? William Letts, her own father. When Rosemary wasn't available, it was thought that William Letts would turn his attention to Fred and Rosemary's daughters, namely seven year-old Anna-Marie.

In October of 1972, Fred and Rosemary hired Caroline Roberts, a seventeen-year-old student, as their children's new nanny. But she quickly vacated the position when Rosemary and Fred asked her to join them in bed. Offended and unnerved by the Wests, Caroline vowed never to return. But when the Wests extended an olive branch the following December by inviting Caroline to dinner at their home, she accepted. Once inside the house, she was violently raped by both Rosemary and Fred. Her release was only granted under the condition that she return to work for them as a nanny. Immediately after leaving the West's home, she reported the rape to police. However, she withdrew the complaint before it made it to the courts. Instead, Fred and Rosemary pleaded guilty to a reduced charge of indecent assault and were fined £50.

It was this brush with the law that prompted the Wests to keep their deviant behavior in the home, away from outsiders. It was Anne-Marie, now eight years old, who now bore the brunt of her father and stepmother's sickness. She was routinely dragged to the basement, bound and gagged, where Fred West would rape her as Rosemary watched. This sickening routine continued on until 1979 when Anne Marie, barely fourteen years old, became pregnant by her father. To add insult to injury, it was speculated that Fred West himself performed an abortion on her. Thoroughly traumatized and unable to cope, Anne-Marie ran away from home, never again having any contact with her family.

Undaunted by his daughter's disappearance, Fred and Rosemary turned their attentions to sixteen-year-old Heather, who now began to endure repeated sexual assaults from her father. Like Anna-Marie, she too seemed to run off in 1987. But in this case, her whereabouts and well being were not known, and the Wests seemed reluctant to actually find her. They filed a missing persons report and that was it. To Fred and Rosemary West's other children, Heather had simply disappeared one night. Eventually, it became a sick joke to Fred and Rosemary, who used to tell their children that Heather was buried under the back patio and if they didn't mind their parents, they'd end up there, too.

In 1992, Fred West's lusts caught up to him. He filmed himself raping one of his daughters, who told friends at school what had happened. Those friends went to their own parents, and the police were called. Again, the Wests were charged with rape, and again, the charge was dropped when the two main witnesses refused to testify in open court. Still, all of the West children were removed from the home, thankfully, and relocated to a safe place in foster care.

But this wasn't the end, for during the child welfare investigation of the West's children, they heard stories from the remaining daughters about how Heather was buried under the patio. Using this statement, police were granted a search warrant to excavate the garden patio. To their complete shock, not only were Heather's remains recovered, but also the remains of two other women as well. The search of the grounds, and the basement of the house itself, yielded more bodies.

Faced with the evidence, Fred West initially confessed to the murders, then quickly recanted, then confessed again, but denied Rosemary was involved. In time, he would confess to nine more murders, including his first two wives, Rena Costello and Ann McFall.

Knowing that Fred had finally confessed to everything, detectives approached Rosemary West and interrogated her as if her husband hadn't said a word. Rosemary's lies came out in gushes, and her stories about the disappearance of her daughter Heather contradicted what Fred had told police. Detective Sergeant

Fred and Rosemary West, in one of many family photographs. At the time this picture was taken, Fred and Rosemary had already raped and murdered their own daughter, as well as 11 other women.

Terence Onions had trapped her in her web of lies and by the time the interview was over, Rosemary West was in tears.

"Fred has confessed to murdering Heather," Onions told her. Rosemary seemed shocked, almost betrayed, yet still managed to stammer out a response. "What?" Onions continued, dropping the hammer full force onto Rosemary West. "And that automatically implicates you."

Knowing the gig was up, Rosemary tried vainly to adhere to the lie of her innocence. "Why does it automatically implicate me?" Onions stared back at her and bluntly told Rosemary West, "Our suspicions are aroused that you are implicated in it."

Both Fred and Rosemary West were charged with a total of ten murders; Fred was charged with eleven murders, and Rosemary with ten. It was apparent that Rosemary had participated in the nine murders that had taken place in the home on Cromwell Street, as well as the murder of Fred's stepdaughter, Charmaine, whose remains were unearthed at the family's first home on Midland Road. According to detectives, Fred and Rosemary would often target young girls or women walking alone. Coaxing them into their car with the offer of a ride, they would either be convinced or forced to return to the house on Cromwell Street. Once there, they would be summarily raped, tortured, and murdered by both Rosemary and Fred West. Fred would then dismember the bodies and bury them, first in the garden and then in the earthen floor of the basement.

The dizzying spiral of depravity was becoming more and more clear as Rosemary's involvement in the murders became more apparent through the recovery of damaging circumstantial evidence. While not conclusive proof of their guilt, the circumstantial evidence, along with Fred's mystifying confessions, would be enough to convict them. Fred West knew this to be true, and he hanged himself in prison while awaiting trial, despite being on a strict suicide watch at the time. Ironically, in life he had fought for Rosemary's innocence from the beginning. But now, he left her alone to take the brunt of the blame for which he was mostly responsible. But unlike Fred, Rosemary had not confessed to a single murder, rape, or assault. She brazenly professed her innocence. All prosecutors had was the circumstantial evidence that placed her at the scene of each crime, but didn't wholly prove that she was 100 percent guilty of murder.

Jurors heard damaging testimony from child welfare advocates who had interviewed the West's surviving children, forensic pathologists who had examined the remains, psychologists who had interviewed Rosemary and her children, and even the mother of one of the victims, Lynda Gough, who testified to seeing Rosemary wearing her daughter's Cardigan sweater and slippers while at the West's home searching for her daughter. Lynda had apparently been seen working as a nanny at the West home prior to her disappearance.

On November 22, 1995, Rosemary Pauline West was found guilty of ten murders and sentenced to life in prison without parole. Though she stubbornly maintained her innocence, she vowed not to appeal the sentence. Rosemary West is still incarcerated at Country Durham's Low Newton prison.

After the trial, the Wests' house was torn to the ground, replaced by a very pleasant walkway complete with plush grass and awe-inspiring foliage. The West children were given new names and sent to live in new homes with new families. But according to British journalist Philip Larkin, the ghosts of their past still haunt them.

"They do not only inherit the guilt of surviving when so many others—including their own siblings—were murdered; they carry the guilt of being the children of their parents, of loving their parents and of being obedient to them and of not stopping them."

The Vile Files

David and Catherine Birnie

David and Catherine Birnie were a couple from Perth, Australia, who murdered women in their home on Moorhouse Street. From October to November of 1986, the two abducted four women and brutally raped and sexually assaulted them before strangling them to death. They would eventually bury most of their victims in Gleneagles National Park in Bedfordale. The duo were apprehended by police after a proposed fifth victim escaped with her life and implicated them. David Birnie would commit suicide in prison, while his wife Catherine would look forward to spending the remainder of her life behind bars for crimes that were most likely his idea from the beginning.

CHAPTER 15

ANDREI CHIKATILO

"THE ROSTOV RIPPER"

Rostov-on-Don, Russia

"What I did was not for sexual pleasure. Rather it brought me some peace of mind."
–Andrei Chikatilo

The blood was in his mouth before he could fully close his lips over the wound. He could feel the flesh yield beneath his teeth, cutting into the softness as the warm, viscous fluid curled into his mouth and nestled among his teeth and tongue. She didn't flail, she didn't even twitch as he ripped the portion of skin and muscle away from her body. The blow to the back of her head rendered her incapable of reacting, which was all part of his plan from the beginning. Andrei Chikatilo slowly raised his head, drunk upon the girl's blood. The taste of the blood, the incapacitated girl, and now, the knife he held in his hand all came together in a shattering symphony of demented lust. Stabbing her repeatedly in the chest before slowly and methodically eviscerating her, Chikatilo reveled and writhed in the process of rendering her into something less than human. Sated by the kill and having relieved his sexual desires, Chikatilo stood up, brushed the dirt from his coat, and walked away, leaving behind an empty container that used to be a little girl. The beast inside him had been placated. But soon, it would demand another sacrifice.

Andrei Chikatilo

In all, fifty-two young people, all under seventeen years of age, would fall gruesomely into death's arms by Andrei Chikatilo, one of the most disturbed and deranged psychopaths to have ever walked the earth. His crimes were horrifying, shocking a country that most believed could never be shocked: Soviet Russia.

Andrei Chikatilo was born in the village of Yabluchne in the Sumy Oblast of the Ukrainian section of the USSR. His parents were both farmers who lived in a one-room house. While they received no wages for their work on the farm, they did hold the rights to cultivate food that they had grown. This isn't to say they had plenty of food. Quite the contrary. Whatever food they grew and harvested was mostly sold to pay for incidental needs. Chikatilo once claimed not to have eaten bread until he was twelve years old, that "he and his family often had to eat grass and leaves in an effort to stave off hunger." To add to this incredible poverty, Chikatilo was told stories by his mother of how his older brother, Stepan, had been kidnapped, murdered, and eaten by their starving neighbors. Chikatilo had no recollection of Stepan; his older brother had supposedly been kidnapped and cannibalized prior to Andrei's birth.

But this wasn't the only time Chikatilo's mother seemed to try and belittle or frighten her son. Incredibly, she was a constant source of berating, nagging, and chastising. She was a harsh disciplinarian, whereas his father was infinitely kinder and gentler.

At the beginning of World War II, Andrei's father was drafted into the Red Army. While his father was off fighting the German Nazi's, young Andrei and his mother were subjected to the horrors of Nazi-occupied Ukraine. Massive bombing raids, fires, indiscriminate executions, and violent rapes were common sights and stories seen and heard all over Andrei's village. Understandably, a frail boy such as Andrei became so upset by the stress and horror he was being subjected to that he became a chronic bed wetter. Because he and his mother shared one single bed, he was subjected not only to the Nazi horrors, but to the the constant beatings and belittlement of his mother.

In 1943, Chikatilo's mother gave birth to a daughter, Tatyana. Because Chikatilo's father was off fighting in the war, most believe that the young girl was conceived after she had been raped by a German soldier. Tatyana's paternity was never solidly confirmed, but it is entirely possible that Chikatilo witnessed the rape of his mother. One has to wonder what went through his mind as he possibly witnessed the brutal denigration of someone he had grown to loathe.

By the time Chikatilo began his formal education in 1944, his eyesight had become so bad that he couldn't even read the blackboard at school. Instead, he began to learn how to memorize facts and figures, and studied incessantly while at home. He was a brilliant student, but his thick eyeglasses and stellar grades got the attention of all the bullies, who delighted in belittling Andrei, picking up where his mother had left off.

But Andrei was driven, nonetheless, to succeed as much as possible, despite what others seemed to want for him. He'd become a model student and an impassioned Communist, organizing rallys and marches. He was the editor of his school newspaper by the age of fourteen and elected chairman of the Student Communist Committee at the age of sixteen. With all of the brightness of a Party-influenced future ahead of him, it was the discovery of his chronic impotence that seemed to bring him down. Already steeped in low self-esteem, Andrei's self-loathing and awkwardness only intensified, effectively canceling out most of the bright spots in his future. If he were a successful Party member, that was great. But if he couldn't father a family, that was not great. His impotence made him terminally shy around women. He didn't date at all during his time at school, focusing attention on his studies and allowing even the most casual crushes to go unrequited.

But the teenaged Andrei would soon unlock the door to his sexuality. One day, he brazenly jumped onto the eleven-year-old friend of his younger sister. As the two wrestled playfully on the ground, Andrei realized that he not only had an erection, but he had also climaxed as the young girl struggled beneath him.

One must go back to the time when Chikatilo possibly witnessed the rape of his overbearing mother, watching this once dominant creature become completely dominated. Perhaps Chikatilo had enjoyed watching his mother suffer, enjoyed it so much that it completely changed his view of both sex and violence to the point where the division between the two was virtually nonexistent. Perhaps his only experience with sex had been the violent assault of his mother, cementing the idea within him that not only was sex violent, but violence was sex.

Chikatilo's life after graduation wasn't exactly what he'd been expecting. His excellent grades, while quite an achievement, failed to net him the scholarship to Moscow State University like he'd hoped. Andrei himself had thought that, because the Party viewed his father as a traitor during World War II (being taken prisoner by the Nazis rather than commit suicide, obviously, was the traitorous thing to do in the eyes of the Kremlin) that had essentially blackballed him from getting into the more excellent colleges. When he didn't make it into Moscow State, Chikatilo simply gave up, working as a laborer in the city of Kursk before enrolling in a vocational college, majoring in communications technology. It was 1955. Chikatilo, after wandering lost a bit after graduation, had finally seemed to regain his footing. He even found himself a girlfriend, a local girl named Natalya. But because of Chikatilo's chronic impotence, the couple was unable to consummate the relationship on the three occasions in which they tried. Though she was certainly understanding, it must have been difficult, and she ended the relationship after eighteen months.

Following Chikatilo's training at the vocational college, he was drafted into the Soviet Army in 1957. He served without incident until 1960, when he officially joined the Communist party, returned to Yabluchne shortly thereafter, and moved back in with his parents as he tried to figure out what he was going to do with his life. Being a member of the Communist party was quite a leap forward, but he and his family were still under an oppressive rule. Poverty and starvation were still quite formidable opponents. In time, Chikatilo would find another girlfriend, this time a young divorcee who lived close to his parents. They dated for three months, then it came to an abrupt halt when the girl began telling her friends that Andrei was impotent. In time, the entire village knew of his shame.

"Girls were going behind my back, whispering that I was impotent. I was so ashamed," Chikatilo related in a 1993 interview. "I tried to hang myself. My mother and some young neighbors pulled me out of the noose... I had to run away from there, away from my homeland."

Chikatilo fled to Rostov-on-Don, where he would spend the remainder of his free life and where most of his crimes would be committed.

In 1961, he was able to get a job as a communications engineer in the large Russian city, renting a small apartment close to his work. Two years later, he married Feodosia Odnacheva, a Russian woman he'd been set up with by his sister Tatyana. Although they'd only known each other for two weeks, it seemed to work out all right. But their sex life, as expected, was minimal to non-existent. By 1969, they had two children: Lyudmila and Yuri. Both were conceived after Chikatilo masturbated, then shoved his semen into Feodosia's vagina. Though hardly romantic, it seemed to suit them both, at least for a time.

While not working at the factory, Chikatilo took part in a correspondence course in Russian literature at Rostov University, taking a job at Novoshakhtinks as a Russian language and literature teacher. But Chikatilo was hardly an effective teacher. His pupils tended to run roughshod over him and he became the target of mockery and bullying for his quiet, almost spineless position. Chikatilo later claimed that the students took advantage of his "modest nature."

But broiling inside Chikatilo was that same hatred for his students that he had felt for his overbearing mother. They berated and belittled him as she had. Chikatilo remembered how satisfying it was to watch his mother be put into her place when the Nazi soldier raped her. He wanted to humiliate and denigrate them all. He began in May of 1973, groping a fifteen-year-old girl at a local swimming pool, and, a few months later, he went so far as to sexually assault one of his female students in his own classroom. Rather than bring charges against him, Chikatilo was ordered to resign quietly so that news of the incident would not stain the school's reputation.

The wheels had begun turning and Chikatilo couldn't stop them. His last teaching job was at a school in Shakhty, which ended following several complaints of child molestation. This time, Chikatilo did not discriminate. He assaulted boys as well as girls.

The beast was loose and with his new job as a supply clerk, he was given freedom to travel all over the Soviet Union by train to either purchase raw materials or negotiate supply contracts for the factory that employed him. It was here, at these train stations, that Andrei Chikatilo would begin his career as one of the most wretched sexual predators to ever have walked the Earth.

Chikatilo took his first victim on December 22, 1978 when he lured nine-year-old Yelena Zakotnova away from the train station and into an abandoned house nearby. He attempted to rape the girl, but failed to achieve erection. When she struggled violently with Chikatilo, he began to choke and stab her repeatedly. As he did, he miraculously achieved orgasm. When he was finished with her, Chikatilo tossed her corpse into a nearby river, where she was found two days later.

After Yelena's murder, Chikatilo would never again be able to achieve an erection and orgasm unless he was brandishing a knife on a struggling victim. His twisted mind had successfully warped his body into working in tandem together and nothing would ever be the same. Of all of Chikatilo's murders, one can almost certainly believe that Yelena Zakotnova would have been Andrei's favorite simply because she was the first.

Over the next five years, Chikatilo's rampage evolved into acts of despicable rage. Simple stabbings evolved into elaborate mutilations. He became fond of biting into the soft flesh of children, drinking their blood, and savoring their final breaths. Evisceration of the organs, intestines, and anus of his victims became common hallmarks of Chikatilo's modus operandi. Though his victims came from different parts of the country, it was his savage killing style that linked them all together and would prove to be his undoing. The press dubbed him "The Rostov Ripper."

Finding him was left to a forensic pathologist named Viktor Bukarov, who had been enlisted by Major Mikhail Fetisov of the Rostov police force. Fetisov was a good ally for Bukarov, who often found his movements and theories limited by Communist party politics. Because some of the victims were young boys, some members of the Party were convinced that the murders were being committed by deranged homosexuals, pedophiles, organ harvesters, or Satanists. They cast a wide net across Rostov-On-Don, interrogating hundreds of known homosexuals and registered sex offenders, brutally questioning them with heavy-handed tactics, using fear and paranoia against them as they fought for their innocence. But while the dragnet didn't find The Rostov Ripper, it did manage to close the books on 95 murders and 245 rapes.

Word of the serial killer in their midst did tend to slip out into the public, however, resulting in numerous false confessions from thoroughly deranged individuals. But the constant influx of Ripper victims proved all of them false and police were forced to turn them loose.

The only evidence the police really had to work with was the semen samples found on several of the victims bodies. Forensic analysis of the semen yielded a blood type of AB. Victor Bukarov had demanded a more thorough test, looking to employ the FBI's tactic of searching for over 200 different parameters of identification. The Soviets, meanwhile, tested for only eleven, creating an enormous margin of error that would call into question the killer's guilt later on.

By mid 1984, more than 25,000 Russians had been interviewed or investigated in connection with the murders, yet none of them withstood the burden of proof. Police were at an impasse and tried a desperate measure. They began stocking the train and bus stations with undercover policemen and women, who had all been briefed about the behavior of their killer. They were told to watch for a man, probably older, most likely carrying a bag. He would be communicative toward younger people but no one else. Finally, they had the eyewitness description of a balding man with a small-to-medium build, wearing large, thick eyeglasses and looking fairly disheveled.

On September 13, 1984, an undercover policeman noticed an odd, nervous man in the Rostov bus station, carrying what looked like an old tool bag factory workers would use to take their tools to and from work. The officer watched the man go from seat to seat, sitting next to young girls or boys, talking to them quietly. Then, he would get up and move on to another seat next to another young person and begin speaking to them. Knowing that this was the established pattern of behavior of their killer, the undercover officer approached the man, announced himself as a policeman, and asked to see the man's credentials. His name was Andrei Chikatilo, a factory worker from Rostov. When he opened the bag, he was aghast at what he found: a large knife and a section of rope.

Andrei Chikatilo was promptly arrested and taken into custody. It was discovered that Chikatilo was currently under investigation from his employers for theft, which allowed the police to hold Chikatilo indefinitely while they put a case for murder against him. But it was over very nearly before it even got started: Chikatilo's blood was Type A. Their murderer, according to Soviet forensic scientists, was, of course, AB. And while Chikatilo wouldn't be charged with murder, he was found guilty of stealing from his employers at the factory, a charge which netted him a year in prison, of which he only served three months. It should be noted that, while Chikatilo was in prison, no other murders of a nature similar to the ones Chikatilo was suspected of were committed. The Soviet authorities refused to consider Chikatilo, citing not only the contradicting DNA evidence, but also the fact that Chikatilo was a member of the Communist Party. They theorized that perhaps the killer had traveled North or perhaps West, continuing his killing spree there.

Burakov, meanwhile, tried a tactic that had never been done in Soviet Russia before: he went to a psychiatrist, asking for help in identifying his killer. Dr. Alexandr Bukhanovsky returned to Burakov a sixty-five page profile of the Rostov Ripper, dubbing him "Citizen X." He described the killer as a man aged forty-five to fifty years old with average intelligence. He would have likely been married or previously married, but was almost certainly a sadist who could only perform sexually if his lovers were in the throes of agony. Bukhanovsky even looked into the times, dates, and locations of the murders themselves, deducing that the killer's work required travel via train or bus, and that he was most likely tied to a set production schedule, such as a factory.

In October of 1990, following the monumental collapse of Communism in the East, Bukarov and Fetisov finally had clearance to implement a massive snare against the Rostov Ripper. Armed, uniformed police officers would be stationed in every major train station, always outside so that people arriving would notice them immediately. Only three stations would not have these guards. They would be filled with undercover officers, with female officers being used as bait for their killer. Essentially, the police were leading an unsuspecting Chikatilo into a spider's web. It was an absolutely brilliant plot, but it forced Chikatilo to vary his timing and to work more quietly than before. Four people would fall under Chikatilo's knife before he would be stopped for good.

It happened on November 20, when Chikatilo left his house with a large jar of beer he'd filled up at a small kiosk in a local park. He was officially arrested by four plain-clothed officers and taken into custody. He hadn't been aware, but the police had been watching him intently for the past six days, noting his movements, collecting evidence to be used against him at trial, and connecting him to the fifty-two murders they had on their dockets.

Chikatilo was a steely suspect, a hard man to break. The evidence against him was overwhelming, but it was all circumstantial. A slam-dunk conviction would only be achieved if Chikatilo confessed. Under Soviet law, they had ten days to wring a confession out of Chikatilo before they would be forced to let him go due to lack of evidence.

Chikatilo held out for eight days, not budging an inch. The prosecuting attorney used harsh, KGB-like tactics that only succeeded in getting Chikatilo to clam up even more. The harder he pressed, the further away Chikatilo drifted. On the ninth and final day, Burakov and Fetisov played their final hand against Chikatilo. They sent in Alexandr Bukhanovsky, the psychiatrist who had written the incredibly accurate profile of "Citizen X," who they now believed was Andrei Chikatilo.

Buckhanovsky did not do anything radical to elicit the confessions from Chikatilo. He merely read the sixty-five page profile of Citizen X to Chikatilo. Chikatilo, in turn, listened and discovered that here was a man who knew him, knew what was driving him, knew what was hurting him. In essence, Buckhanovsky showed a clinical empathy for Chikatilo, something no one had ever done for him. Finally, here was a man who understood him, who *knew* him. And it brought Andrei Chikatilo to tears as he confessed to fifty-three murders of young girls and boys over a twelve-year period.

On October 15, 1993, Chikatilo was found guilty of fifty-two of the fifty-three murders and sentenced to death for each offense. Chikatilo kicked his bench across his cage when he heard the verdict, swearing loudly in Russian. On February 14, 1994, Andrei Chikatilo was taken to a soundproof room in Novocherkassk Prison and executed with a single gunshot behind his right ear. Much like his victims, he never saw it coming. But perhaps, in the interest of true justice, maybe he should have.

The Vile Files

Mikhail Popkov

(March 7, 1964-)

From 1992 to 2000, Russian serial killer Mikhail Popkov stalked, raped, and brutally murdered twenty-nine women in Angarsk, Russia. What distinguished Popkov from other serial killers is that he was also a policeman, using his patrol car and uniform to intimidate or influence women into leaving with him. Once they were in his car, Popkov would drive his victims to secluded areas of the forest where he would viciously rape them before bludgeoning them with an axe, or stabbing and strangling them to death. He was arrested on June 23, 2012, when his DNA was matched to DNA found on twenty-nine of the murder victims. He confessed to twenty-four of the murders and was sentenced to life in prison.

CHAPTER 16

GARY HEIDNIK

"THE HOUSE OF HORRORS KILLER"

Philadelphia, Pennsylvania

"You people think I committed murders that I have not committed. And I have refused to appeal my case. I still refuse—even though I can prove my innocence, right, I still refuse to appeal my case. I resent this kind of shit being done to a disabled veteran."
—**Gary Heidnik**

Heidnik watched her from above, tapping her chains as she dangled in the shallow pit. The water was up to her calves now, ice cold and numbing her flesh. The shackles and chains had rubbed her brown skin raw, yet she still tried to climb them, anything to alleviate the pressure of her weight pulling her down. She watched Heidnik, pleading with her eyes, for only her eyes hadn't been taped shut.

Heidnik, in return, brought the electrical cord slowly closer to the chains, his unblinking, placid, black eyes fixed on the woman in the pit. The connection between them was undeniable, but whereas hers pleaded for mercy, his responded with serene coldness and it didn't change a bit as he brought the open end of the electrical cord to the chains. Stoically and quietly, he watched the African-American woman convulse as the electricity flowed down the chains and into her body, conducted beautifully by the stagnant water beneath her. Her insistence on defying him was done, over, finished. In the morning, he would replace her. It wouldn't be difficult. He'd done it before three times, and it just seemed to get easier. Deborah Dudley was dead, and he would enlist one of the others, his favorite, to help him discard the body. Probably out in the Pine Barrens of New Jersey. It was a quick trip and the chances that it would be found were slim to none.

It's hard to believe, but Gary Heidnik's idea of a new utopia was taking shape in the basement of his home at 3520 North Marshall Street in North Philadelphia, Pennsylvania. It had been a long road, but he still saw a light at the end of the tunnel.

Gary Heidnik was born November 22, 1943, in the Eastlake suburb of Cleveland, Ohio, to Michael and Ellen Heidnik. Gary was barely three years old when his parents divorced, living at first with his mother, then with his father and his new wife about four years later. Ellen Heidnik would commit suicide shortly after, poisoning herself with arsenic.

Heidnik would allege later on that his father was incredibly emotionally abusive, a tactic some might have thought was used to toughen young Gary up. But to Gary himself, it was just torturous and wrong. A chronic bed wetter, Michael Heidnik would humiliate his son by hanging Gary's urine-stained sheets from his bedroom window where all the neighbors could see.

Shannon Heidnik, Gary's niece and the eldest daughter of Gary's older brother, Terry, would later tell *Philadelphia Magazine* that, "The whole family was screwed up and weird. My mom told me how their dad beat Gary real bad with a toy wooden airplane because he peed his pants. His dad was an alcoholic, and his mom took poison. They found her in the basement. She was tired of the abuse. They were really sick parents, and they gave their kids some serious problems."

But one mustn't dwell on the parents for too long. Another childhood symptom of serial killers is disturbances to the brain, whether it be a chemical imbalance brought on genetically, or a traumatic brain injury brought on by a serious accident. Both are true in Gary Heidnik's case. Gary's brother, Terry, would find himself in and out of mental institutions for the rest of his life, battling depression and paranoia, leading one to see mental illness as a genetic link in the Heidnik family. But Gary also had the misfortune of suffering a brain injury; he had fallen out of a tree when he was very young, smacking his head violently on branches as he fell twenty feet onto the hard ground.

The accident changed Gary considerably. He became withdrawn and more antisocial than before, refusing to make eye contact with his fellow students. Other kids teased him about his oddly shaped head, another result of his fall from the tree. If you were a student who *did* manage to get Gary's attention, chances were pretty good that you would regret it, finding an angry, conceited boy who would respond to their interest with a caustic and menacing rebuttal such as, "You're not worthy enough to talk to me!"

Despite Gary's thoroughly antisocial behavior, it didn't keep him from excelling in school. He did exceptionally well in all of his subjects and was even tested with an IQ of 130, near-genius levels. Encouraged by his father, young Gary dropped out of public schools and entered the now-defunct Staunton Military Academy in Virginia, a stint he followed through on for two years before returning to public schools. Much like many brilliant young men, however, Gary was bored with the rigmarole of public education and most likely thought that he was better than what they were offering. Had he been promoted a grade or two in advance, Gary Heidnik may well have finished his education and gone on to great things. In the end, he dropped out completely and enlisted in the Army in 1960 at the age of seventeen.

In the Army, like his schooling, Gary excelled during basic training, and when he graduated, he set out to become a field medic, training in San Antonio, Texas, before being transferred to a medical surgical hospital in West Germany. While there, he not only completed his medical training, he also managed to earn his general education diploma for high school.

In August of 1962, Heidnik called in sick to his job at the hospital, complaining of headaches, dizziness, blurred vision, and nausea. The official cause was listed as gastroenteritis, but an eagle-eyed neurologist also noted that Heidnik seemed to display symptoms of some kind of mental illness or psychosis. Upon further testing at a military hospital in Philadelphia, the neurologist's suspicion was confirmed. Gary's outrageous behavior, a hallmark of his personality from the time he fell from the tree, finally had a name. Schizoid personality disorder. Gary Heidnik was honorably discharged from the Army and sent home.

From that point on, truthfully, Gary no longer needed to work. He was given a monthly pension of $2,000 from the Army that more than covered his living expenses in the mid- to late-1960s. But Gary still pursued a life in medicine, becoming a licensed practical nurse. He took a job at a Veteran's Hospital in Coatesville, but was let go for constantly being absent and exhibiting rude behavior toward the patients.

Heidnik was getting as much help as he wanted for his condition, which was minimal. Usually, it was only as much as taking medication to keep his outbursts under control. But there were times when he would lose all hope and attempt suicide, only to wake up in a sanitarium where he would receive a battery of tests, therapy, and treatments.

The last time he was released from a mental hospital, in 1971, Gary Heidnik had a plan, one that would hopefully give him purpose, but also keep him out of the hospitals. Secretly, it would be a way for him to develop his own vision of Utopia where he could be in complete control.

In October of that same year, Heidnik founded his own church, the United Church of the Ministers of God. The church struggled along and, by 1975, Heidnik was able to finally open an account under the church's name with powerhouse brokerage firm Merrill Lynch. He deposited $1,500 initially, but through his incredibly smart financial sense, was able to increase his investment by 500 percent, making a cool $500,000 tax-free. In today's environment, that would be well over $1,250,000. Investing and reinvesting the dividends made the church Heidnik created both prosperous and affluent. His congregation grew and grew, comprised of mostly retarded and mentally-ill parishioners, handpicked by Heidnik because of their willingness to fall for his rhetoric and their ability to be easily controlled or influenced. He quickly began to take advantage of many of the women in his congregation, mostly African-Americans, and routinely staged orgies with three or more women and himself.

But with the new church came Heidnik's first arrest and incarceration in a prison. In 1978, Heidnik was seeing a girl named Anjeanette Davidson. Her sister, Alberta, was living in a mental institution, and Heidnik convinced Anjeanette to sign Alberta out for the day. Once back at his house, Heidnik raped and repeatedly sodomized Alberta before she was rescued and returned to the hospital. It was later found that Heidnik had also given her gonorrhea.

Gary Heidnik was arrested and charged with kidnapping, unlawful restraint, false imprisonment, involuntary deviant sexual intercourse, and interfering with the welfare and custody of a committed person. He spent three years in a mental institution. When his first parole hearing came up, Heidnik refused to speak, writing a note that informed the parole board that the devil had lodged a cookie in his throat to keep him from speaking.

"He comes up for parole on that prior assault," recalledChuck Peruto, Heidnik's attorney. "These are the people with the power to grant your release. And they ask him a question at the parole board hearing. And he doesn't answer them. He writes on a piece of paper: 'The devil put a cookie in my throat.' Are you gonna release him on society?"

The answer, apparently, was yes, for Heidnik found freedom despite his obvious lack of sanity. He returned to his church and set about continuing his work. Despite being a veteran of several mental institutions and flaunting a thoroughly spotty character to boot, Heidnik remained both a successful businessman and certifiably whacko street preacher who drove about town in Rolls Royces and BMWs. His astonishing financial prowess had made him a force to be reckoned with in the religious communities of North Philadelphia. Now, Heidnik set his sights on marrying. He chose to use a "mail order bride" type of service that connected him with Betty Disto, a Filipino woman who he corresponded with for two years before finally proposing to her. Betty arrived in the United States in September 1985 and married Heidnik the following October.

To say the marriage deteriorated quickly is an understatement. It didn't deteriorate; it imploded. Betty Disto often found her new husband in bed with multiple women at a time, sometimes forcing her to watch him as they had sex. Other times, Heidnik would randomly assault his wife, using brute force to subdue her. Disto was done with Heidnik, but had little recourse until she was able to connect with the influential Filipino community in Philadelphia who helped her escape Heidnik and file for divorce in January of 1986. Heidnik didn't know it at the time, but Betty Disto was pregnant with his child, a fact that he uncovered when Disto filed for child support payments. She gave birth to a son, Jesse John Disto, and wisely kept her distance from Heidnik. Jesse certainly wasn't his first child. He'd had three children prior to his marriage to Betty Disto, all born to mentally challenged women and as a result, each child was removed from the mother's care and placed into foster care.

But Betty Disto's escape was probably more of a relief to Heidnik than it was to Betty. She had been too strong willed, too possessive. If she hadn't left, he would have probably left her. Or worse. But Gary Heidnik had other plans for his legacy. He still dreamed of a Utopia filled with subservient women and obedient children, but all of the women he had under his thumb were now gone, as were his children. He had to start from scratch and he had to make sure that the population of his Utopia was ensured. Heidnik concocted a ghastly plan to kidnap multiple women, chain them in his cellar, and use them as brood mares for his Utopia.

Heidnik went to work immediately, abducting his first victim, Josefina Rivera, on November 25, 1986. By January 1987, five women were being held captive in a large pit dug out of his basement. All were African-American, all were mentally challenged or had a history of mental illness, and all were being habitually raped, beaten, and tortured. On a daily basis, Heidnik would pull one girl after another out of the pit, assault and rape her, then toss her back in before covering the hole with several thick wooden boards. It was his plan to impregnate all of them with his seed, then raise the children on his own, populating his sick, deviant Utopia with sick, deviant children bred and raised by a madman.

Lisa Armstrong, another of Heidnik's victims, went willingly to Gary Heidnik's home following a meal at TGI Friday's. "We was watching a movie, then we went upstairs, and then we had sex. Afterwards, he got up and strangled me. I couldn't hardly breathe. And I told him that he could do whatever he want, and that's when he got the handcuffs and took me down to the basement. He had the chains and clamps, the car clamps. He put them on my ankle, and he had to count the links so, you know, the amount to open my legs wide to have sex."

Of the five women held by Heidnik, surprisingly only two of them died. Sandra Lindsay succumbed to starvation, torture, and a massive fever that essentially cooked her brain. Heidnik, who hadn't planned on any of his "baby machines" to die, quickly dismembered her corpse. "I'm sitting there, you know, trying to figure out what the hell to do, you know," he would tell police. "I started chopping up the body. It makes me sick just thinking about it."

He stuffed her arms and legs into his freezer, marked them "dog food" and went about taking care of the rest of Sandra. He cooked her ribs in an oven and boiled her head in a pot on the stove. Police came to the house due to the complaints of a bad odor, but left the premises after Heidnik's explanation: "I'm cooking a roast. I fell asleep and it burnt."

It was widely circulated after Heidnik's arrest that he had ground up portions of Sandra's flesh, mixed it up with dog food, and fed it to his other women in the cellar, but this has turned out to be a false story, made up by Heidnik's defense attorney in an effort to drum up support for an insanity defense. No evidence of cannibalism was ever found in Heidnik's home, nor was there any corroborating testimony.

The other woman who died, Debra Dudley, was found to have been electrocuted as she hung in the pit by her hands. Josefina Rivera, Heidnik's favorite, recalled the events leading up to her death on March 18, 1987.

> Gary went out, and when he came back, the girls were making noise. Gary told me to hook the hose up to the sink so he could fill the hole with water. While the water was filling the hole, Gary went over to the electrical extension and he started to touch their chains with the hot wire. The girls were screaming and hollering, begging him to stop. Gary said he would stop if everybody got quiet, but Debbie refused to get quiet. Gary gave me the wire and told me to hold it on Debbie's chain. Debbie was still hollering, and then he took the wire from me and held it on Debbie's chain for a few minutes. Then everything went quiet.

Josefina knew that time was running out. If she didn't act fast, all of the women would be dead soon. She used her clout as Heidnik's favorite to whip up a plan of action. A lot of times, Josefina was allowed to walk around the house unbound, and she often accompanied Gary on errands. Josefina became so close to Heidnik that he even trusted her to let her visit her family on March 23, 1987. Heidnik, along with his best friend Cyril "Tony" Brown, drove Josefina to a gas station close to her home and they waited for her there while she met with her family. But once she got a few blocks from Heidnik's house, she used a pay phone to first call 911, then to call her boyfriend.

Responding officers, however, were hesitant to believe her story at first. But once she repeated the story with no deviations, and noting the brutal chafing the chains had made on her legs, the police officers went to the gas station and took Heidnik and Brown into custody. Cyril Brown, who admitted to seeing Sandra Lindsay being dismembered by Heidnik, would eventually be released on $50,000 bail with the agreement that he would testify against his best friend.

When police descended upon the house, they quickly realized that it was much worse than they could have ever imagined. Everything Josefina Rivera had told them was true. The windows were all barred. The wooden doors had been replaced with steel doors, creating a truly intimidating, almost prison-like atmosphere. Inside, they found the television had been turned up very loud, drowning out the screams of the women in the pit below. Police found Lisa Thomas, nineteen, Agnes Adams, twenty-four, and Jacqueline Askins, eighteen, lying on the cellar floor, still chained to the pipes and sitting on a mattress. All were naked, beaten, and clearly in a state of deep shock. Upon seeing the police coming down the stairs, they joyously kept shouting, "We're saved! We're saved!" Police ultimately had to rush down to the local firehouse and borrow a pair of bolt cutters to free the women from their bonds.

As news of Heidnik's ghastly doings spread across the country, and indeed, the world, it should come as no surprise that the media quickly descended upon the house of horrors on North Marshall Street. Local anchors such as Dennis Woltering and Bill Baldini spent numerous hours reporting from the scene of the crime. They would soon be joined by media outlets from England, Germany, and Japan.

Gary Heidnik's arraignment and trial was just as bizarre as he was. During his arraignment, Heidnik claimed that the women chained in the cellar were already there when he moved in. His defense attorney, Charles Peruto, attempted to prove Heidnik was legally insane, even going so far as making Heidnik look like Charles Manson by advising him to not shave or cut his hair. But Heidnik's wealthy bankroll proved otherwise when Merrill Lynch financial adviser Robert Kirkpatrick called Heidnik "an astute investor who knew exactly what he was doing." Peruto attempted to refute the claim by bringing in his own psychiatrist, Jack Apsch, who testified that Gary was, in fact, obviously insane, citing Heidnik's numerous mental health incarcerations and his medical discharge from the Army.

On July 1, 1988, Gary Heidnik would be found guilty of two counts of murder in the first degree. He was sentenced to die by lethal injection at the State Correctional Institution in Pittsburgh. In the interim, Heidnik attempted suicide a number of times, all without success.

To the lay person, nothing Gary Heidnik did could ever be mistaken for something rational or sane. Many students of the law and those in the mental health community pointed to the judge in the case, Lynne Abraham, and accused her of overlooking the obvious and sending a mentally ill man to his death. But the prosecution, headed up by Charlie Gallagher, had posited a strong case for sanity and proved it to the judge and the world.

"Judge Abraham was fair and impartial," says Charlie Gallagher today. "The trial record completely refutes any claim now by Peruto to the contrary. No such complaint about bias was ever made in the eleven years of appeals. And the trial was reviewed and affirmed by the Pennsylvania Supreme Court and all levels of the federal court, including the Supreme Court prior to Heidnik's execution in 1999."

It all comes down to this: if Heidnik were actually insane, if he were not in his right mind, if he was not thinking clearly, would he have tried to cover up the deaths of Debra Dudley and Sandra Lindsay? No. Take the case of Ed Gein, the pleasant little man from Wisconsin who murdered two women and robbed the graves of numerous others. When police found him, their body parts were strewn all over his home. It was a normal thing for Ed, and it showed that he really had no sense of right or wrong. He never tried to cover up what he did. Heidnik, however, did try to obscure the truth and save himself from getting caught, which are the actions of a sane man with a twisted agenda who wanted to conceal what he knew was wrong.

But aside from all the evidence to the contrary, there were many who believed that Gary Heidnik was insane, including his own daughter, Maxine, who tried to uphold her father's execution but failed when it reached the federal level. Heidnik, meanwhile, had constantly asked the courts to waive all appeals and forego proceedings that would delay his execution. His lawyer, Chuck Peruto, abided by his client's wish.

"As a lawyer, it was very frustrating that Heidnik didn't want to appeal," says Chuck Peruto. "But he was smart enough to know he was not getting acquitted. He had a motive not to fight the death sentence. Look at the type of crime he committed and all of his victims were black. He was getting his ass kicked every single day in jail. So it was either a lifetime of getting your ass kicked—and I'm not talking about punched—or the death penalty."

On July 6, 1999, Heidnik got his wish, as he succumbed to the needle in the death house at State Correctional Institution, Rockview, in Centre County, Pennsylvania. Several members of his victims' families were present, but he never spoke to them, never acknowledged them.

"I went to the execution, but it was too calm and serene for me," said Tracey Lomax, Sandra Lindsay's sister and one of Heidnik's victims. "I'm thinking execution is something like, turn around and let me shoot you. Instead they just stuck a needle in his arm. He never looked at us. Never acknowledged us. Never said he was sorry. He didn't say anything. He didn't even look in our direction."

To those people seeking closure, Gary Heidnik denied it to them and took everything with him to the grave. Following the declaration of the medical examiner that he was in fact deceased, relieved applause broke out in the witness room of the death chamber. His body was cremated, his ashes scattered over the Potter's Field at the prison, and Gary Heidnik would become the last person to be executed by the State of Pennsylvania.

Today, the survivors of Gary Heidnik have moved on with their lives, yet the memories of that summer of horror still haunt them. Survivor Jacqueline Askins had so much trouble coping with the ongoing terror that she developed a multiple personality disorder. She called her other self "Donna," a stronger version of herself who would take on all of the leftover trauma created by Heidnik in his basement on Marshall Street. For Josefina Rivera, nightmares come easily and she still sleeps with a light on. "It is a constant struggle to deal with normal life. . . For a long time I was haunted by Heidnik, by the women who died next to me. But not any longer. I hope I can inspire other victims to feel positive about the future."

The Vile Files

Giorgio Orsolano

While only guilty of three murders, the crimes of Italian murderer Giorgio Orsolano were incredibly brutal and horrific. After serving eight years in jail for the violent abduction and rape of a young girl, Orsolano was released back into society to kill once more, raping and murdering three more women before finally being caught and hanged in 1835.

CHAPTER 17

EDMUND KEMPER

"THE CO-ED KILLER"

Santa Cruz, California

"One side of me says, I'd like to talk to her, date her. The other side says, 'I wonder how her head would look on a stick.'"
—**Edmund Kemper**

It's hard not to like Edmund Emil Kemper III. He's a likable guy, amiable, and even at his full imposing height of six-foot-nine, he's still a guy you'd want to have with you when you go out drinking, start telling dirty jokes, or even have an incredibly intellectual conversation. His genius-level IQ of 145 would ensure that.

But when he was alone and he was able to think and feel quietly on his own, in the darkness of his tortured heart lay a sickening secret life; those who have seen it are already dead, and by the time the source of his anger was squashed out, ten people's lives would be tragically cut short by his prodigious hands.

Kemper's life began normally enough in 1948 in Burbank, California, the only son born to Edmund Emil Kemper and Clarnell Stage. His early years were uneventful, though he was noted to be extremely bright, yet thoroughly antisocial. But in keeping with the patterns of other serial killers, his personality changed when he reached twelve or thirteen years of age. As puberty set in, his antisocial moods and behaviors became increasingly psychotic. His brutal treatment of animals, now a staple behavior in the genesis of a serial murderer, was unparalleled, even for a serial killer. He would capture and bury small animals alive, then dig them up later when they were barely alive, only to torture them further. It wasn't enough that he had buried them alive. They also had to suffer the pain and horror of being dismembered, burned, and systematically broken down into gelatinous pieces before Kemper would be satisfied.

Edmund Kemper was the only boy of three children. His older sister had been a lot of trouble for him for most of his youth, abusing him randomly and, according to Kemper, attempting to kill him at least twice. The first instance was when Edmund was five and she pushed him into the family's swimming pool. He came close to drowning several times before his father finally rescued him. The other incident occurred when Edmund and his older sister were playing near some train tracks and she pushed him into the path of an oncoming train. Edmund was able to jump out of the way in time, but it became evident that Edmund's sister had quite the sadistic streak in her, possibly one that was passed down to him from her. But unlike Edmund, who nurtured that sadistic streak into a career of killing, his older sister seemed to outgrow it and become a normal citizen.

We all know that "hand me downs" come in all forms, whether they be clothes, cars, toys, or even books. When it came to questionable behavior towards siblings, this too was handed down to Edmund, who in turn tried to pass it on to his younger sister. For Kemper, his trusting younger sister was the perfect victim to abuse and tease, and as he got older, it became apparent that he began to covet more than her trusting nature. His mother Clarnell seemed to pick up on his bad ideas almost immediately, forcing her son to sleep in the basement of their house behind a locked door for fear that he would rape his younger sister in the night. To some, and indeed to Edmund, this might seem a bit overprotective and borderline abusive. But Clarnell must have sensed Edmund's bad intentions and believed in them so much that it made her go to such drastic lengths to protect her daughter. Ask any mother and they'll tell you that they know their child better than anyone. In this case, I believe Clarnell saw the evil inside Edmund and did what she could at the time to protect her family. What an awful atmosphere it must have been in that house when a mother could not trust her only son with her youngest daughter.

But Clarnell was no saint either. She was a vicious, scathing woman who routinely drank herself into rages where she would belittle and humiliate Edmund. Like Henry Lee Lucas before him, Edmund had a rather fond hatred for his mother, yet a fairly docile relationship with his father. When Edmund Sr. and Clarnell divorced in 1957, Edmund was devastated, not only because his father was gone, but also because he was forced to stay behind with his mother. Six years later, at the age of fifteen, Kemper ran away from home to Van Nuys, California, intent on finding his father. So fed up was Kemper with his mother that he hitchhiked and stowed away on train cars, traveling from Helena, Montana, to sunny California.

But when Kemper arrived in California, he was met with a devastating truth. His father had remarried and had new children with his new wife. But it wasn't all bad. Edmund's father allowed his son to stay with them for a while before sending him home, at least giving his son a bit of respite before having to contend with his mother once more.

But Clarnell Kemper's door was closed for Edmund; she refused to allow him to come back home, instead ordering him to live with his paternal grandparents.

Edmund Kemper I and his wife, Maude, lived on a seventeen-acre ranch on the mountains of North Fork, California. Though the area was serene and alive with nature, Edmund hated living there. His grandparents were incredibly out of touch with the current reality; Edmund would describe his grandfather as "senile" and his grandmother as "constantly emasculating [Kemper] and [Kemper's] grandfather."

If we pause now to look at Edmund's emotional surroundings, we begin to see the foundations for his long-running hatred of women in general. There is a saying "Mother is the word for God on the lips and hearts of all children." As men, our general tendencies are to embrace and protect women, but if we are taught at a young age to despise them, then the worm turns and they become something that needs to be destroyed, an infection that needs to be cut from the flesh. This is what Edmund's mother, and now his own grandmother, seemed to be teaching him: how to really hate women. But we can't place all the blame onto their shoulders. While he was an impressionable child who seemed to be looked down on by the most beloved women in his life, Edmund Kemper's own altered chemistry made it seem right to follow a murderous path opened by his mother. His actions, whether they were voluntary or not, were still actions of his own doing.

He was about to trudge alone down that path and he would take two people with him, whether they wanted to go or not.

On August 27, 1964, fifteen-year-old Edmund Kemper fatally shot his grandmother in the head as she sat at her kitchen table. When his grandfather returned from the grocery store, Edmund met him in the driveway and shot him as well. Then Edmund did something odd: he called his mother, Clarnell, who urged her son to turn himself in. Even after the years of humiliation his mother had put him through, Edmund still ran to Clarnell Kemper seeking her advice. Shockingly, in a shade of things to come, Edmund did as he was told, calmly calling the police and waiting for them to arrive. During questioning, Edmund was markedly remorseful about murdering his grandfather, who was killed by Edmund so that he would be spared the sadness of having lost his wife. In relation to the murder of his grandmother, however, Edmund's motives were cold and to the point: he'd murdered her just to see what it would feel like. Her murder was Edmund's test upon himself to see if he really was capable of committing such a heinous act, and he found it quite easy to do so.

Initial screenings of Edmund's mental health revealed a very telling diagnosis of paranoid schizophrenia, which had gone untreated for Edmund's entire life and provided an answer as to why Edmund had always felt different and antisocial. His IQ was also tested, with results in the 130-145 range, generally considered to be borderline genius. However, it was because of his level of mental illness that he was recommended for a mental health facility rather than a juvenile detention center, and he was remanded to the Atascadero State Hospital which, at the time, was used to house mostly criminally insane sex offenders.

While Edmund's crimes were atrocious, they never bordered on sexually deviant and as his own blossoming sexuality began to show, his ideas of what sex was began to adapt to his surroundings.

In Atascadero, he was surrounded by pedophiles, child killers, necrophiliacs, and some who practiced all of the above all at once. Edmund went into Atascadero having no idea of what sexuality was, but by the time he was released in 1969, he had an altogether unwell view of sex in general. The deviant nature of necrophilia especially played a significant role later on in his career as a serial killer.

Against the wishes of his doctors, Edmund was released from Atascadero into the care of his mother, who had moved to California during his time in the hospital. Edmund assured his doctors that it was fine, and he backed up his certainty with a more loving attitude toward his mother. Convinced, the state psychologists expunged his juvenile record and set him off on his way. Now standing six-foot-nine inches and weighing 280 pounds, the "gentle giant" with the genius IQ began to work toward a normal life, finding employment with the California Department of Transportation paving roads. Though Kemper was supposed to report to a parole officer and a court-appointed social worker following his release, he never did. "I didn't have the supervision I should have had once I got out... I was supposed to see my parole officer every other week and a social worker the other week. I never did. I think if I had, I would have made it."

Eager to be in compliance and stay out of trouble, Kemper finally called the district parole office and asked if he was supposed to check in with his parole officer, or would the parole officer come to him.

Kemper said the man on the phone asked him, "What's the matter, you got a problem?" When Kemper told him, "No," the man replied, "Well, we're awfully busy with people who have; we'll get to you."

Adjusting to life outside Atascadero was a daunting task for Edmund. He'd gone from the straight arrow 1960s directly into the new hippie movement that was enveloping California, and specifically the San Francisco, Berkeley area. "When I got out on the street it was like being on a strange planet. People my age were not talking the same language. I had been living with people older than I was for so long that I was an old fogey."

He moved into an apartment building in Santa Cruz with Clarnell Kemper, which was a stipulation for his release from Atascadero. Clarnell had taken a job at the University of California at Santa Cruz as an administrative assistant. Co-workers and students found her to be charming and lovely, but Edmund couldn't think less of his mother in any capacity. Cohabiting with his mother was not the best of situations and Edmund tried to do his best, but he couldn't avoid the frequent arguments he and his mother had, usually dealing with his so-called "uselessness" as a person.

"She loved me in her way and despite all the violent screaming and yelling arguments we had, I loved her, too. But she had to manage your life. . . and interfere in your personal affairs."

Her interference also included Edmund's dating life. An old-school disciplinarian and control freak, Clarnell Kemper took to setting her son up with women she approved of, but her taste in women differed greatly from his.

"My mother was a big, ugly, awkward woman who was six feet tall and she was always trying to get me to go out with girls who were just like her . . . friends of hers from the campus. I may not be so much to look at myself, but I have always gone after pretty girls."

Edmund's rage toward his mother built up inside of him like a volcano and it wouldn't be long before he began to ponder how he could vent that rage.

The madness within Edmund wasn't gone. Like life in Atascadero had taught him, it was better to adapt to the madness than allow it to continue unchecked. He began to devise ways in which he could murder a woman and get away with it. He entrenched himself in books and television shows on the subject, teaching himself what not to do as a career criminal. For Edmund, getting away with murder was merely an equation with relatively simple answers: don't talk about the crime with others, don't leave any witnesses, don't leave any evidence, don't hit the same area twice, and more important than anything, always trust your gut instinct. He hearkened back to the years he spent listening to the criminals at Atascadero tell tales of their crimes and noting the mistakes that had landed them behind bars. These factors allowed Edmund to begin a killing spree in the Bay Area of California that would terrify the nation. He practiced dry runs daily, kidnapping imaginary women and driving them to secluded places in the mountains. Every aspect of the act was taken into consideration and Edmund shaped and smoothed the process into a very fluid routine that was free of mistakes. By the time summer of 1973 came around, Edmund Kemper III was ready.

From May of 1972 to February of 1973, Kemper murdered six women, most of them college coeds who he would pick up as they hitchhiked back and forth between Berkeley and San Francisco. Eighteen-year-old Fresno State students Mary Ann Pesce and Anita Luchessa were Edmund's first victims, followed by fifteen-year-old high school student Aiko Koo, nineteen-year-old student Cindy Schall, and University of California, Santa Cruz, students Rosalind Thorpe, twenty-four, and twenty-three-year-old Alice Liu.

His method, perfected over months of intense practice runs, consisted of picking up the unsuspecting hitchhikers, driving them to a remote area, and either stabbing, shooting, or strangling them. But death was not the end of the nightmare.

Edmund would take each body back to his apartment in Santa Cruz. He would take photographs of their naked corpses, often raping their dead bodies before

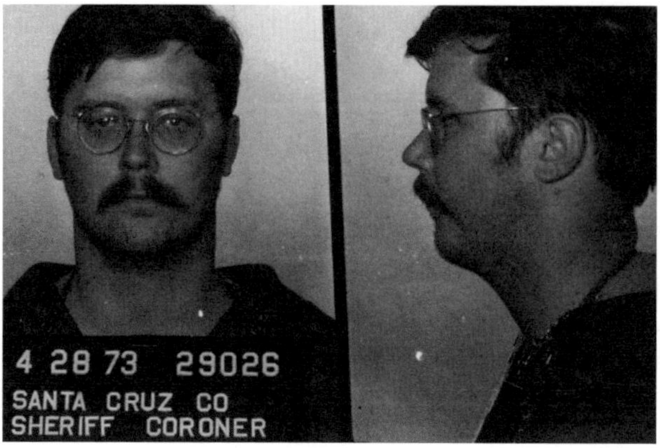

Edmund Emil Kemper III.

dismembering them. He relished the act of decapitating his victims and having sex with the headless body, or using the woman's severed head to perform oral sex on himself. Once the sick fantasy had played itself out, Edmund would gather up the pieces of the body and drive them out into other removed sections of the California wilderness to dispose of them. But alongside his methodical, cold-blooded treatment of his victims lay a very sick sense of humor. In the case of Cindy Schall, Edmund buried her severed head in his mother's garden, facing his mother's bedroom, to which he later remarked that his mother had "always wanted people to look up to her."

Edmund Kemper even took to hanging out with off-duty policemen at a local bar near the courthouse called the Jury Room. There he was known as "Big Ed," a gentle giant of a man who was well liked and often bought rounds of beer for his new friends. It was an attempt not only to glean information about what the cops knew about the coed murders, but also to place himself directly into the spotlight of his own story.

Kemper's last two murders, committed on Good Friday, April 20, 1973, were murders that Edmund had spent the better part of his life practicing. The women he'd murdered before were mere prologues leading up to the climactic end of his career as a killer. It all began that day at around 5:15 a.m. when Kemper's mother returned home from a party. He'd been waiting up for her most of the night and when he heard her arrive home, Edmund went to her. He found her in her bedroom, reading a paperback book after getting ready for bed. Noticing her son walking into the bedroom, she looked up from her book, sighed heavily, and said,"I suppose you're going to want to sit up all night and talk now."

Kemper, near tears, replied, "No, good night."

He raised the hammer he'd been holding in his hand and brought it down upon his mother, repeatedly bashing her skull in with the blunt end. Screams came but were choked by blood and the mutilation the hammer had caused so the screams sounded more like grunts packed in wet towels. Enraged and unloosed, Kemper took his mother's dead body and beheaded her with one of his long knives. He ripped the larynx from her ravaged corpse and tossed it into the spinning garbage disposal. He eventually raped her headless corpse and used her severed head as a dartboard. Kemper would put the head onto his fireplace mantel, where he would yell and scream at his mother, letting out years of anguished rage, taking full advantage of the fact that she could no longer argue back. It was a little past 9:00 a.m. when he decided to clean up. Kemper stowed her body under fresh sheets inside her bedroom closet, and flipped the bloodstained mattress so that the crimson pool would not be immediately evident. He even left a note under the mattress, which read: "Sorry gents for the mess but really had no time."

Edmund was stuck now, for he knew that he would be linked to the murder almost immediately. He had broken one of his own rules for committing murder by killing someone he knew. In an attempt to hide his involvement, Kemper invited his mother's best friend, Sara Hallett, for a surprise dinner. When she arrived, he put his plan into motion.

"I came up behind her and crooked my arm around her neck, like this," he said in a 1974 interview. "I squeezed and just lifted her off the floor. She just hung there and, for a moment, I didn't realize she was dead . . . I had broken her neck and her head was just wobbling around with the bones of her neck disconnected in the skin sack of her neck."

Afterwards, he placed Sara Hallet's body into the closet with his mother, stole her vehicle, and began a 1,500-mile, three-day journey to Pueblo, Colorado. He drank caffeinated soda, popped No-Doz pills like Pez, and kept himself awake for all three days, stopping only occasionally to refuel and gather up more coffee and soda. As he drove, he thought about his crimes and reflected on the reasons why he had shed so much blood. By the time he reached Pueblo, Colorado, Edmund Kemper III had gained an understanding of his psychosis, of his desire to murder the images of his mother wherever he found them, of his need to quiet her nagging voice that haunted his every step. That voice was gone now, her murder had quieted her. But it wasn't just his mother that Edmund had been trying to kill. His social skills were horribly underwhelming and he was always terrified of rejection from a girl he liked. "If I killed them, you know, they couldn't reject me as a man," Kemper once said. "It was more or less making a doll out of a human being. . . and carrying out my fantasies with a doll, a living human doll."

Edmund, realizing he was free of her, but remorseful for every murder that led up to that point, decided to give up. He stopped at a roadside pay phone and phoned the Santa Cruz police.

"I killed my mother and her friend. And I killed those college girls," he told the dispatcher. "I killed six of them and I can show you where I hid the pieces of their bodies."

He was still sitting by the phone when he was eventually picked up and arrested by Pueblo police. The local police chief, Robert Mayber, noticing Kemper's hulking size, remarked to the Associated Press, "I'm glad he didn't decide to resist arrest. He's big enough to beat a mountain lion with a switch." Two rifles, a shotgun, and a pistol were recovered from his car following his arrest. Once he'd been extradited back to California, Kemper spilled his guts, giving the police thoroughly graphic and detailed descriptions of the murders he'd committed and even took them to the places where he'd dumped the bodies.

The murder of his mother had been a long time coming. But her murder was also the one that Kemper found the most difficult to accomplish. According to Kemper, he loved his mother so much, but hated the way she treated him. He didn't want to kill her, but she couldn't be left alive. Perhaps Kemper realized that if he had only murdered his mother first, the lives of nine other people might have been spared, that all along he had been seeking to murder his mother in each and every killing he performed. He did to those women, as well as his grandparents, what he always ached to do to his mother. What kept Kemper from doing it, of course, was the fact that Clarnell Kemper essentially had Edmund trained to be submissive. Years of belittlement and humiliation had turned him into a cowering mama's boy who was afraid to truly confront the demon haunting his life, so he did the next best thing. He murdered six women in effigy, transferring the rage he felt toward his mother on to them, then punishing them for it.

But like most killers in that position, he feared the punishment from others and attempted to take his own life, severing an artery in his right wrist with a sharpened ball point pen in his prison cell, screaming at first responders that he would kill them if they tried to save his life. He bled out for four minutes before passing out, allowing EMT's to patch him up and get him into the infirmary.

Edmund Kemper III pleaded not guilty by reason of insanity, placing blame for the murders on his bouts with schizophrenia and his incredibly dysfunctional family life. But Dr. Joel Fort, a psychiatrist working for the prosecution, refuted the defense's claim of insanity. Fort had spent hours upon hours with Kemper, interviewing the killer about his previous life at Atascadero and even garnering new bits of information about his sexual practices with the corpses of his victims. Kemper understood his actions and why he did what he did, which is one thing an insane killer would not be able to comprehend. Kemper may have been obsessed with sex and violence, but he was not insane. Fort even called Kemper's diagnosis of paranoid schizophrenia into question, finding no evidence of that condition whatsoever.

The jury would deliberate for only five hours before they returned with eight first-degree murder convictions. Each conviction garnered him a consecutive life sentence, which he still serves today at Folsom Prison, one of California's more notorious maximum-security penitentiaries. He is known as the "genius serial killer" and has spoken at length about his crimes in hopes that he can help bring more monsters behind bars. He looks much the same as he always has, perhaps a bit heavier, and his incredible intelligence is still very evident each and every time he opens his mouth to speak. But behind the eloquent speech and meticulous manners lies the soul of a raging demon who is glad to have been finally stopped.

The Vile Files

The Servant Girl Murders

During the course 1885, a silent killer stalked the rural homeowners of Austin, Texas. While the newspapers of the time labeled the deaths "The Servant Girl Murders," the victims weren't all employed as servants. In all, six women were brutally butchered in the middle of the night, as well as two married women of the homes and the young daughter of one of the victims. The killer would usually sneak into the homes and drag his victims into the yard where he would viciously rape them before stabbing them or bludgeoning them with an axe. Other times, he would simply strike them with his axe as they slept. Police searched in vain for the duration of 1885, taking casts and photographs of footprints found at the scene, but after December of that year, no other murders matching the Servant Girl Murderer ever occurred. Detectives would later link nineteen-year-old Nathan Elgin to the murders. Elgin, an African-American servant himself who had been killed in a bar fight in February 1886, was pinned to the murders when his footprints matched up to the bloody footprints found at the scene of most of the murders.

CHAPTER 18

JACK THE RIPPER

Whitechapel, London

"I am down on whores and I shant quit ripping them till I do get buckled. Grand work the last job was. I gave the lady no time to squeal. How can they catch me now. I love my work and want to start again."

–Excerpt from the notorious "Dear Boss" letter

Mary Jane Kelly was a true busybody the night of November 8 and the early morning hours of November 9, 1888. As a so-called "Lady of the Night," she was accustomed to such hours. She'd been up at the Ten Bells with Elizabeth Foster, another prossy, drinking and trying to hook in some more money to pay her rent. The little room at 2 Miller's Court wasn't much, but there were four walls, a roof, a fireplace, and a bed, which is all she needed, yet not nearly as much as she wanted. She'd been at the Ten Bells since 8:00 p.m. that evening, and with nary a customer or two, the time had been wasted pretty quickly. Now home, Mary Jane Kelly had just finished up a small meal of meat and potatoes when she set out into the streets again, intent on making her rent for the week. Normally, the blonde-haired, blue-eyed stunner would not be lacking in attention. Were it not for her beauty, then the Irish lilt in her voice and the soft touch of her hand would make most men crumble before her. How awful and tragic it was that the man who had escorted her back to Miller's Court would be the last one to see her alive.

Jack the Ripper

Mary Kelly had known the risks her job as a Whitechapel prostitute entailed, especially in these last few months of 1888. She and her friends had been beaten, raped, and robbed before. But now, there had been a bona-fide madman on the loose, striking out indiscriminately at prostitutes all over the city. His crimes had frightened them all to their very core, but with little other prospects for survival, they had no choice but to weather the terror and go about their business. It was a way of life the Ripper of Whitechapel counted upon.

The crimes of the man dubbed "Jack the Ripper" are said to have begun in August 1888 with the murder of local prostitute May Ann Nichols, but most "Ripperologists" claim that murders matching the Ripper's *modus operandi* began as early as December 1887, as mutilation-style murders of various women began turning up in the Whitechapel area. It is thought that as many as thirteen murders were committed by Jack the Ripper before the accepted list of murder victims even began.

Looked upon in hindsight, women such as Martha Tabrum, "Fairy Fay," Alice McKenzie, and Carrie Brown all bore the tell-tale signs of an encounter with the Ripper, which included a slashed throat, various facial mutilations, and meticulously performed vivisection. They were also committed, strangely, under a veil of silence in dark, empty streets. No screams were heard by neighbors in the area and very few actually saw the victims with their killer. It was as if he were a phantom, silencing their screams before they even knew the terror was upon them.

In the time of Jack the Ripper, London was seeing an influx of immigrants, mostly from Ireland, Russia, and many other smaller Eastern European countries. Whitechapel, in particular, saw an enormous jump in population; the cheap lodgings and good factory and masonry jobs kept the streets and tenement buildings packed full. But anyone who lives in a big city can tell you: for every 100 honest, hardworking citizen there are twenty who are in it for the crime. Burglars, rapists, murderers, and muggers all claimed the streets of London and its surrounding districts. Whitechapel was, indeed, the worst of them. Poverty flourished in epidemic-like proportions and women who had no prospects found themselves working as prostitutes to pay the rent. A census performed by the Metropolitan Police Department in 1888 counted nearly sixty-two brothels and over 1,200 women working as prostitutes in Whitechapel alone. Anti-Semitism, brought on by the sudden appearance of thousands of Eastern European Jews, became a common source of tension in the neighborhood.

In the midst of all this social unrest in the East End of London, a gentleman clad in black with a heart filled with dark imaginings, wandered amongst the denizens of Whitechapel, eyes fixed upon the "Unfortunates," those women of the night selling their bodies for gin and rent. The level of violence against women in Whitechapel in 1888 was staggering and an accurate count of how many women fell to Jack's blade is truly unknown, though most believe the murders began on

August 7, 1888, with the savage murder of Martha Tabram, whose body claimed thirty-nine stab wounds. The murder fit within the timeline of Jack's rampage, yet lacked the same wound pattern he would utilize on the rest of his confirmed victims; Martha had been stabbed, whereas the others had been slashed, or "ripped," viciously, yet meticulously. I believe that Martha Tabram *was* Jack's first murder in Whitechapel, due mostly to the fact that he would have been nervous about his first time. He would have approached her timidly and tried to take her out as quickly as he could, exploding upon her like a caged beast. It wouldn't be until after the murder that he'd realized how sloppy it truly was and that he hadn't accomplished what he set out to accomplish. His goal with Martha Tabram's killing would have been to just see if it could be done, how much time he would have from beginning to end before he would have to flee, how nosy the neighbors were, and what would be the best way to disappear from the scene. Those factors, along with many others I'm sure, were swirling about in Jack's head in the orgasmic haze following Tabram's murder. His next one would be more to his liking. Martha Tabram's murder would be the mere prologue to a three-act play performed in the dark, gritty streets of Whitechapel.

The task of finding the Ripper went to Inspector Frederick Abberline, a seasoned Scotland Yard detective who not only had to find a killer of women, but also maintain and quell the vengeful mobs of people who felt as if the police weren't doing enough to protect them. Abberline and his task force faced a daunting task, one nearly devoid of clues, yet rife with theories and speculation, none of which would support a prosecution against the murderer should he be found. Abberline, instead, began to rely on the very early art of criminal profiling, building a portrait of who he thought may have been the type of man who could do such a thing to another person, an art that wouldn't see fluid perfection for at least eighty more years when the Federal Bureau of Investigation would make it a part of their line of work.

The Ripper's first confirmed victim would be Mary Ann Nichols, whose body was found lying on Bucks Row at about 3:40 a.m. on Friday, August 31, 1888. Her throat had been slashed to the spinal cord and her abdomen had been partially ripped open, leaving a deep jagged wound. Several other cuts were found dotting her abdomen as well, all caused by the same knife. Nichols's murder was a clear evolution from Tabram's murder. There were still elements of the savage stabbing that Martha had endured, but here now were the first elements of what would be Jack the Ripper's staple attack: slash the throat so that they couldn't scream and so that their blood would literally gush out of them, then go to work on them once they were in a severely weakened state after having been bled almost to death. It's almost exactly how a lioness or a cheetah attacks and subdues its prey on the Serengetti: weaken them to the point of exhaustion or death, then tear them to shreds. In that way, Jack is exactly like the animal we now know him to be and nothing else.

Jack continued his rampage with the murder of Annie Chapman on September 8, 1888, one week after the murder of Mary Ann Nichols. Annie Chapman's body

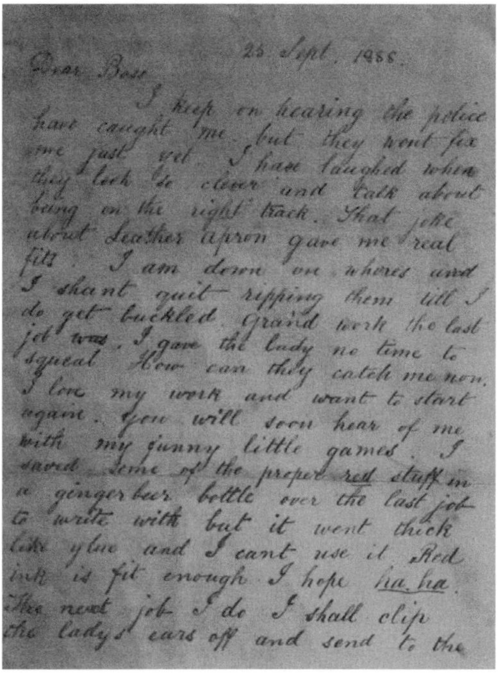
25 Sept. 1888.

Dear Boss

I keep on hearing the police have caught me but they wont fix me just yet. I have laughed when they look so clever and talk about being on the right track. That joke about Leather Apron gave me real fits. I am down on whores and I shant quit ripping them till I do get buckled. Grand work the last job was. I gave the lady no time to squeal. How can they catch me now. I love my work and want to start again. You will soon hear of me with my funny little games. I saved some of the proper red stuff in a ginger beer bottle over the last job to write with but it went thick like glue and I cant use it. Red ink is fit enough I hope ha. ha. The next job I do I shall clip the ladys ears off and send to the

had been found in the backyard of a house on Hanbury Street in Spitalfields. Her throat, like Nichols, had been slashed to the bone, but her attack was even more brutal. Her abdomen was completely flayed open and the killer had removed her uterus, which he left lying near her head.

The Metropolitan Police Department, as well as the Whitechapel papers, began to receive numerous letters from "the killer" and, while many were imaginative and interesting, none of them seemed connected to the true murderer stalking Whitechapel—that is, until police received the so-called "Dear Boss" letter.

Dated September 25, with a postmark of September 27, 1888, the "Dear Boss" letter was received by the Central News Agency and was forwarded to Scotland Yard like all the others had been. As written:

> Dear Boss,
>
> I keep on hearing the police have caught me but they wont fix me just yet. I have laughed when they look so clever and talk about being on the right track. That joke about Leather Apron gave me real fits. I am down on whores and I shant quit ripping them till I do get buckled. Grand work the last job was. I gave the lady no time to squeal. How can they catch me now. I love my work and want to start again. You will soon hear of me with my funny little games. I saved some of the proper red stuff in a ginger beer bottle over the last job to write with but it went thick like glue and I cant use it. Red ink is fit enough I hope ha. ha. The next job I do I shall clip the ladys ears off and send to the police officers just for jolly wouldn't you. Keep this letter back till I do a bit more work, then give it out straight. My knife's so nice and sharp I want to get to work right away if I get a chance. Good Luck. Yours truly
>
> Jack the Ripper

> Dont mind me giving the trade name
>
> PS Wasnt good enough to post this before I got all the red ink off my hands curse it No luck yet. They say I'm a doctor now. ha ha

Inspector Abberline and the other investigators from Scotland Yard initially dismissed the letter as a hoax, one in a million they'd already received. But their interest in the letter was renewed when, three days later, Katherine Eddowes's body was discovered with one ear partially cut off.

The murders on September 30, 1888, shouldn't have been a double murder. Jack had targeted Elizabeth Stride as his victim of the night, but a possible interruption from an innocent bystander kept him from exploiting his bloodlust in full. Elizabeth Stride sustained only a cut throat, that of a severed artery on her left side. Police and criminologists, especially those who have studied the patterns of serial killers, speculate that not murdering Stride in the way he had become accustomed drove Jack to find another victim to satisfy that unquenchable thirst for blood. He would find Katherine Eddowes forty-five minutes after Elizabeth Stride's murder, and she would be the recipient of his fury for having not finished the job on Stride. Katherine's body was found in Mitre Square in the city of London, a brisk walk or jog from Whitechapel. Her throat had been cut, her torso had been torn open, her left kidney was ripped out and taken, and most of her uterus had been excised. Also, chillingly, as the Dear Boss letter had predicted, one of her ears had been clipped. Nearby, a note had been scrawled in chalk on the wall on Goulsten Street. Directly below the note was Katherine Eddowes' bloody apron, torn from her by the Ripper himself, a calling card implicating himself as the author. The note said:

> The Juwes are the men that will not be blamed for nothing.

But it seemed out of place for a murderer, having just committed his second homicide of the night amidst a volatile police presence, to scrawl a note as cryptic as this. To some officers, the note seemed faded, as if it had been there for some time, possibly scrawled there during one of the many past incursions of anti-Semitic protesting prior to the Ripper's rampage. Other officers maintained that, until proven otherwise, it was a clue from the Ripper himself and should have been logged as evidence. The debate raged until about 5:30 that morning when Police Commissioner Charles Warren arrived on the scene and immediately ordered it removed. His decision was radical, but his reasons were tight: in the largely Jewish populated area in which the note had been scrawled, it would only serve to increase feelings of Anti-Semitism, a problem that was already a boiling kettle in the East End. It also couldn't be proved that the note was new and from the Ripper himself, calling into question its authenticity as a clue in the investigation. Warren chose to have it removed simply to keep the peace.

Police at the time doubted a connection, mostly due to the fact that the two bodies had been found so far apart and both had been murdered in less than an hour. Clues began pouring in from people who remembered seeing the murdered women walking either with a well-dressed gentleman or a shabbily dressed one.

It brings to mind a theory many Ripperologists have about there possibly being two killers. As said, all of the witnesses who had seen the girls that night testified to last seeing them with either a well-dressed man, or a shabbily dressed one. Perhaps Jack the Ripper was a part of a ghastly duo, comprised of a psychotic killer, and a demented coachman who would get him where he needed to go. Such a theory isn't out of the realm of believability and it could also explain how the Ripper managed to murder one woman and get all the way across London to murder another, all in less than an hour.

Shortly after the double murder of Eddowes and Stride, the police received yet another letter, one that proved that they were dealing with the actual killer. The handwriting was similar to the Dear Boss letter and it referenced not only the unpublished previous letter, but also the infamous double murder of Katherine Eddowes and Elizabeth Stride: As written:

> I was not codding dear old Boss when I gave you the tip, you'll hear about Saucy Jacky's work tomorrow double event this time number one squealed a bit couldn't finish straight off. Had not got time to get ears off for police thanks for keeping last letter back till I got to work again.
>
> Jack the Ripper

The final accepted correspondence from the Ripper came as a postcard and cardboard box received by George Lusk. Lusk was a rather loud voice in the Whitechapel Vigilance Committee, a boisterous group formed as a sort of neighborhood watch program in Whitechapel. Dubbed the "From Hell" letter, it included with it a portion of a human kidney, much like the one missing from Katherine Eddowes's body on the night of her murder. It read (as written):

> From hell
>
> Mr Lusk
>
> Sor
> I send you half the
> Kidne I took from one women
> prasarved it for you tother piece
> I fried and ate it was very nise I
> may send you the bloody knif that
> took it out if you only wate a whil
> longer.

signed
Catch me when
you Can

Mishter Lusk.

The Ripper was obviously aware of George Lusk's position in Whitechapel and with little response from the police, he was turning to the leader of what was essentially a loose-cannon posse. Lusk was a powder keg, easy to ignite into action, and he didn't let the Ripper down. His Vigilance Committee tried vainly to find the Ripper themselves, following up on anti-Semitic rumors and questionable theories posed by newspaper writers. All they managed to do was make life difficult for police, which is what the Ripper had planned all along.

The final murder attributed to the Ripper was that of Mary Jane Kelly, a pretty Irish woman who'd arrived in London with high hopes for her future, but found herself, like her friends, working the streets for a living. But Mary, unlike the others, had somewhat stable lodgings and a brighter future than most ahead of her. Her beauty alone had taken her to Paris and back, posing for nude paintings by well-known artists. But when her body was found on November 9, 1888, all traces of her beauty had been scoured away with a knife.

Neighbors had seen Mary's suitor for the evening, describing him as having a pale complexion, a slight mustache, and dark hair and eyes. He wore a heavy waistcoat with a large gold chain, standing five-foot-six inches or five-foot-seven tall, and carrying a parcel under his arm. Such a sight wasn't uncommon at Miller's Court. Mary's reputation and employment was hardly a secret, as were the facts that men came and went often from Mary's apartment. It was because of this, that no attention was paid to their goings-on at 2 Miller's Court until much later that morning.

A rent collector named Thomas Bowyer, hired by Mr. John McCarthy, had come to gather Mary Kelly's rent for the week and, after receiving no answer at the door, peered in the window. To Thomas Bowyer, it was as if he had looked in a window to hell. Blood drained from his face and his body went cold as the true horror of what had happened to Mary Jane Kelly finally sank in.

She was lying naked in the middle of the bed, her head turned on the left cheek. Portions of skin and muscle had been torn from her body, arms, and legs. Her entire abdominal cavity was devoid of any organs or intestines. Her breasts had been cut off and her throat slashed down to the spine. Her face had literally been torn away, revealing the horrid skull beneath.

Her heart, which was noticeably missing, would be found later boiling in a tea kettle over the fire in her apartment.

It was said that the only way she could be positively identified was by the color of her blonde hair, one of the more defining characteristics of Kelly outside her glowing personality. To the hardened detectives and constables, even this murder

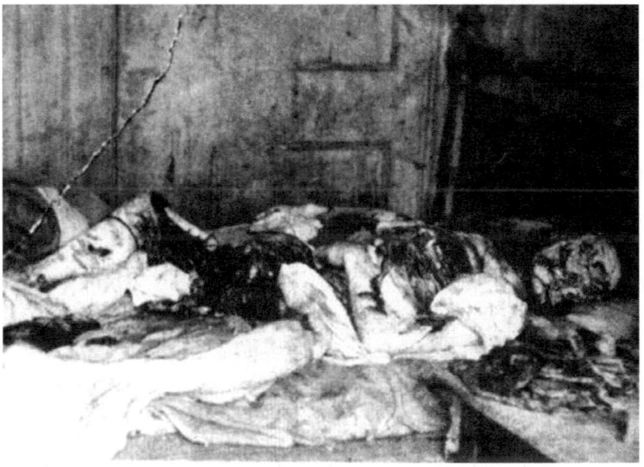

In life, it was said that her beauty was unparalleled. In death, however, Mary Jane Kelly's obliterated corpse shocked and sickened even the most hardened policemen in Whitechapel.

was too much to handle. It was savagery defined, a brutal death perpetrated by a vicious madman who finally had the time and privacy to construct his ultimate work of art. Sheltered by Mary Kelly's apartment, the Ripper had been free to do whatever he pleased without any fear of discovery.

Mary Kelly is generally considered to be the Ripper's final victim, yet four other murders occurred after hers that some believe were also committed by the Ripper: those of Rose Mylett, Alice McKenzie, the Pinchin Street torso, and Frances Coles. But the deaths of these unfortunate women, while tragic, bore no resemblance to Jack the Ripper's method. Adding to the confusion were the differing opinions of several doctors and pathologists; some maintained they were Ripper victims and some argued that they weren't.

The newspapers, meanwhile, were more than happy to keep "RipperMania" going, so any and all connections, whether genuine or not, were published and exploited.

The list of suspects, meanwhile, became as lively and as colorful as one might expect from such a scandalous age. The list included Royalty (Prince Edward Albert Victor and Sir William Gull), doctors (such as Dr. Francis Tumblety and Dr. Neill Cream) and social deviants from the neighborhood (such as Aaron Kosminski, an insane Polish Jew; and Michael Ostrog, a certifiably mad doctor from Russia). Later theories linked Lewis Carroll, author of the *Alice in Wonderland* books, to the Ripper murders as well.

Aaron Kosminski was a paranoid schizophrenic and a true misogynist. He was placed into a London insane asylum after the last-known Ripper murder was committed. No other Ripper-like murders were ever committed after his incarceration. He was at the top of Scotland Yard's list of suspects and had no alibi for any of the murders. One of the eyewitnesses placed him in the company of Elizabeth Stride shortly before her murder.

Montague John Druitt was a failed teacher and lawyer who shared in a family history of mental illness. What kept him from being a serious suspect was his location away from Whitechapel; his family home was in Dorset, several miles from Whitechapel. While some scholars believe that his location made him ineligible for being a Ripper suspect, his family's wealth would have ensured him plenty of ways to navigate to Whitechapel any time he pleased. In fact, his own family suspected him of being the Ripper. Ironically, he committed suicide by drowning in December 1888, one month after the last Ripper murder.

Michael Ostrog was a Russian-born con man and petty thief who had been named as a suspect by Assistant Chief Constable Sir Melville Macnaghten, who joined the case in 1889. Though known for thievery and not murder, Ostrog was still considered a candidate due to the fact that he was thought to be clinically insane and had once claimed to have been a surgeon in the Russian Navy. French prison records, recovered only recently, however, place Ostrog in prison in France during the time of the murders.

James Kelly was first identified as a suspect in Terence Sharkey's *Jack the Ripper: 100 Years of Investigation*, published in 1987. Kelly is said to have murdered his wife in 1883 by stabbing her in the neck, after which he was committed to Broadmoor Asylum. He would escape the asylum in early 1888, remaining completely hidden from authorities for almost forty years until he unexpectedly turned himself in to the Broadmoor Asylum. He would pass away only two years later. Kelly fit the bill for Jack the Ripper given his quickness with both his temper and a knife, both of which seemed to target women. Following the Ripper murders, Kelly emigrated to the United States and settled in New York City; many point to the Ripper-like murder of a prostitute named Carrie Brown as well as one or two additional murders of prostitutes while Kelly was there as evidence of his guilt. The profile written by doctors from Broadmoor Asylum is said to have matched the Ripper profile almost exactly.

Walter Richard Sickert was a German-born artist of British and Danish ancestry, first mentioned as a Ripper suspect in Donald McCormick's 1959 book *The Identity of Jack the Ripper*. Sickert had been fascinated with the Ripper murders, which wasn't uncommon for the time. A number of people were fascinated by the crimes, but Sickert seemed to take his obsession to the extreme. He was rumored to have stayed in a room that had once been used by the Ripper himself as a lodger, though this can hardly be counted as evidence, seeing that the true identity of the Ripper is still a mystery to this day. Being a fairly exceptional painter, Sickert would later depict a good number of the murders in his paintings. It was also rumored he had known some of the women who had been killed, namely Mary Kelly, when he'd paid for her to pose for several of his paintings and drawings. In 2002, crime novelist Patricia Cornwell, in *Portrait of a Killer: Jack the Ripper—Case Closed,* claimed to have matched Sickert's DNA recovered from one of his letters to DNA evidence recovered from one of the Ripper letters sent to police in 1888.

One of the more chilling theories was that the Ripper was notorious American serial killer and con man, H. H. Holmes. Holmes was a doctor and his handwriting very nearly matched the writing on the Dear Boss letter almost perfectly. In addition, eyewitness descriptions of the Ripper seem to favor the look of Holmes.

Holmes also had the time, the money to travel, and the opportunity. However, Holmes's motives were driven by money and no evidence exists that he would have benefited monetarily from the murders of five poor, homeless women. Was Holmes, already a ruthless killer, honing his craft in London before returning to the States to open his infamous "Murder Castle" hotel?

In my opinion, I must downplay and almost eradicate the assertions that the killer had to have had medical knowledge; the murders were brutal, savage, and were not nearly as clean as some theorists like to maintain. Compare the clinical dissection a doctor would make upon a body to the butchery a slaughterhouse worker might commit and one can see that the deaths of the five prostitutes resembled a butchered pig more than they did a dissected corpse. During slaughter, the pig's throat is cut first, allowing it to bleed out and die quickly, followed by the systematic disemboweling of the animal. This method is similar to that which was played out upon our five victims. Add to this the fact that the organ system of a pig very closely resembles the organ system of a human, and you have a killer who may not be the brightest man in the world, but he could know his way around a body very well.

Premier FBI criminal profilers John Douglas and Roy Hazelwood have gone on the record stating that, given the evidence and taking the profile into consideration, they believed someone like Aaron Kosminski best fit the profile of Jack the Ripper. In a 1988 BBC special commemorating the 100-year anniversary of the Ripper murders, both Douglas and Hazelwood appeared and gave their take on who they believed Jack the Ripper to be.

"Jack the Ripper was a white male, in his mid-to-late twenties, with very average intelligence," said John Douglas, "and Roy [Hazelwood] and I both believe that he wasn't really that clever as he was lucky."

"He was most likely single, never been married. In fact, he probably never socialized well with women at all," continued Hazelwood. "We believe that Jack the Ripper lived very close to the murder sites because killers of this nature begin killing within very close proximity to their homes. He was obviously very familiar with the area." The two compounded their view by stating that he had to have been single because, given that the murders were committed late at night or very early in the morning, he would have had to have no one to answer to, like a wife who'd be suspicious of his nocturnal activities.

Douglas and Hazelwood went on to say that, if he were employed, it would be as a laborer, the doer of some sort of menial task that would have kept him away from other people, such as a butcher or mason. He would have been raised in a broken home with a very dominant mother who would have abused him either sexually or physically as a child. This abuse would have led Jack to become both hateful and fearful of women in general, which is why he would have killed the women quickly on the streets. The killing itself was not the objective, but the mutilation would be his impetus for dispatching them. The slashed throat took their screams and their lives quickly, leaving them vulnerable to his intrusive knife.

In extracting their private parts, he would no longer see them as women and therefore, they would no longer be seen as a threat or as a dominant force to oppress him.

To this end, of all the suspects the Ripper case had generated, it would seem that someone like Michael Ostrog or Aaron Kosminski would fit the criminal profile generated by the FBI. They wouldn't have minded getting their hands dirty and they would have been able to blend into the crowds of people in Whitechapel easier than a gentleman killer would have. But it would be discovered later on that Ostrog had been prison in France during the duration of the killings, leaving only Kosminski, who had no alibi and was not out of the city or country at the time.

"If he didn't do it," said Douglas, "someone just like him, living in Whitechapel, did."

The Vile Files

The Real Sweeney Todd?

The tale of Sweeney Todd revolves around a vengeful barber who joins forces with Mrs. Lovette, a wily baker, to murder clients in his chair so that their flesh can be harvested for her "Meat Pie" emporium beneath his tonsorial salon. He first appeared in a penny dreadful serial in London newspapers called "The String of Pearls," in 1847, and has become the basis of numerous films and plays since then. While there is no evidence that the "Demon Barber of Fleet Street" existed in real life, it is possible that he was inspired by a real set of killers in Paris, France. In reality, the sinister murders and the grievous making of human meat pies happened in an area of Paris known as *Rue De La Harpe* in the early 1400s. French histories of the time tell of Bernabe Cabard and Pierre Miquelon, a barber and a baker who conspired to kill, rob, and make meat pies of the barber's dead clients. Unlike Fleet Street in London, there actually is a place on *Rue De La Harpe* where two buildings used to stand; a marker on the site forbids anyone from building upon the empty lot where most believe the inspiration for Sweeney Todd was born and has become the final resting place for hundreds of victims.

CHAPTER 19

TOMMY LYNN SELLS

"THE CROSS COUNTRY KILLER"

Huntsville, Texas

"I went in and, and I don't know if it was her room, don't know if it was his room, I just knew I wanted to go in there and hurt someone."

–Tommy Lynn Sells

Tommy Lynn Sells was everything the FBI looked for in a serial killer. Embroiled in a broken childhood marred by tragedy and sexual abuse, he found himself becoming a remorseless loner with nothing in him but hatred. He was a perfect predator with no roots, no boundaries, and no regrets. Before his execution on January 3, 2014, Tommy Lynn Sells took the lives of twenty-two men, women, and children, though his reach extended far beyond his grasp; Sells would eventually confess to almost seventy murders, and authorities found it difficult to argue with him. Sitting in his prison cell, regaling reporters with stories of his exploits, Sells' crooked, endearing smile showed the world a man who was not only proud of his work, but was finally happy that the world had finally taken notice of him; he seemed to enjoy his notoriety, another classic facet of the serial killer persona.

Tommy was, and still is, the perfect example of a conventional serial predator.

Born June 28, 1964, Tommy Lynn and his twin sister, Tammy, began life in utter pain. Both contracted meningitis at eighteen months of age and only Tommy survived. But the bacterial brain infection left him with learning disabilities and a penchant for fits of rage. He never knew his mother; she'd been in prison since his birth and he spent his earliest years being shuttled from home to home, living with various relatives off and on with no permanent place to call home. He lived with his Aunt Bonnie for the longest period of time, who later said that his favorite activity was riding his tricycle up and down the sidewalk in front of her house. Tommy himself would later call this the "one bright moment" in his entire life.

Tommy's mother was released from prison when he was six years-old and finally, he was able to call a place home and call a woman his mother. Living in Missouri with his mother and his grandfather, Tommy thought that his dreams of a stable family life had finally come true. But his happiness was short lived. Her unfathomable indifference to Tommy resulted in him abusing alcohol by age seven and becoming a constant truant from school. No one in the house cared where he went, what he was doing, or who he was with; he was, in essence, a cross for them to bear. They didn't even try to disguise it.

The final nail in the coffin that sealed Tommy's fate as a burgeoning serial murderer came when he befriended a man named Willis Clark. Tommy, not realizing that he was a notorious pedophile, began staying at Clark's house in nearby Frisbee, Missouri, when he was eight. He began smoking marijuana with Clark, which led to Tommy being molested by the man on numerous occasions. Tommy was eventually able to pull himself away from Clark, but never reported the molestation.

Of course, he was never the same afterwards and the disgust he felt would follow him for the rest of his life. It also began to infect his daily life. Small animals faced his brutal wrath. He began to exhibit sexually inappropriate behaviors with his own grandmother, and, at age thirteen, was sent to a mental hospital for evaluation after he attempted to rape his mother.

After being repeatedly abandoned by his family, Tommy Lynn Sells left home in 1978 at the age of fourteen, hitchhiking and train-hopping his way across the country. He shoplifted, burglarized homes, and blatantly stole to support himself on his jaunt across America. He worked menial manual-labor jobs and abused alcohol and drugs constantly; but, until he was sixteen years old, Tommy had resisted the urge to actually kill anyone.

According to Tommy himself, he had been staking out a house to rob when he claims to have seen an older man performing fellatio on a young boy. Disgusted and enraged, Tommy killed the man by cutting his throat. Police later indicated that there was no evidence of molestation and the boy would refute Tommy's story to authorities. Obviously, in Tommy's mind, the murder of a pedophile made the act more acceptable, almost justified. Whether or not there was any molestation or not, it awakened a beast inside Tommy Lynn Sells that would never, ever, be quieted until the day of his execution twenty-five years later. He'd murdered and gotten away with it. As a child, being invisible to others was a curse. As a killer, it was a blessing. For the first time in his life, Tommy Lynn Sells felt unflinching power over others.

And he liked it.

Over the years, he would abuse drugs, fight, kill, and rape his way across the country. He was in and out of prison constantly, and doctors were finally able to properly diagnose him. The list of disorders read like a laundry list of psychological terms: he was antisocial, suffered a borderline personality disorder, was highly schizophrenic, bipolar, and suffered from severe psychosis and depression. In a bizarre twist, Tommy managed to marry while in prison, exchanging vows with a Tennessee woman named Nora Price. Once out of prison, he moved to Tennessee to be with her, but subsequently left her to continue his murderous travels across the country.

Sells would go on to father two children, one with Nora Price, and the other with a woman named Jessica Levrie, a single mother of four from Del Rio, Texas. While living with Jessica, Sells would continue his rampage unabated, eventually committing possibly more than twenty murders. Traveling as far north as Madison, Wisconsin, Sells cut a bloody swath of murder and rape across the Panhandle the likes of which softened even the most hardened policemen. No one was off limits. Entire families, hookers, teenage girls, innocent bystanders, and even children fell at Tommy's hands. His sheer brutality and incredible bravado stunned police and communities alike, and his willingness to murder anyone kept people from describing or identifying him in every single instance. Once the beast was loosed, no one stood a chance. In one instance, Sells told of how he came upon Keith and Elaine Dardeen and their three-year-old son, Peter. Breaking into their home, he murdered the young boy and his father, then viciously raped the boy's pregnant mother. The trauma of the assault caused Elaine to give birth to the baby in the midst of the rape. After strangling her, Tommy Lynn Sells took a baseball bat and bludgeoned the newborn baby to death. His need for blood now became more important than any kind of personal gain.

Detective John Kemp, who originally investigated the case, once told CBS News, "How you can kill a three-year-old and also kill a newborn infant? That just goes beyond explanation."

Tommy's downfall would come on New Year's Eve, 1999, when he made his way to Del Rio, Texas. He'd returned to the area and was once again living with Jessica Levrie and her children. But domestic life hardly slowed him down. The nights of December 30 and 31, 1999, were Sells' first forays into murder in almost six months. He'd held it in as long as he could, but on this set of nights, this New Year's holiday, Tommy Lynn Sells would not have been able to stop himself even if he'd tried.

He started by murdering Danny and Kathy Freeman in Welch, Oklahoma. Police discovered their bodies inside the burning remains of their mobile home. Hauntingly, the couple's daughter, Ashley, and her best friend Lauria Bible were missing from the scene. The two teenaged girls would never be seen again. Sells confessed to their murders as well, telling police that he dumped the bodies near the Texas-Mexico border close to the Red River.

Returning home to Del Rio, Sells skulked into the nearby Guajia Bay subdivision. He settled on a remote little double-wide trailer, one belonging to Terry and Crystal Harris, a married couple he and Jessica had met while attending services at Grace Community Church.

The night of the last murder, Sells had been at one of the local bars, hitting on the female waitress until he was chased off by a chivalrous man at closing time, who saw that the bartender had grown increasingly agitated with the scruffy truck driver. It was believed that Sells then went to the Harris's home and entered it through an open window in the bedroom of fourteen-year-old Justin Harris, a blind boy who thought his sisters had been sneaking in and out of his room. In the dark, he called out, "Will y'all stop coming into my room?"

Sells moved out of Justin's room and looked into the next bedroom, using the small flame of his cigarette lighter for guidance down the unfamiliar hallway. Sells made his way quietly through the house, checking bedrooms until he found the one for which he'd been searching. He saw Kaylene "Katy" Harris, thirteen, sleeping in the bottom bunk, but did not notice Krystal Surles, ten, sleeping in the top bunk. Sells laid down next to Katy and nudged her awake.

"What are you doing here?" she asked him.

Sells put his hand over her mouth and pulled a twelve-inch boning knife he had brought with him, cutting Katy's shorts, panties, and bra off as he fondled her. Unnerved and finally wriggling free of Sell's lecherous advances, Katy stood up and yelled at Krystal to "Go get Mama!"

Sells turned on the light and moved to block the door. Katy was bleeding and she exclaimed, "You cut me!"

Panicked, Sells moved behind her, put his hand over her mouth, and cut her throat not once, but twice. Limp and weak, Katy dropped to the floor as blood gurgled in her throat. Not content with merely cutting her throat, Sells stabbed her an additional sixteen more times.

Once the frenzy with Katy was over, Sells turned his attention to Krystal and he moved toward her quickly, slashing her throat. Sells' knife had missed the artery, though it had still cut deep enough to render Krystal speechless. The young girl immediately dropped to the floor and pretended to be dead.

"I just lay there and pretended I was dead," Krystal said later. "If he knew I was alive, he would come back and kill me for sure."

Sells turned off the light, wiped his fingerprints from the doorknob, and took two window screens he thought might contain his fingerprints. He then walked out through the front door and drove home. He stopped along the way to discard the knife and screens.

It was uncharacteristic of Tommy's style in that he zeroed in on the two girls and ignored the parents sleeping next door, though it fits with the same kind of blood lust that all serial predators feel: the need to kill will eventually overwhelm all rational thought and behavior.

Sadly, Kaylene succumbed to her wounds, dying that night in her bed. But her friend Krystal miraculously survived her attack and was able to provide police with something no one else could: a full description of their attacker. Her description was so detailed and so meticulous that, within three days, Tommy Lynn Sells was spotted, arrested, and charged with the capital murder of Kaylene Harris and the attempted murder of Krystal Surles. Sells copped to the whole murder and forensic evidence such as fiber and blood samples recovered from the scene corroborated his confession. Tommy would plead innocent to capital murder charges, mostly because he knew that a capital murder conviction was the expressway to an automatic death sentence. Tommy himself even played up the idea that he was not mentally sound, and while most people agreed, his own defense attorney, Victor Garcia, shot them down, saying:

> I don't think he's a Charles Manson. In fact, I know he's not. He's not crazy. He didn't sit in the court and stare down the jurors or make funny faces or be disruptive. The reason he's not mentally insane is as soon as he does it, he knows it's wrong. That's why he wipes off the fingerprints.

The beastly, brutal Tommy Lynn Sells was no match, however, for the absolute courage and undaunting bravery of Krystal Surles, who faced down her attacker in court with iron-bound resolve. The ten year-old girl, bearing a hideous scar across her throat, took the stand and tearfully recalled the night she met the Boogeyman.

To no one's surprise, he was convicted and sentenced to die after only three hours of deliberation. Sells would appeal the conviction numerous times, all to no avail. Sells became known as prisoner number 999367, a number, like other monsters before him, that became his name.

Krystal Harris's mother told reporters at the conclusion of the trial, "I believe with all my heart the reason why this man was apprehended is because it was time for God. God wanted it done. And I believe the reason why he did not get everyone in my house killed that night is because every angel of the people he killed was put there to make sure this man was caught."

Soon, police agencies from across the country were flying into Texas to see if Sells could close the books on some of their more brutal cold-case murder investigations. Sells found his worth, and, like Henry Lee Lucas, used his reputation of viciousness to stave off the death sentence. As long as he was alive, more cases could be closed. He finally had something that someone else wanted, and while on death row, Sells would confess to more than seventy murders, closing the books on cold cases from Idaho, Nevada, California, Arizona, Illinois, and as far east as

New York. He even took credit for a number of murders that had been pinned on another serial killer, Angel Rafael Resendez, nicknamed "the Railway Killer," who had been stalking portions of Illinois, Oklahoma, and Texas at the same time. It is both chilling and fascinating to think that Resendez and Sells may have crossed paths during their respective murder sprees.

Authorities in Texas began to wonder if Sells had actually killed as many people as he claimed, citing Henry Lee Lucas's questionable confessions twenty years earlier. Indeed, according to Victor Garcia, Sells had confided in him that he was actively trying to pursue a sentence commute, saying that it was Henry's constant confessions that had gotten him his life sentence. It was a deranged, cruel play of the hand to make people believe he had information about killings when, in reality, he didn't have a clue. In the end, none of his "confessions" could be substantiated and, having already fallen for Henry's wild games, the State of Texas continued with their goal to have Sells executed.

Lieutenant Larry Pope, one of the detectives who had arrested Sells, spoke with him one last time from Sells' death row cubicle. "He said, 'I'm going to Jesus, I'm going to see my maker,' and I'm thinking, you've got the directions mixed up," Pope said.

On January 3, 2014, fourteen years and a day after his apprehension, Tommy Lynn Sells was executed by lethal injection at the Texas State Penitentiary in Huntsville. He had no final words and the lethal potion of pentobarbital, pancuronium bromide, and potassium chloride killed him quietly in thirteen minutes.

The beast had finally been quieted.

In one of his final interviews, Tommy Lynn Sells reflected on his past life as a savage murderer, saying, "My life don't make a lot of sense . . . . It don't make sense that I go around the country killing people. Period. It don't make sense doing that."

The Vile Files

Angel Rafael Resendez

(1959-2006)

Nicknamed "the Railway Killer," Angel Rafael Resendez was a Mexican serial killer responsible for as many as fifteen murders across the United States and Mexico from 1986 to 1999. Like Tommy Lynn Sells, he was a migratory serial predator, bludgeoning, stabbing, and raping his way across the Midwest. His main method of transportation was the railroad, which he used as a getaway car before and after his crimes. After a particularly successful profile on *America's Most Wanted,* Resendez surrendered to Texas authorities on July 13, 1999. Following a lengthy and oftentimes bizarre trial, Resendez was sentenced to die by lethal injection in Huntsville. "I want to ask if it is in your heart to forgive me. You don't have to. I know I allowed the Devil to rule my life," Resendez said in his final statement. "I just ask you to forgive me and ask the Lord to forgive me for allowing the devil to deceive me. I thank God for having patience in me. I don't deserve to cause you pain. You do not deserve this. I deserve what I am getting."

CHAPTER 20

DARREN DEON VANN

"THE LAKE COUNTY STRANGLER"

Hammond, Indiana

"This is all unbelievable to me. A total shocker. I never knew him to be violent, never."

–Darren Deon Vann's ex-wife

The city of Gary, Indiana, was known for Michael Jackson and the birthplace of the Jackson 5. That was back in the 1960s. Since then, the city did little to capitalize on the renown of their most famous alumnus. The main source of employment was the enormous steel mill and much of the city became known for its rampant poverty and beefy crime rates. Abandoned businesses and foreclosed homes were as plentiful as gang members on the streets. Struggling to survive, but doomed to a life of notoriety, the citizens of Gary, Indiana would face yet another setback in their quest to redeem themselves when serial killer Darren Deon Vann was arrested in nearby Hammond, Indiana.

Darren Deon Vann is currently in prison awaiting trial for the vicious murders of seven women. Because he has yet to stand trial, many facts surrounding his case have not yet been released. All I, or anyone else has at the moment, are a series of sterile facts and allegations. Everything in this chapter is taken from public record.

It is believed that Vann began his career in murder with the brutal strangling of nineteen-year-old Afrikka Hardy. Contacting the woman through her job at an escort agency, Vann, using the moniker "Big Boy Appetite" and reportedly arranged to meet her at a Motel 6 in Hammond, Indiana, ten miles west of his hometown of Gary. Once in the motel room, Vann allegedly assaulted, beat, then strangled the young woman. Returning home, police believe Vann dumped Afrikka's body into one of the many abandoned houses in the residential area of Gary.

Afrikka Hardy had recently moved back to the Chicago area after graduating from high school while living with her mother in Aurora, Colorado. Her own mother had no idea she had been working as an escort, but Afrikka had long-term plans for the future, with designs on returning to school. "But I guess she started hanging with different people and it took her towards another way," reported one of her cousins.

Vann would allegedly take advantage of the poverty-stricken city multiple times, using the abandoned homes to hide his kills. Afrikka Hardy's murder would soon be followed by twenty-eight-year-old Teira Batey, who left home one night to meet up with a friend. Teira's mother, Gloria Cullom, got a phone call the next day from Teira, who was crying and sounded scared over the phone. She was begging for someone to come pick her up, but before she could divulge a location, the line went dead. Teira's mother never heard from her daughter again. Teira was a very vulnerable young woman, trusting to a fault, a trait her killer most likely took advantage of very quickly.

Police, meanwhile, used Afrikka Hardy's cellular phone records to track down the one unfamiliar number in her phone, one which belonged to "Big Boy Appetite." The phone number led directly to Darren Deon Vann, and according to police, Vann was found to have several pieces of Afrikka's personal property on his person. Shocked at how quickly he'd been found, but obviously relieved, he willingly confessed to not only murdering Afrikka Hardy, but also to the strangulation murders of six other women. Though police doubted the validity of his confession at first, they were quickly convinced when Darren Deon Vann led them to each and every body.

Anith Jones and Christine Williams, in addition to a third, unidentified body, were found in the 400 block of East 43rd Avenue. Teaira Batey's body was found in the 1800 block of East 19th Avenue. A sixth and seventh body were found in the 2200 block of Massachusetts Street and on the 4300 block of Massachusetts Street. The bodies had lain there in relative anonymity for close to six months without detection, and the discovery of the bodies, naturally, had a disturbing effect on the residents of Gary. They were understandably upset that a suspected serial killer was dumping his victims in several of the over-10,000 abandoned homes in the city.

"It disgusts me because it's seven bodies," resident Ronnie Williams told CNN. Williams lived next door to one of the homes where a body was recovered and claimed to have not had a single clue what was going on, which wasn't at all suspicious; no one in any of the neighborhoods ever claimed to have seen anything, leading police to believe that Vann mostly worked at night when most law-abiding citizens were at home behind locked doors.

As the bodies of the seven women were recovered and examined, police did much of the same to Darren Deon Vann, looking into his background intently.

Born in Gary in 1971, Darren Deon Vann was a product of the poverty plaguing Gary, Indiana. He accrued a lengthy arrest record quickly, but nothing to really indicate the life of murder he would eventually carry out. In the mid-1990s, he married very young to a woman who was almost thirty years older than he, a woman who has since asked to remain anonymous. The marriage was frowned upon by most every one of her children, who saw Vann as "bad news" and found it odd that a twenty-one-year-old man would find love with a fifty-one-year-old widow. Her son, who also has asked for anonymity, got a bad vibe from Vann right from the start and he worried for his mother.

"The guy is a nutcase. He is," he would tell CNN's Ashleigh Banfield. "And I'd watch him. I'd never allow him near my kids or in my home because he just freaked me out."

In an attempt to find work, Vann and his wife moved to Austin, Texas, but found little success. He was forced to return to Gary, moving home as a failed hero who was unable to support his wife in the way he wanted. Vann turned to alcohol and infidelity during this time, picking up a girlfriend on the side. His frustration at not finding decent work came to a head when he was fired from a temporary employment agency. He took his frustration out on his girlfriend, beating her within an inch of her life. Arrested and convicted of felony battery, Vann began his first real stretch in prison, doing ninety days behind bars. Through it all, his wife remained with him, insisting that Vann never showed her any violence or even the slightest bad temper.

Following his release, Vann again returned to the Austin area where, in December 2007, he was arrested for the aggravated sexual assault of a woman at his apartment. The victim was a twenty-five-year-old woman who was responding to a service call from her employer when she met Vann at the apartment, attempting to assess the problem he'd been having with the apartment. Once inside the apartment, Vann asked her if she was a police officer and when she told him that she was not, Vann viciously attacked her, choking, beating, and raping her. Indicted in July 2008, Vann pled guilty and was convicted in September 2009 and sentenced to five years in prison. He and his wife divorced while he was doing this stretch in prison; she ultimately returned to Gary to be with her family while he finished out his sentence in Texas. Released in July 2013, Vann returned to Gary, Indiana and, over the course of fifteen months, Vann would strangle and rape his way through seven women, dumping their bodies like garbage into the abandoned homes of Gary.

During the course of the initial police interview with Vann, he alluded to a connection to one of his victims, that of thirty-five-year-old Anith Jones. He intimated that he had been paid $500 to make the woman disappear, the result of a longstanding drug debt. Such a boast lacks corroboration and it only solidifies the idea that serial predators like Vann feel a need to justify their actions; it isn't enough that they feel a compulsion to do it. There *has* to be a deeper need to murder these women so their own morality won't turn against them.

But Vann wasn't finished with police: he would eventually confess to other murders he had committed, some going back as far as twenty years across the state of Indiana, and even after interviewing the confessed murderer, police still had no idea why he started killing. To them, there wasn't a whole lot of the stereotypical elements of your classic serial killer, yet when you ignore the stereotypes, you start to see the personality anomalies. In this case, I personally see a good possibility that Vann lashed out at the weakest of the species because of wounded pride or a skewed sense of personal vanity. Low self-esteem and an inability to keep even the most menial of jobs compounded with a devastating sense of hopelessness can drive a proud man mad.

Today, Vann sits in a Lake County jail cell in Crown Point, Indiana, anxiously awaiting his day in court where he will learn if he will live in prison for the remainder of his life or face the executioner. As the prosecuting attorney builds his case against Vann, police are also struggling to still identify three of the women Vann claims to have murdered whose bodies were found along with the others. It is certain that a great portion of Vann's story has yet to be told, but to us, it will be a familiar story, not unlike that of Tommy Lynn Sells, Jeffrey Dahmer, or Richard Ramirez. Some men find the taste for killing to be similar to the same rush as shoplifting, and for most serial predators, it is indeed a familiar path that leads from petty crime to vicious homicide. For Darren Deon Vann, his propensity for violence against women and his utter contempt for the law meant that it was only a matter of time before he took his first life.

But instead of focusing on what makes a man like Vann tick, we should focus on the type of prey he chose, for like many before him, he culled the weak from the herd. Trust, good natures, and friendly personalities aren't weaknesses to humans, they are assets. But to an animal looking to kill you for sport, those three traits are essential when picking a victim. They take the most trusting, most vulnerable women and men that they can find and use their trusting natures against them. That is the most horrific aspect of their crimes, for using good against itself truly is the work of devils. But do we trust no one, or trust everyone? Do we eyeball everyone with a scrupulous eye, or do we gloss over our gut instincts in favor of finding the good in people? The answer, of course, lies somewhere in the middle where we must trust our own primal instincts and act accordingly. That, and only that, is our one similarity to these monsters.

The Vile Files

Anthony Sowell

(1959-)

Known as "the Cleveland Strangler," Anthony Edward Sowell was convicted July 22, 2011, for the kidnapping, rape, and strangling murders of eleven women whose bodies had all been found in his Cleveland-area home. Like John Wayne Gacy, visitors to his home often complained of an overpowering stench, which Sowell first wrote off as first his stepmother, then as a result of the sausage shop next door. He was eventually caught and arrested when a girlfriend reported him to police after he attempted to choke her. Sowell received the death penalty and currently resides on Death Row at the Chillicothe Correctional Institution in Chillicothe, Ohio.

CHAPTER 21

ED GEIN

"THE BUTCHER OF PLAINFIELD"

Plainfield, Wisconsin

"She isn't missing. She's at the farm right now."
—**Ed Gein,** adding his own theory
on the disappearance of Bernice Worden

Billy liked Ed, despite what everyone used to say about the little weird man. Sure, he was kind of a hermit, opting most times to keep to himself rather than associate with most people his own age. From what he could tell, Ed liked him, too. They'd gone to the movies a lot, took in a few baseball games during the summer. But what Billy really liked about Ed was his house. Packed to the brim with antiques, private detective magazines, old toys, and World War II memorabilia, Ed's house was a fascinating, yet slovenly, museum of the odd.

Especially the shrunken heads, hanging in a line down the front of one of Ed's bedroom doors. Ed had told him a cousin had sent them to him from somewhere in the Philippines, and it was just like something out of one of the old death-cult magazines Ed had laying around. Ed had even told him how they used to skin the heads properly and boil them until they diminished in size. But these shrunken heads weren't that diminutive.

In truth, they weren't shrunken heads at all, but faces peeled from the corpses Ed Gein had stolen from the graveyard, fashioned just so that he could wear them as a mask and be someone else for a little while. And when the full moon came about, he'd wear those masks and dance in the bluish black moonbeams as they shone down upon his remote, very private farm.

The tale of the "Butcher of Plainfield" has been told numerous times, prompted countless nightmares, frightened young children, and inspired horror films such as *Psycho*, *Deranged*, *The Texas Chainsaw Massacre*, and *The Silence of the Lambs*. But nothing is as frightening, or tragic, as the quiet little man behind those legends. Ed Gein can barely be called a serial killer; his total number of victims counts as only two. But if one were to count the nearly forty bodies he stole from the area's graveyard, if you were to take into account all of the things he'd done with their skin and bones, then Ed Gein victimized countless others by desecrating the bodies of their loved ones. The horror in his own backyard was nothing compared to the horror in his own mind.

Edward Theodore Gein was born on August 27, 1906, in the town of La Crosse, Wisconsin, to George and Augusta Gein. At the time of his birth, he also had a brother, Henry, who was seven years older. His father George was a timid and weak man with a taste for alcohol. His mother Augusta, on the other hand, was a strict, iron-fisted woman whose utter contempt for her husband was matched only by her utter contempt for her boys. A fanatical Christian, Augusta Gein taught her boys the puritanical way of life, depicting all other women but herself as corruptive whores in a Godless country bent on sin and degradation. She routinely preached to her two boys from the Bible, often choosing verses from the Old Testament that dealt with death, murder, and divine retribution.

It was also these puritanical views that kept her from divorcing her husband, probably much to her husband's chagrin as well, for it was not the most loving household in any regard.

The Geins had purchased a small grocery store in Plainfield and found a rather large, very private farmhouse located nearby. Augusta Gein's rationale for purchasing such a remote home was mainly to keep the destructive influence of outsiders away from her family. Augusta discouraged her sons from having friends and was absolutely against the idea of dating from the very beginning. As a result, both Ed and Henry became fairly reclusive, quiet, odd boys. But whereas Henry tended to allow his mother's influence to lapse once he left the home for the day, Ed carried it with him all of his life. He spent so much time with her that he even developed slightly effeminate mannerisms, actions that made him a target of playground bullies.

Throughout their teens and early twenties, Henry and Ed pretty much depended on each other for company as friends weren't allowed at the house and each of them was scolded rather harshly if Augusta Gein had discovered that they were making friends outside the family. Henry, being the oldest, would try and test his mother every so often, yet Ed went out of his way to try and please her, doing whatever he could to gain favor in her eyes. But despite his best efforts, Augusta Gein was very rarely, if ever, pleased with anything her sons did.

Edward Gein, leaving the police station following his arrest in 1957. (*Photographer unknown, courtesy of the Library Of Congress.*)

Henry and Ed's father died in 1940 of a massive heart attack. Ed was thirty-four at the time, Henry nearly forty-one, and neither of them had any concept of anything outside the farm. They took on odd jobs around town to help with the expenses. Henry found a lot of work as a tradesman and handyman, while Ed frequently babysat for his neighbors, preferring the company of children to adults. When Ed wasn't babysitting or fixing a neighbor's fence, he was at his mother's side, listening to her read from the Bible or tending to her every need. Ed's attachment to their mother frequently disturbed Henry, who had finally begun to forsake his mother's old world view of modern culture. Though he never defied her to her face, Henry frequently spoke ill of Augusta to Ed, who seemed to take it rather personally each time, driving a thick wedge between the two brothers.

On the day of May 16, 1944, a brush fire started by Ed and Henry near the farmhouse began to burn out of control. As they went about extinguishing it, the smoke and flames became too intense and thick. Eventually, the two brothers were separated and Ed lost sight of Henry as darkness fell. Once the fire was out and Ed could no longer find Henry, he called the police, who found Henry dead on the ground. But police immediately suspected something was amiss when bruises were found on his head and the ground around him had gone unburnt. Most investigators suspected Ed in the death of his brother, but no charges were ever brought against him.

A year later, Ed lost his mother after a series of devastating strokes, an event that left Ed in a fog of unending sadness and profound loss. He boarded up her bedroom, leaving it exactly as she left it. Immaculately clean, it soon paled in comparison to the horrid filth and clutter that would soon overtake the rest of the house.

Shortly after his mother's death, Ed became fixated on becoming a woman, a misguided attempt to bring his mother back into his life by any means necessary. He perused the daily newspaper's Obituary section every day, seeking out those who fit his profile; most all of the corpses he sought, in some way, tended to resemble his mother. So Eddie Gein began to visit the local graveyards, unearthing the freshest female corpses, committing these acts under what he would later describe as a gauzy haze, almost as if he were dreaming it rather than doing it. He would steal the body back to the farmhouse where he would harvest the skins, preserve them by tanning them, and very soon began to stitch together a suit of skin that allowed him to transform into a woman whenever he donned it.

The remaining body parts would find their way around his home in a variety of different and macabre ways. He would fashion a belt made out of nipples. There was a lampshade and several chairs that he'd crafted out of human skin. A bisected skull served as a makeshift soup bowl. A string of human ears hung from one of the doors like a grisly necklace. He'd even fashioned a window shade pull out of a pair of dissected lips. All of these morbid, grotesque artifacts lay about his home as if they were part of the scenery, meaning as much to him as a knife and fork did, which is why sheriff's deputies found them all in plain sight once he and his nocturnal activities were uncovered.

Ed Gein's strange behaviors and odd collections piqued the interest of some of the kids who had befriended him and stories of Ed's odd tales and shrunken heads began to circulate about the town of Plainfield. They saw no harm in his weirdness, but still couldn't help but eyeball him just a little closer once they realized what was in his farmhouse.

In the late 1940s and early 1950s, there had been a rash of disappearances around the La Crosse, Plainfield, and outlying Jefferson County areas, instances where people simply up and vanished without a trace. Much has been written about these disappearances and Ed's connection to them, but the victims had all been little girls or older men, two victim profiles that were definitely not within Ed's wheelhouse.

But one missing person was: fifty-four-year-old tavern owner Mary Hogan. By most accounts, Mary Hogan was a fun-loving, down-to-earth gal who enjoyed the drink and enjoyed the attention men gave her. A sweet person with a bawdy personality, Mary Hogan was loved by just about everyone who came to her bar. To Ed Gein, she was both sinner and saint, a reflection of both his mother and the whores she'd warned him about. Mary Hogan was Ed's inner conflict made flesh. He made up his mind to not only cleanse the world of her, but to preserve and keep her for himself.

On December 8, 1954, a customer named Seymour Lester walked into Mary Hogan's tavern and found it to be empty. A trail of darkening blood led out the front door, prompting Lester to run to the nearest farmhouse to call police. Responding sheriff's deputies found the blood trail, a spent shell casing from a .32-caliber handgun, and nothing else. Mary Hogan's disappearance would go unsolved for nearly two years.

While at the tavern drinking one night, some of the men were talking about Mary and her disappearance that night in 1954. Ed, who'd been essentially eavesdropping the whole time, said, "She's not missing. She's at the farm right now." The men burst out laughing, thinking Ed was joking in that odd little way that Ed did. A collective chill would go down their spines later when they realized Ed had been telling them the truth.

Almost three years passed by and Mary Hogan's case was still ice cold. No other clues, no other witnesses, nothing had turned up during that time. The latest, and final disappearance, that of Plainfield hardware store owner Bernice Worden was the big break police had been needing. Her disappearance was directly linked to Ed Gein, who'd been the last to see her the night before and the first to see her the next morning. Written receipts for Ed's antifreeze was the last one she had written on the morning she disappeared from the store.

Sheriff Art Schley was able to retain a search warrant for Ed Gein's property and immediately went to expedite it. Though Ed wasn't at home at the time, Schley executed the warrant anyway and discovered Worden's decapitated body in a shed, hung upside down with rope and a crossbar piercing her ankles. She resembled a gutted deer, left alone to drip dry. Once the search entered Ed's house, the full realization of Ed's madness finally came to light.

They found all of the morbid, handcrafted items Ed had made from the skin and bones of cadavers, as well as the heads of both Bernice Worden and Mary Hogan. A total of nine masks made from the faces of dead women were also recovered. Human bones, in whole and in fragmented parts, were littered all over the house. A human heart was even found in a closed kettle.

Ed Gein made no bones about it: between 1947 and 1952, he admitted raiding the graves of at least ten women. In an attempt to prove or disprove his ghastly admission, sheriff's deputies exhumed two of the graves Ed had admitted robbing and found they were empty, corroborating Ed's confession of grave-robbing.

He admitted to the murder of Bernice Worden, which he obviously couldn't refute even if he wanted to, and to the shooting death of Mary Hogan. Though Gein admitted to coveting their skins and their motherly personalities, he denied having sex with any of the corpses he stole.

"They smelled too bad," he was reported as saying.

Sheriff Art Schley, who conducted much of the initial interrogation, was so disgusted by Ed Gein that he assaulted him during his confession, slamming Gein's head against the brick wall. The assault led to Gein's confession being ruled inadmissible. Undeniably, Schley had been traumatized by what he'd found at Ed's farmhouse and the mental anguish he was under obviously got the better of him. Truly, the horrors found in that house were unlike anything that had ever been seen before and rivaled even Jeffrey Dahmer's apartment in terms of horrific.

Gein was found incompetent to stand trial and was remanded to the custody of Central State Hospital for the Criminally Insane in November of 1957. He would later be transferred to the Mendota State Hospital in Madison, Wisconsin. Over the course of eleven years, Gein received intensive psychiatric therapy, finally feeling a sense of normalcy for the first time in years. His attachment to his mother seemed to dwindle as well. When he was informed that his house had burned down in 1958, he simply shrugged and said, "Just as well." Knowing that his

Ed Gein's headstone shortly before it was stolen from a Plainfield cemetery.

mother's carefully preserved room was now nothing but cinders, and replying as he did, showed a great deal of growth in Ed, away from the clutches of his domineering mother and more toward rectifying what he had done.

By 1968, Ed was finally determined to be sane enough to stand trial. Ironically, he was found guilty but insane and was returned to Mendota where he would live out the remainder of his life. Life for Ed in the hospital was fairly blissful. He found a peace of mind he'd never had before and, according to the resident physicians and orderlies, Ed Gein was a model patient, prompting Superintendent Schubert to declare that he wished all of his patients could be as good as Ed. However, some nurses recalled feeling unnerved when they would catch Ed staring at them.

Ed was protected from the outside world in the institution, much in the same way his mother had sheltered him. Doctors routinely turned away reporters and television news crews. Ed received an occasional fan letter, but little else. He was completely oblivious to the fascination the world held for him and he couldn't be happier.

On July 26, 1984, Edward Gein succumbed to respiratory and heart failure brought on by his aggressive battle with lung cancer. In a fitting twist, his grave site in Plainfield was frequently vandalized and tourists began chipping away parts of the tombstone to take as souvenirs. In 2000, someone simply stole the entire 350-pound tombstone. It would be recovered in June 2001 in Seattle, Washington, and returned to Plainfield, where it is currently on display in a museum.

While Ed Gein may not be classified as a serial killer, his morose, grotesque lifestyle lends itself to inclusion here and, had he not been stopped, the body count would no doubt be considerably higher. Like Albert Fish and Carl Panzram before him, the cause of Ed Gein's massive troubles lay in his childhood. Most scholars have speculated that his childhood, while tragic, was far from unique, begging the question: How did Ed, Albert, or Carl become such deranged killers when other children suffered as much and overcame it without falling prey to the darkness within?

That may be the question of the ages, pondered over and debated for decades. But somewhere out there, steeped in darkness and raised on terror, another child is growing into the large shoes left for him by his murderous forefathers and the mystery of why we kill will continue to deepen. As modern medicine clamors for the answer, there will always be that person filled with dark imaginings, standing outside your house at night, whispering...

THE BOOGEYMAN
IS REAL . . .
AND YOU FOUND HIM.

Appendix

In Memoriam
Those we love don't go away,
They walk beside us every day...
Dedicated to the lives
lost at the hands of monsters...
You are not forgotten.

AnetheChristensen
DayleOkazaki
MaxineZazzarra
MaryLouiseCannon
LelaKneiding
StephenDeanHolmes
BillySutherland
GrahamAllen
Frieda"Becky"Powell
WalkerCountyJaneDoe
SueLuna
TeresaWatson
"EklutnaAnnie"
DelynnFrey
RoxanneEasland
MaryThill
NelsonWinslow
MariaFasching
SereenaAbotsway
BrendaAnnWolfe
JacquelineMcDonell
JenniferLynnFurminger
HeatherChinnook
IngaMoniqueHall
CynthiaFeliks
DebraLynneJones
AndreaFayBorhaven
FrancisMcDonnell
Catherine"Rena"Costello

KarenChristensen
Tsai
William"Bill"Doi
JoyceLucilleNelson
ChainarongKhovananth
KennethOckendon
MalcolmBarlow
StephenSinclair
KateRich
LisaFutrell
TamiPederson
PaulaGoulding
LisaFutrell
JoannaMessina
CeciliaVanZanten
AlvinGothea
WalterCollins
JoseCollozo
MonaLeeWilson
MarnieLeeFrey
DianneRosemaryRock
HelenMaeHallmark
TanyaHolyk
TiffanyDrew
AngelaRebeccaJardine
WendyCrawford
CaraLouiseEllis
BillyGaffney
LyndaGough

JennieVincow
"Veronica"LanYu
MableKeller
MaxKneiding
ElyasAbowath
MartynDuffey
JohnHowlett
ViolaLucas
"OrangeSocks"
MalaiLarsen
AngelaFeddern
SherryMorrow
AndreaAltiery
"HorseshoeHarriet"
MeganEmerick
LewisWinslow
RobertWarnke
JosephKallinger Jr.
AndreaJoesbury
GeorginaFaithPapin
HeatherKathleenBottomley
PatriciaRoseJohnson
SherryIrving
SarahDeVries
DianaMelnick
KerryKoski
GraceBudd
CharmaineWest
CarolAnnCooper

Appendix

LucyKatherinePartington
JuanitaMarionMott
HeatherAnnWest
LyubovTiryuk
OlgaKuprina
OlgaStalmachenok
LyudmilaKushuba
VeraShevkun
MartaRyabenko
SvetlanaPetrosyan
SvetlanaTsana
AkmaralSeydaliyeva
NatalyaPokhlistova
IlanBilovetskiy
YevgeniyMuratov
AlexeyMoiseyev
AndreiKravchenko
ViktorPetroy
ViktorTishchenko
SandraLindsay
JamesDoxtato
RaymondSmith
DavidThomas
TonyHughes
JeremiahWeinberger
KatherineEddowes
AnnieChapman
MathildaKemper
AnitaLuchessa
RosalindThorpe
SallyHallett
LouisMasgay
PeterCalabro
HarveyDubs
LonnieBondSr.
CliffordPeranteau
KathleenAllen
JamesGibson
ThereseSiegenthaler
ShirleyAnneRobinson
YelenaZakotnova
LyubovVolobuyeva
IrinaKarabelnikova
LauraSarkisyan
IgorGudkov
SergeyMarkov
DmitriyPtashnikov
YelenaBakulina
NatalyaGolasovskaya
AlexanderChepel
IrinaGulyayeva
YuriTereshonok
TatyanaRyzhova
HelenaVarga
YaroslavMakarov
IvanFomin
SvetlanaKorostik
StevenHicks
RichardGuerrero
EdwardSmith
CurtisStraughter
KonerakSinthasomphone
OliverLacy
MaryJaneKelley
PollyNichols
EdmundEmilKemper,Sr.
AikoKoo
AliceLiu
PaulHoffman
DanielDeppner
MaryHogan
DeborahDubs
BrendaO'Connor
JeffreyGerald
ScottStapley
DeborahEverist
ShirleyHubbard
AlisonChambers
LarisaTkachenko
OlegPolzhidayev
SergeyKuzmin
IrinaDunenkova
ValentinaChuchulina
NatalyaShalapinina
TatyanaPetrosyan
AnnaLemesheva
LyudmilaAlekseyeva
IrinaLuchinskaya
OlegMakarenkov
AlexeyVoronko
AlexanderDyakonov
AlexeiKhobotov
LyubovZuyeva
VadimGrovov
DeborahDudley
StevenTuomi
AnthonySears
ErnestMiller
ErrolLindsey
MattTurner
JosephBradehoft
ElizabethStride
MarthaTabrum
MaryAnnPesce
CindySchall
ClarnellKemper
GarySmith
GeorgeMalliband
BernieceWorden
SeanDubs
LonnieBondJr.
MichaelCarroll
MarkKilroy
SimoneSchmidl

Vile

GaborNeugebauer
JoanneWalters
MariaMolotkova
MinnieGotthardt
MasamiYoshizawa
TinaCribbs
ChristineMartenson
MaryRamey
SusanHancock
SusannahCandy
JoeSowers
HenryMcKenzie
MaryAnnLongcor
JimmyRayPayne
MariaCiallella
WilliamWard
LouiseLenzen
IdaReuter
FrancescaTonso
AnjaHabschied
MarinaLyzhina
TatianaMartynova
JuliaTurner
ErikaNamba
MollieSmith
ElizaShelly
GracieVance
EulaPhillips
NoelenePatterson
BenBrown
JohnnyBoyle
DrWilliamYork
NathanialCarter
DeborahOsbourne
BetsyBacon
GertrudeAlbermann
TeresaPignocco
VincentZazzara
CarolineClarke
LiliaPashkovskaya
YuliaKuprikova
MariKonno
AyakoNomoto
ClaraStrand
IreneCross
OrangeWashington
MaryNeilson
DeniseBrown
W.F.McCrotty
GeorgeNewtonLongcor
JohnGreary
StephenSladowski
AnnaOlesiewicz
ChristineKlein
RosaOhliger
CatherineGivogre

Acknowledgments

The notorious Jeffries and Yuill families, especially my father, Arliss, who will always be the reason I started writing, and my mother, Linda, who is one of the reasons why I continue to write.

Kathi Sceggell and her daughter, Bella Evans (the true Dynamic Duo); the indestructible Brandi Diley; my 765 Paranormal brothers and sisters; the founding members of my unofficial Book Club, Valerie Mahan, Heather Marshall Letizia, Crystal Marshall Brant; Traci Emerson and Hope Inman; Jordan Hofer, for the support during my various author crises and for being my brotha from an alien motha.

John E. Douglas, Roy Hazelwood, John Borowski, Katherine Ramsland, and the late Philip Carlo for the inspiring work they've done in this thoroughly complicated field.

Dave Schrader and Tim Dennis from *Darkness Radio* for having me on their show and not sandwiching me between the lady who married Satan in a trailer park and the guy who summoned his dead sister's best friend's cousin's boyfriend using a Ouija board made out of an old pizza box and a mason jar.

Pete Schiffer, for continuing to gamble on me, and my ever awe-inspiring editor, Dinah Roseberry, who always seems to get saddled editing my manuscripts and kills it every single time.

Everyone in the world who bought my books and either enjoyed them, hated them, or used them as coasters. Thank you all for the tremendous support and helping keep this boy's dream from dying;

And finally, to all bookstores and libraries, both physical and online, who not only carry my books, but continue to hold faith in the power of reading, the miracle of writing, and the eternal wonderment of knowledge.

Bibliography

The following resources were instrumental in the research of this book.

Borowski, John. *Albert Fish in His Own Words: The Shocking Confessions of the Child Killing Cannibal.* Waterfront Productions, 2014.

Carlo, Philip. *The Ice Man: Confessions of a Mafia Contract Killer.* New York, New York: St. Martin's Press, 2009.

Carlo, Philip. *The Night Stalker: The Life and Crimes of Richard Ramirez.* (Paperback ed.). New York, New York: Kensington Publishing Corp., 1996

Douglas, John E. and Mark Olshaker. *Mindhunter: Inside the FBI's Elite Serial Crime Unit.* New York: Scribner, 1995.

Douglas, John E. and Mark Olshaker. *Journey into Darkness.* New York: Scribner, 1997.

Douglas, John E., Mark Olshaker. *Obsession: The FBI's Legendary Profiler Probes the Psyches of Killers, Rapists and Stalkers and Their Victims and Tells How to Fight Back.* New York: Scribner, 1998.

Douglas, John E. and Mark Olshaker. *The Cases That Haunt Us.* New York: Scribner, 2000.

Fiorillo, Victor. "Inside the House of Heidnik." *Philadelphia Magazine*, July 2007.

Google News Archives. http://news.google.com/news/advanced_news_.

Mudede, Charles. "Death Farm: The Geography of Pig Farmer Robert Pickton, the Man Suspected of Having Killed Over 60 Vancouver, BC, Sex Workers." October 30, 2003. Seattle, WA: *TheStranger.com*

Newton, Michael. *The Encyclopedia of Serial Killers (Facts on File Crime Library).* Checkmark Books, 2006.

Ramsland, Katherine. *The Devil's Dozen: How Cutting-Edge Forensics Took Down 12 Notorious Serial Killers.* Berkley, 2009.

Rumbelow, Donald. *The Complete Jack the Ripper. UK*: Virgin Books; Revised edition, 2013.

Schechter, Harold. *Deranged: The Shocking True Story of America's Most Fiendish Killer!* NY: Simon and Schuster, 1998.

Schechter, Harold. *Deviant.* Simon and Schuster, date unknown.

Schechter, Harold. *The Serial Killer Files: The Who, What, Where, How, and Why of the World's Most Terrifying Murderers.* NY: Ballantine Books.

Schreiber, Flora Rheta. *The Shoemaker: Anatomy of A Psychotic.* Signet, 1984.

Thaxter, Celia. "A Memorable Murder." Originally printed in *Atlantic Monthly*, May 1875.

Weitz, Katy. "Real life Silence of the Lambs: 'I was caged, beaten and raped by deranged cannibal.'" *UK Daily Mirror*, March 31, 2014. www.mirror.co.uk.

www.crimemuseum.org/crime-library.

www.MurderPedia.com.